Business studies in practice

Business studies in practice

David Needham
Robert Dransfield

McGRAW-HILL BOOK COMPANY

London · New York · St Louis · San Francisco · Auckland · Bogotá · Guatemala
Hamburg · Lisbon · Madrid · Mexico · Montreal · New Delhi · Panama · Paris
San Juan · São Paulo · Singapore · Sydney · Tokyo · Toronto

Published by
McGRAW-HILL Book Company (UK) Limited
MAIDENHEAD · BERKSHIRE · ENGLAND

British Library Cataloguing in Publication Data
Needham, David
   Business studies in practice.
   1. Business studies – For schools
   I. Title   II. Dransfield, Robert
   658
   ISBN 0-07-084978-1

12 34 WL 898

Typeset by Eta Services (Typesetters) Ltd, Beccles, Suffolk
Printed in Great Britain by Whitstable Litho Printers Ltd, Whitstable, Kent

Contents

Acknowledgements

Many people have helped to bring this book together. We would particularly like to thank *The Independent*, *The Economist*, the *Barnsley Chronicle*, the *Harrogate Advertiser*, the *Aberdeen Press and Journal* and the *Reading Standard* for their willing contributions free of charge.

Many other groups and individuals went out of their way to help us including: Derek Chapman (The Prudential), Alan Robinson (Huntley, Boorne & Stevens), Maureen Coombes, Christopher Rowney, Peter Radband, Frageo's, the Bank Information Service, the Ford Motor Company, Burton Group plc, the *Guardian* Pictures Desk, the Women's Press, Friends of the Earth, Greenpeace, John Warner (Understanding Industry), British Nuclear Fuels, British Telecom, British Gas, Corby Industrial Development Centre, Hampshire Development Association, the Export Credits Guarantee Department, Geoff Hale, Scottish Whisky Association, Ashbourne Water, Leigh RLFC, Steve Hodkinson, Roland Peck & Co., Margaret Walsh, Benn Cribb, Eva Tutchell and Paul Clarke.

1 Introduction to business studies

Seeing business in its wide setting

The aim of this book is to introduce an enquiry-based approach to business studies in a modern setting. The study of business life can only be done against a wider background of interdependence and interrelationships. In the modern world no individual or group can make decisions which are not affected by a wide range of outside factors. In the UK we are particularly aware of how other groups and individuals influence our everyday lives. We are still very much a trading nation and as such are heavily dependent on the world market. When world prices rise for products such as oil, copper, other raw materials and foodstuffs we soon feel the effect and the same applies to a fall in prices.

Business life therefore takes place against a much wider setting and when we look at the individual business we will have to focus it against the following:

1. The international setting
2. The national setting
3. The local setting
4. The influence of government
5. The influence of competitors
6. The influence of buyers
7. The influence of suppliers
8. The influence of the local community and environment
9. Other influences

The modern approach to business studies is to tackle issues and problems through direct student activity. With this in mind this book has been structured in the following way. Each chapter is made up of a section of text, followed by case studies, questions and coursework activity. The exception is this opening chapter where the case studies have been written into the text.

Introduction to the coursework

Coursework activity is based on a number of approaches to business investigation. Business investigation is concerned with an awareness of business in its wider setting; i.e. a setting in which the business is only one amongst many groups or bodies with claims to scarce resources. Business investigation is therefore concerned with examining the alternative ways in which a community can allocate scarce resources, particularly focussing on the way in which business units operate.

You will find that there are many ways of carrying out an investigation. Some of these methods can be explored within the classroom whilst others must be based on investigation outside the classroom.

A coursework task must be posed as a question or problem. This gives you scope to ask questions, enquire, select and order information and make some sort of judgement or recommendation.

An important coursework skill is learning to ask the right questions. One of the aims of this book has been to introduce problems and situations which will encourage you to think about the sorts of questions that should be asked in the business-studies setting. Once you have selected the right sort of questions to ask then the questions need to be structured in a sensible way for delivery. If a questionnaire is being used this will involve setting up simple and direct questions that can easily be understood. The data should be collected in such a form that it is easy to break down to make sense of it. You must show a clear understanding of the material gathered and the purpose for which it was gathered.

Having collected the information and set it out in an understandable way, you should then develop a clear statement or argument from it. You might then make some recommendation to deal with the problem. For example, you could ask the question, 'Why does the XYZ Business find it difficult to recruit labour?' You should then decide on a set of appropriate questions to ask and techniques of asking questions. Who would you ask? How would you ask? What would you ask? You would then have to decide how to make sense of the information gathered. This would include assessing whether the information is reliable and meaningful. How much weight should you give to particular opinions? You might decide to look at alternative employers and alternative employment. Having built up an effective data base and decided how to make sense of it you could then go on to draw some conclusions. For example, you might argue that because the XYZ wages are very low, the hours inconvenient and the work unpleasant, few people are prepared to do the job.

Presenting information

As a result of a business-studies investigation you will build up a bank of information. It is crucial that this information is presented in a manner that is direct and easy to understand both for the student and for anyone else reading the report. Charts and tables are a very useful method of presenting information.

Tables

This is a simple way of presenting information. Tables can be used for a variety of purposes and can present information very clearly, whilst being simple to set up.

An example of a table that gives a lot of information and is easy to read is a football league table including the names of teams, games played, games won, drawn and lost, the goals scored for and against and the number of points each team has (see Fig. 1.1).

Saturday
Premier League

	P.	W.	D.	L.	F.		Pts
Centre 17	11	6	3	2	18	10	15
Birdwell Rov	10	6	2	2	14	5	14
Barugh Green	10	5	3	2	24	16	13
Honeywell Soc	9	6	1	2	21	17	13
Royal Oak	7	5	2	0	18	7	12
Royston Cross	11	3	5	3	15	16	11
Ward Green	10	5	0	5	23	14	10
The Star	10	4	1	5	16	16	9
High Green	6	2	1	3	9	13	5
Holyland Neth	7	1	2	4	13	17	4
Gr'thorpe M.W.	12	1	2	9	10	34	4
Gr'thorpe Ex.	9	1	0	8	7	23	2

Figure 1.1 A football league table—an example of a table that gives a lot of information.

Flow charts

These show the individual stages of a process from beginning to end. The simple flow chart in Fig. 1.2 shows how a mail-order catalogue works.

Pie charts

These can be used to present data in

Start

Customer chooses goods

↓

Agent visits customer

↓

Agent orders goods

↓

Goods delivered to agent

↓

Agent delivers to customer

↓

Payment made

Stop

Figure 1.2 Flow chart showing how a mail-order catalogue works.

a clear and often dramatic way. A circle is made up of 360 degrees. If you wanted to show that three-quarters of a firm's costs were labour costs and one quarter were transport costs you would give labour a value of 270 degrees and transport 90 degrees (see Fig. 1.3). You must be careful to set a pie chart up accurately if it is to have real meaning.

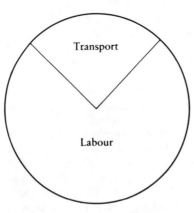

Figure 1.3 Pie chart showing how a firm's costs are divided between labour costs and transport costs.

Bar charts

These are also known as block graphs and are useful not just for showing proportions, but particularly for comparing amounts. You can easily see how one amount 'stands' in relation to another. For instance you could compare the male/female employee ratio in two firms (see Fig. 1.4).

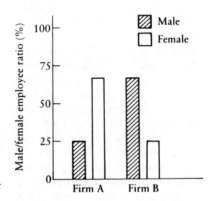

Figure 1.4 Bar chart showing the proportions of male and female employees in two firms.

Line graphs

Line graphs need to be drawn on graph paper so that the scale is accurate. They are particularly useful for showing how things change over time. The line graph in Fig. 1.5 shows the sales of a firm's products in the first six months of the year.

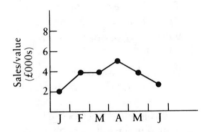

Figure 1.5 Line graph showing the sales of a firm's products over six months.

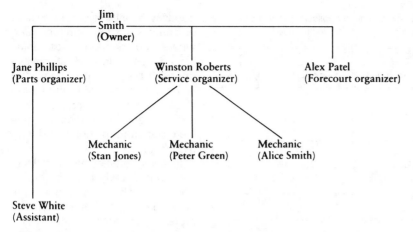

Figure 1.6 Organization chart of Jim Smith's garage business.

Organization charts

An organizational chart is used to show the relationship between members of an organization. Jim Smith has a small garage business in London. He was asked to draw an organizational chart to show how roles were structured in the organization (see Fig. 1.6).

Evaluation

Once the information is set out, organized conclusions can be drawn. At this stage you must be very careful not to simplify. You should be aware that data is often limited and biased by the value judgements of the people that have supplied the information. You should be aware that there are various ways of looking at things. An example of this would be that there are different ways of evaluating the success of an organization.

In looking at data you should try to identify trends. For example, you may notice from the sales figures of a company that over the years there has been an upward trend. You might then try to identify the causes of this improvement in sales. You should be cautious, however, about making statements like, 'The firm is

much better off because sales have increased,' when in fact the firm's costs may have increased by more than its sales.

You might also find out that the data you have collected is poor. This often happens when you have not asked very good questions in the first place or the people to whom you have put the questions have not understood them clearly. You should always be prepared to change your questions and an important part of your evaluation might be an understanding of the fact that you did not carry out your investigation as well as you could, so that if you started again you might go about it in a different way.

EXAMPLE OF QUESTIONNAIRE DESIGN

The following assignment was set up to test whether students could collect, select, analyse and interpret data and whether they could use language, simple data, tables, diagrams and graphs to explain an argument. The task was to answer the question: 'Why do people shop

in the different supermarkets in Chichester?'

One of the main aims of the group assignment was to find out whether the same factors are important for all supermarkets or whether people shop at their supermarket for a special reason.

SUPERMARKET QUESTIONNAIRE

Be polite
Explain what you are doing

1. On average how often do you shop in this supermarket?

| More than twice a week |
| Twice a week |
| Once a week |
| Once a fortnight |
| Once a month |
| Less than once a month |

2. How did you travel to this supermarket?

Walk	
Car	
Bus	
Train	
Other	

3. How far did you travel to shop?

Less than 2 miles	
3–5 miles	
6–10 miles	
Over 10 miles	

3

4. Why did you shop at this store? (Please say whether the following factors were very important, of some importance or not important in your decision to shop here.)

	Very important	Of some importance	Not important
(a) Low prices			
(b) Easy car parking			
(c) Good-quality products			
(d) Wide range of goods			
(e) Good service			
(f) Better opening hours			
(g) Advertising			
(h) Habit			
(i) Convenience			
(j) Good value for money			

Thank you for your help

Figure 1.7 Questionnaire used to interview supermarket shoppers.

Questions

Do you think that the students set up an effective and simple questionnaire? What modifications, if any, would you make to the questionnaire?

CASE STUDY—SETTING UP YOUR OWN BUSINESS

In February 1986, two young women were sitting in a pub thinking, 'Why are we in the jobs we're doing?' Since childhood Frances Stott had wanted to run a boutique. Frances had met Georgie Bateman whilst working for a computer firm in Henley. They had talked about setting up a combined coffee shop and boutique and had gradually realized that it was not impossible

to do so. They decided to sell their homes and take out a combined mortgage to purchase suitable business premises.

They found that the biggest problem was to raise enough capital to set up the business because they had to convince their bank managers that the venture would be a success. To do this, they had to prepare a cash-flow forecast, showing the money that the business expected to take in against the money they expected to pay out. In total they needed to raise £120 000 to buy premises and £20 000 for decorating and stocking the shop.

One of the first decisions was choosing a location. They were looking for a small market town in the Thames Valley, where there would be a good market for their

goods, where there would be a lot of tourists in the summer, and where competition was fairly limited. They looked at several towns before deciding on Abingdon. They had found that in Henley the price of property was too high and in Hungerford there were not enough shoppers during the week.

In Abingdon they had found that there had already been a petition from local traders asking for the development of a coffee shop and more clothes shops. They investigated the town in greater depth and discovered that it was busy every day of the week as well as at weekends. There were no other coffee shops and there was no direct competition for a boutique.

> **Direct competition** exists when there are businesses producing highly similar products appealing to the same group of people.

Having chosen their location and arranged finance, Georgina and Frances looked at the legal position. They had to apply to the local council for permission to change the use of the existing premises to include a coffee shop. They then had to make sure that the premises fitted in with the regulations requiring them to be 'fit for use' as a coffee shop.

Georgina is 26 and Frances 25 years old. They arrived at the name 'Frageo's' for their business simply by combining their two names. They set about redecorating and stocking their shop. The boutique (see Fig. 1.8) obtains stocks from four main suppliers who are well known in the fashion business. The coffee shop (see Fig. 1.9)

Figure 1.8 The boutique part of Frageo's. (*Source:* Kim Hooper, Reading)

Figure 1.9 The coffee-shop part of Frageo's. (*Source:* Kim Hooper, Reading)

obtains stocks from London as well as from local sources. The target market for the coffee shop is all ages, whereas the boutique is aimed at the 20–35 age group. To launch the shop in January 1987 it was decided to advertise in seven newspapers and a story about the business made the front page of two papers. The main expense of the business is the mortgage repayment but other considerations are insurance, lighting and heating.

The biggest hurdle in their first year is to build up the turnover of the two lines between the winter months and the summer when demand from tourists will boost sales. The story of this business is a classic example of the build-up of a new enterprise. With luck and good management it will flourish.

Questions

1. What was the biggest problem in setting up this business?
2. What sort of location were they looking for?
3. Why is it important to choose a good location?
4. What groups of people and organizations did they have to consider in setting up their business? (This is an important question because in business studies we are concerned with business and its environment.)
5. Who do you think would benefit from the setting up of Frageo's?
6. What did Georgina and Frances find out about their market?
7. What will be their main types of costs and revenue?
8. What will the success of the business depend on?
9. From studying the Frageo's case study, what questions would you ask if you were going to carry out a business investigation of a local enterprise?
10. For Frances Stott and Georgina Bateman the main business problem they are faced

5

with is that of making a success of the business in their own terms. Quite clearly there are a number of ways in which they could judge their own success. How would you define a successful business?

11. If you were going to set up a small florist's business, list five important decisions that you would have to make.

Resources

In any society resources will be scarce relative to the need for them.

A **resource** is a means of support. A resource from the point of view of business studies can be regarded as any feature of our environment that helps to support our well-being.

There are two main types of resource:

1. *Physical or natural resources*—such as soil, climate, water, minerals, forests and fisheries.
2. *Human resources*—people and their various skills.

Opportunity cost

Businesses use up resources which are scarce. If society had all the land, labour, raw materials and other resources that it needed to make all the goods that people could possibly want, then we could produce goods without making sacrifices. However, resources are scarce and therefore when we produce an item we are preventing the resources which we use to make it from going to produce something else. This is a major problem for any society. The real cost of using resources for a particular purpose is the next best use to which they can be put.

The **opportunity cost** of any activity is the next best alternative given up.

CASE STUDY—HOUSES VERSUS A SHOPPING PRECINCT

This case study (adapted from an article in *The Independent*) represents a classic business problem from society's viewpoint.

You live in an area in which there are 1300 homeless families. There are 12 500 people on the council-house waiting list.

Within this area there is a 17 acre site which is the last large piece of land available for council development. This land has been derelict for ten years.

A property-development company has asked to buy this land for £15 million to build a shopping precinct, a car park and 150 houses for sale.

Housing groups are angry about this scheme. They put forward the following arguments:

1. It would fail to provide cheap housing at a time of real need.
2. There is no proof of the need for a shopping precinct.
3. The property-development scheme will not make full use of the land.
4. There is an alternative housing plan that would involve building 410 houses, two-thirds of which would be for rent.

A council spokesperson has said that public opinion over the two plans is 'neck and neck', but a spokesperson for a homeless-families campaign says the local public are firmly in favour of the 410 houses plan.

Questions

1. What alternative uses of the land are mentioned in the case study?
2. What would be the real cost if the land was used as a shopping precinct and private housing estate? (This issue is a very useful discussion topic.)
3. Which scheme would you favour?
4. Who would benefit from a new shopping precinct and who would lose out?
5. What is the best use of the land for the people in the area?
6. What else do you need to know to answer question 5?

The aims of a business

In the chapter on business organization (Chapter 2) we shall see that there are many different types of business. Some of these are in the hands of a few owners, some are owned by a large number of shareholders and others are owned by the government. What are the aims of a private organization?

In the long run firms need to make a profit. People as a rule will only tie up their money in a business if they are satisfied with the return they get from it. This would suggest that profitability is a major business aim, although it is not the only one. Individuals will often set up in business because of the freedom it gives them to make decisions for themselves. It is not surprising, therefore, to find people who are willing to take a drop in earnings in order to own their own business.

A business is made up of many people each with his or her own ambitions and aims. Motivations in the running of a business might include, apart from profit:

1. *Maximization of sales.* In some large companies the salaries earned by managers may depend on the size of the business. Thus their objective may be to make the business as large as possible.
2. *Prestige.* For other people the image and name of a company may be very important. The company may spend a lot of money on public relations so that it is well thought of.
3. *Survival.* In some businesses, the aims of the firm may just be about surviving. An old-established company may, for instance, have the objective of keeping the business in the family.
4. *As a hobby or interest.* Some people can afford to run a small business at a loss. There is enjoyment in running the thing for its own sake.

CASE STUDY—JOSEPH ROBINSON'S GROCERY STORE

When Joseph Robinson retired from the Civil Service, he hoped to buy a small book shop in Harrogate where he lived. However, he found that there was already too much competition in this field and in any case town-centre rates were too high. Instead, he bought a small corner shop with living quarters at the back for £42 000. It cost him £1000 to stock his shop and a further £800 for fixtures. He sold his existing house for £50 000 and had additional savings of £22 000, which were invested in the building society at a rate of interest of 10 per cent.

Joseph has made some calculations based on his monthly business:

Cost of new stock each month	£800
Value of sales each month	£1300
Expenses per month	£400

He opens the shop, which sells general groceries, at about 9 a.m. on most days. He closes for an hour at midday and then works to any time between 6 p.m. and 8 p.m. He has made many friends and plans to run the shop for at least five years.

Questions

1. Is Mr Robinson's business venture financially sound?
2. What are the problems he will face?
3. How will other people benefit from Mr Robinson's activity?
4. Do you think that this is the best use of Mr Robinson's capital?

The government and business

So far we have been looking at some of the reasons why private firms operate in the way they do. We must also remember that in most countries the government also plays a big part in business life.

1. It lays down rules and laws setting out some of the things that individuals and groups such as businesses can and cannot do.
2. It charges taxes on firms and individuals and it pays out subsidies to some firms and individuals.
3. It runs and has shareholdings in some business organizations and other bodies.

The **public sector** is that part of the economy that is government-owned. The **private sector** is that part of the economy that is owned by private citizens.

CASE STUDY— GOVERNMENT AND A DENTISTS' PARTNERSHIP

Claire Lindsay is a member of a successful dentistry partnership consisting of three partners. They have a large group of patients and their numbers have been growing steadily. Many of the patients pay for treatment (although part of the cost may be borne by the NHS), but others get free treatment and the partnership claims the fees back from the NHS. Patients whose fees are paid by the NHS include pensioners on supplementary benefit, students, children and pregnant women. Like doctors and some other groups dispensing health-care treatment, dentists are restricted by government regulations as to how they can advertise.

In order to keep accurate figures for tax purposes, the partnership must keep detailed records of money coming into the business from fees and of the cost of running the business.

Question

How is Claire's business affected by the roles the government plays in the economy?

Economic systems

In all societies the problem of scarcity exists. This leads to the problem of deciding how scarce resources will be used:

1. *What* will be produced?
2. *How* will it be produced?
3. *For whom* will it be produced?

Questions

Look at the following newspaper headlines and split them up according to whether they raise a 'what?', a 'how?' or a 'for whom?' issue:

1. 'New technology boosts production'
2. 'UK to produce more machine tools'
3. 'Pensioners to get higher benefits'
4. 'Teachers to lose out in new pay deal'
5. 'Textiles in decline'
6. 'Bring back craft industry'

Some sort of system must exist to sort out the three types of problem. In the past they were resolved by custom and tradition. For example, the way that crops were grown and shared out was decided by folk tradition. In many parts of the world traditional economies are giving way to three major systems:

1. The centrally planned system
2. The free-market system
3. The mixed system

Central planning
In a centrally planned system many of the decisions are made by a central planning organization. Smaller groups such as factories and other business units submit their plans to a local committee. The local plans are then fed back for approval at the centre. The central organization might then decide what resources will be made available to each local area, which in turn allocates resources to each factory, farm or other productive unit. (See Fig. 1.10—factor-

ies, farms, cinemas and shops are just some examples of units that might use up economic resources.)

The free market
In a free market the decisions about *what, how* and *for whom* are made by consumers and producers; the government does not intervene. Consumers decide what they want to do with their incomes and they vote with their money for the products they want to buy. (Some people think that it does not work quite like this; they think that producers often decide what they would like to make and then persuade consumers to follow their wishes through advertising.) If a product sells well firms will be inclined to produce it. But if no one buys the product firms will stop making it, since under the market system firms will seek to make profits from the goods they sell.

Producers are forced to pay attention to the wishes of consumers in order to survive.

Questions

1. In recent years the demand for videos and take-away meals has increased. How have producers responded?
2. In recent years the demand for black and white television sets and push along lawn-mowers has fallen. How have producers reacted?
3. Every year the fashion industry

spends a lot of money on advertising clothes. How do consumers react?

The mixed economy
A mixed economy combines elements of both the free-market and the central-planning systems. Some decisions are made solely through the private sector whilst other decisions are made by the government. The UK is an example of a mixed economy: some parts of industry are owned and operated by the government but large chunks of the business world remain in private hands.

Questions

Which of the following products are made mainly by government-owned business and which by private-owned business?

1. Coal
2. Bread
3. Cinema entertainment
4. Electricity
5. Fish
6. Insurance
7. Railway journeys
8. Banking services

Production

The concern of production is to add value to things so that they become goods or services that people will want. Production includes a wide range of occupations including acting, playing professional football, selling ice-cream, running a flower shop, working as a buyer in a department store, acting as a paid child-minder and thousands more. Each of these occupations is concerned with adding a bit more value to something to turn it into the product that is finally purchased by a consumer who derives satisfaction from it.

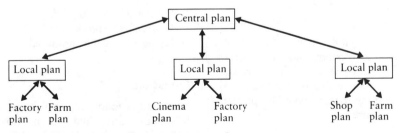

Figure 1.10 How a centrally planned system works.

Table 1.1 Examples of occupations in the different sectors of industry—add to these lists yourself.

Primary	Secondary	Tertiary	
		Commercial services	*Direct services*
Mining	Building	Insurance	Police
Fishing	Chemicals	Banking	Hairdressing
Forestry	Food processing	Advertising	Photography

It is important to stress this definition of production because some people mistakenly associate production just with manufacturing. In fact one of the most important trends in Britain in the twentieth century has been that of deindustrialization. The 1984 Census of Employment showed that whilst jobs in manufacturing have been disappearing, service industries like tourism, catering, finance, banking and leisure pursuits have boomed.

> **Deindustrialization.** The number of workers employed in manufacturing in the UK fell from just over 6 million in September 1981 to just over 5 million in September 1986. In the same period service-sector jobs increased from 15 million to 16 million.

Much of the growth in jobs has been centred in the south-east of England although there are pockets of growth in some areas hard-hit by the decline in heavy industry. In Scotland, for instance, many jobs in the computer industry have been created around Stirling in an area now known as 'Silicon Glen'.

Production is normally classified under three headings: primary, secondary and tertiary. *Primary industry* is concerned with taking out 'the gifts of nature', i.e. extracting natural resources. The *secondary sector* is concerned with constructing and making things. The *tertiary sector* is made up of services. There are two parts of this sector:

1. Commercial services concerned with trading activity
2. Direct services to people

Table 1.1 shows occupations in the different sectors—you should add to these lists.

CASE STUDY—THE EMPLOYMENT STRUCTURE IN BARNSLEY AND A JOB FOR JOHN DRAVSKY

The changing structure of employment has profound implications for individuals in different parts of the UK. John Dravsky left school in June 1985 with five CSEs and 'O' levels in Maths, English and Technical Drawing. He had hoped for a job in the local colliery as an electrician but just before he left school the mine where his father and brother worked was closed down. His brother was given work at a neighbouring colliery and his father took redundancy pay. There were no new opportunities for school-leavers in mining. Since 1981, six Barnsley collieries have closed or amalgamated, with a loss of 10 000 jobs. John managed to get work experience on a Youth Training Scheme. He spent six months working as a storeman at the Co-op and a further six months doing a brick-laying course. In July 1986 the training scheme ended and since then he has been out of work. At the end of 1986 the unemployment level in Barnsley was 20.3 per cent and there was very little prospect of work.

Table 1.2 shows the breakdown of employment (for selected employment categories) in Barnsley compared with the national figures.

Questions

1. In what sorts of employment is Barnsley under-represented compared with the national figures?
2. In what sorts of employment is Barnsley over-represented compared with the national figures?

Table 1.2 Breakdown of employment for males in Barnsley compared with the national figures, for selected employment categories. (*Source:* Census of Employment, 1981)

Employment category	Barnsley (%)	National (%)
Banking, finance	2.8	7.8
Energy and water supply	32.2	4.5
Metal goods, engineering, vehicles	5.5	16.3
Transport and communication	4.7	8.8

3. Would you expect this to cause problems for Barnsley?
4. Why might a business be attracted to Barnsley?
5. Why might a business be discouraged from moving to Barnsley?
6. How might these problems affect John Dravsky?
7. What would you do if you were in John's shoes?
8. Does John Dravsky have a problem? If he does, is it a national, local or personal problem?

Interdependence

By 1990 it is estimated that a further 3400–6000 jobs will have been lost in the Barnsley area (see case study above). This will have knock-on effects on other industries dependent on mining.

The interrelationship between different individuals, groups, businesses, industries and nations is very important in business life. On a simple level this is seen in the division of labour within a firm and the interdependence between different types of business activity.

An example of interdependence— Inputs, processes and outputs at Huntley, Boorne & Stevens

If we look at the workings of any business we will notice interdependence both within the firm and between the firm and its wider environment (see Fig. 1.11). Huntley, Boorne & Stevens makes a wide range of tin boxes of many different shapes and sizes. These boxes are used for packaging biscuits, sweets, tea, commemorative chocolates and many other things.

Huntley, Boorne & Stevens also have an aerosol line which is highly automated. As well as specialist management staff there is a wide range of other specialist jobs resulting from extensive division of labour. Specialist staff include:

1. Salespeople
2. Design artists
3. Engineering designers
4. Printers
5. Factory-floor workers
6. Engineers
7. Buyers
8. Office workers
9. Cleaners
10. Lorry drivers
11. Canteen workers
12. Secretarial staff

If we then go on to study the inputs of the business we can see that inputs come from various

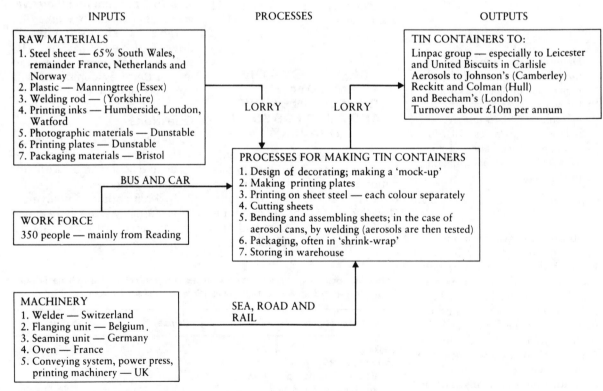

Figure 1.11 Inputs, processes and outputs at Huntley, Boorne & Stevens Ltd.

10

parts of the UK and the world. If we look at the processes involved in production we can see a wide range of specialist yet interdependent tasks. If we look at the outputs of the firm we notice that many outlets are supplied and eventually products will be distributed all over the world.

We can see that the process of manufacture and distribution is held together by a transport network. In addition the firm will have to use a wide range of specialist business services including banks, insurance services, import/export agencies, translation services, and postal and telecommunications facilities. Business takes place in a very wide setting and Huntley, Boorne & Stevens will have as much interest in changes taking place in Bristol and Belgium as in those occurring in Reading.

The internal structure of a business

The internal organization of a business is usually illustrated by an *organigram* which shows the lines of control within a business. The organization of a business will vary greatly according to the size and nature of a business. A small firm will have fewer posts of responsibility and different organizations will have different officials. It would be very unlikely for a firm that concentrated on selling, for instance, to have the same group of managers as one that concentrated on production.

Because small firms employ fewer people they cannot be organized so easily into departments, and management will have more general functions. In large firms specialist officers will be appointed who concentrate on narrower areas.

Departmental organization in large businesses

Large organizations in the UK will normally be private companies, public companies or public corporations (see the chapter on ownership and control—Chapter 2). In this section we will concentrate on the sort of organization structure which we might expect in a large public company.

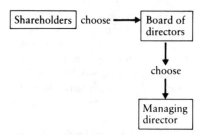

Figure 1.12 The control structure of a large public company.

The company will be owned by shareholders who appoint a committee known as a board of directors to represent their interests. The board of directors then appoints a managing director who, like a head-teacher or the principal of a college, has the job of making sure that all the various departments are running effectively. (See Fig. 1.12.)

Every organization is different and any organizational structure will be aimed at meeting the particular needs of that body. The organigram in Fig. 1.13 may be found in some company structures but you are more than likely to find something completely different.

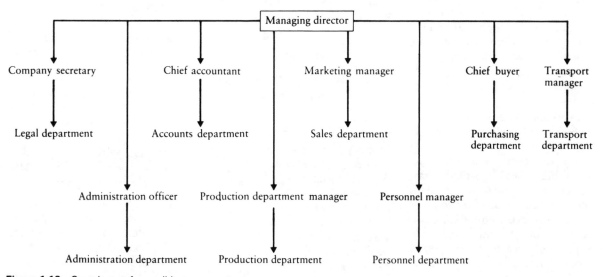

Figure 1.13 Organigram of a possible company structure.

11

The company secretary and the legal department

The company secretary is responsible for all the legal matters of the company. If paperwork is not done properly, the company secretary could end up in court. He or she must fill in the documents that set up the company and keep the share register. Other departmental managers may consult the company secretary on legal matters.

The administration officer and administration department

Many large firms have a central office which is responsible for controlling the general paperwork of the firm. This department might handle the filing of materials, the company's mail, word-processing and data-handling facilities. The modern office is increasingly using computers and information technology.

The chief accountant and accounts office

The chief accountant is responsible for supervising the accounts department. The accounts section must keep a detailed record of all money paid in and out and present the final balance sheet at the end of the year. Modern accounts are stored on computer files and accounting procedures are greatly simplified by the use of computers.

The production department manager and production department

The production manager is responsible for making sure that raw materials are provided and made into finished goods effectively. He or she must make sure that work is carried out smoothly, and must supervise procedures for making work more efficient and more enjoyable.

The marketing manager and sales department

The content of the marketing department will vary from firm to firm. Sometimes sales and marketing are split. In a combined marketing/sales department the manager will be responsible for market research, promotions, advertising and the organization of product sales.

The personnel manager and personnel department

The personnel department is responsible for the recruitment and training of staff. It is also responsible for health and safety at work, trade-union negotiations and staff welfare.

The chief buyer and the purchasing department

The buying department of a firm is responsible for all items bought by the firm. It sends for quotations from suppliers, issues orders and keeps track of the delivery of goods. It also checks that the prices, quantities and quality of goods received are as expected.

The transport department

This department is responsible for obtaining supplies and ensuring delivery of goods.

QUESTIONS

1. Complete the following sentences using the words below.

Mixed economy
Centrally planned economy
Free-market economy
Opportunity cost
Specialization
Interdependence
Division of labour
Resource
Public sector
Private sector

(a) A .... is a 'means of support'.
(b) The .... involves each member of the workforce concentrating on a specialized task.
(c) By .... we mean the next best alternative that is sacrificed.
(d) In a .... major decisions are fed through a planning agency.
(e) In a .... decisions about what, how and for whom are made by prices.
(f) A .... combines elements of central planning and the free market.
(g) The .... is the government-owned sector of the economy.
(h) The .... is made up of privately owned businesses.
(i) The .... of economic units is one of the basic facts of business life.
(j) .... involves individual workers concentrating on given skills.

2. Table 1.3 shows employment by sector in a town in the Midlands.

Table 1.3 Employment by sector in a Midlands town, 1967–87. (The table does not include the unemployed.)

Sector	% employed 1967	1977	1987
Primary	8	6	4
Secondary	45	41	37
Tertiary	47	53	59

(a) Give examples of occupations that would be included in the primary, secondary and tertiary sectors respectively.
(b) Draw a bar graph to show

the distribution of employment between sectors in 1987.

(c) Draw a line graph to show the change in employment in the three sectors over time.

(d) Analyse the above information to explain the way in which the employment pattern has changed over time.

(e) What further information would you require to make a more detailed analysis?

(f) What use could be made of statistics dividing the work-force into employment by sector?

3. Draw an organigram to illustrate the line of command in a small bank branch with three counter clerks, a supervisor and a branch manager.

4. Who would you expect the following employees to report to in a large public company?

(a) A salesperson
(b) A machine minder
(c) The production manager
(d) A buyer
(e) The managing director
(f) A word-processor operator
(g) A legal clerk
(h) A trainee accountant
(i) A lorry driver

5. Which of the following are centrally planned economies?

(a) Tanzania
(b) Kenya
(c) The UK
(d) South Africa
(e) India
(f) Hungary
(g) The Soviet Union
(h) Hong Kong
(i) Italy
(j) East Germany
(k) Jordan
(l) Mexico
(m) Albania

6. Explain how the principle of specialization applies in a department store.

7. Sarah Jones has set up a small florist's business. List the main aims the business may have. Do any of these aims conflict with each other?

8. Why is it easier for large businesses to organize into departments than for small business?

9. What would you consider to be the five main departments of the following?

(a) An insurance company
(b) A chocolate manufacturer

COURSEWORK

1. Study the passage below which is based on an article that appeared in a national newspaper:

Central Football Club and Royal Park Rangers will cease to exist in their present form at the end of the season, when they are to be amalgamated. Under the terms of the deal agreed, third-division Central FC is to merge with its first-division neighbours, playing on possibly as Central Park Rangers at Royal Park, the ground of Rangers.

Multi Estates, a property development company, which already owns the land on which several London football clubs have their grounds, including Central FC, yesterday gained control over Royal Park by buying up the greater part of the club's shares from the present chairperson.

Central FC has been a football club for 89 years and now Multi Estates will develop the land into new luxury apartments overlooking the River Thames. The chairperson of Central FC is also the chairperson of Multi Estates and he

told this paper yesterday: 'The small number of fans we still have at Central FC will appreciate that it is not very economical, in the long run, for the club to continue on its own.' A spokesperson for Multi Estates confirmed that Central's ground will be converted into luxury flats probably using the name 'Boat Race Towers'.

Commenting on this development, the Football League secretary, Graham Kelly, said: 'Obviously this is a blow, but there has been talk of rationalization for a long time. Perhaps there are too many clubs in the league and we might be able to operate better with a smaller number.'

(a) Find out the meaning of the following terms used in the passage:

(i) Amalgamated
(ii) Merge
(iii) Property-development company
(iv) Gained control
(v) Chairperson
(vi) Develop the land
(vii) Spokesperson
(viii) Rationalization

(b) Make a table showing the people and groups you think will benefit from the change and those who will lose out by it.

(c) How did Multi Estates gain possession of Central Football Club?

(d) What is Multi Estates going to do with the site of Central Football Club?

(e) The chairperson of Central Football Club is quoted as saying, 'The small number of fans we still have at Central FC will appreciate that it is not very economical, in the long run, for the club to continue on its own.' Do you agree with this statement? Give reasons for your answer.

(f) What do you think are the implications of the above statement for types of organization other than football clubs?

(g) Using your local newspaper find a local issue involving alternative uses of land. Develop a questionnaire to interview the public to gauge the extent of feeling in the local community. What are the main groups involved in the issue? Write a report summarizing their views. Why do you think they have these views?

2. Pick a local business and describe how it is organized. This could be done as a piece of groupwork. The class could be split up to find out the organizational structure in different types of business organization. It could be used as a basis for comparing the organization structure in different sizes of firms or in firms dealing with different types of product.

2 Ownership and control

There are various types of business organization and each of these types is subject to different kinds of control. The UK has a mixed economy and this means that, as well as many businesses being privately owned, many organizations are run by the State. (See Fig. 2.1.)

Private limited companies and *public limited companies* have limited liability whereas *partnerships* and *sole traders* have unlimited liability. Limited liability means that, if the business goes bankrupt because it is unable to meet its debts, the shareholders/owners will not be liable to lose their personal possessions to pay the money that is owed. They will only lose the value of their investment.

Private enterprise

The sole trader

This is the most common form of business ownership and the easiest to set up. A sole trader is a business owned by one person though, of course, this business might employ a large number of people. A sole trader might be a removal firm, gardener, window cleaner, small retailer, electrician, etc.

Table 2.1, on page 16, outlines some of the advantages and disadvantages of this form of business ownership.

The pressures of competing with larger units cause many sole traders to go out of business. In order to overcome the risks of being small, an owner may look to expand his or her organization by taking in partners.

Partnership

Partnerships generally have to have

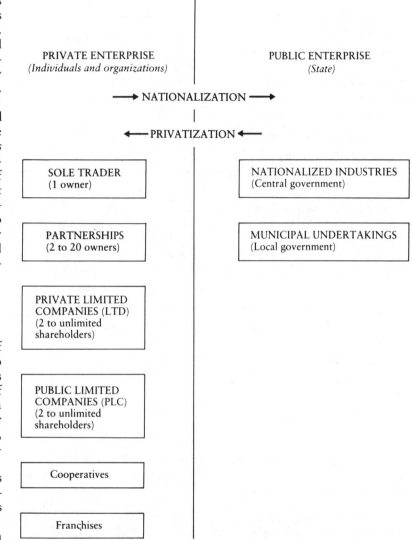

Figure 2.1 The different types of private and public enterprise.

between 2 and 20 members, though there are some exceptions. The Partnership Act of 1890 established rules which partners could refer to as a last resort; these related to agreements between partners. Most partnerships draw up some form of partnership deed which refers to financial matters affecting each partner, e.g. capital contributed, drawings, salary, etc., as

15

Table 2.1 Advantages and disadvantages of being in business as a sole trader.

Advantages	Disadvantages
Easy to set up as no special paperwork is required.	Having unlimited liability endangers personal possessions.
Generally these are small businesses, so less capital required.	Finance can be difficult to raise.
Speedy decisions can be made as few people are involved.	Small scale limits discounts and other benefits of large-scale production.
Personal attention is given to company affairs.	Prices are often higher than those of larger organizations.
Special services can be offered to customers.	Ill-health/holidays etc may affect the running of the business.
Cater for the needs of local people.	
Profits do not have to be shared.	
Business affairs can be kept private.	

Table 2.2 Advantages and disadvantages of a business partnership.

Advantages	Disadvantages
Capital from partners.	Unlimited liability (except for sleeping partners).
Larger-scale opportunities than for the sole trader.	Disagreements between partners.
Spreads responsibilities and decisions.	Limitation on number of partners.
Members of family can be introduced to business.	Partnerships have to be re-formed if partner dies.
Affairs can still be kept private.	
Reduces the responsibility of a one-person business.	

well as the general rules and guidelines for running the business–the introduction of new partners, disputes, etc.

Limited or sleeping partners may be introduced to a partnership and have limited liability as long as they take no active part in the running of the business. However, there must always be at least one partner with unlimited liability.

Table 2.2 outlines some of the advantages and disadvantages of this form of business ownership.

Private limited company ('Ltd')

The owners of limited companies are called shareholders because they each own a share in the business. Private companies must have at least two shareholders but there is no upper limit to the number of shareholders and companies can expand by selling more shares. However, the shares of private companies are not quoted on the Stock Exchange and they are not allowed to advertise the sale of shares publicly. There is also a danger of issuing too many shares and thus having to divide the profits between large numbers of shareholders. The liability of shareholders is limited to the value of their shareholding and, to warn creditors about the dangers of dealing with these companies, 'Limited' (or 'Ltd') appears after their name.

All limited companies must comply with the Companies Acts of 1948 and 1980 and register with the Registrar of Companies. In order to register a prospective company, two documents have to be completed. These are the *memorandum of association* and the *articles of association*.

The memorandum of association outlines the relationships of a company with the outside world. For example, it would state the name of the company, the purpose of the company, and what the company does.

The articles of association state the internal rules determining the company's organization, including rules regarding meetings and the voting rights of shareholders, and include the list of directors, etc. Shareholders can vote to change the articles.

Once the articles and memorandum have been received by the Registrar of Companies, together with a number of legal declarations, the Registrar will provide a Certificate of Incorporation and the private limited company will start trading.

Table 2.3 outlines some of the advantages and disadvantages of this form of business ownership.

If a company needs to get more capital in order to expand, it may consider 'going public' and having its shares quoted on the Stock Market (see Fig. 2.2). This became easier to do in 1980, when the Stock Exchange created the Unlisted Securities Market (USM) to enable smaller businesses to sell shares to the public.

Public limited company ('plc')

These have the opportunity to

Table 2.3 Advantages and disadvantages of the private limited company.

Advantages	Disadvantages
Money from shares.	Cannot sell shares on the stock market.
Firm grows bigger.	Accounts not private.
Limited liability.	Limitations on capital.

Table 2.4 Advantages and disadvantages of the public limited company.

Advantages	Disadvantages
Limited liability for shareholders.	Formation can be expensive.
Easy to raise capital.	Decisions can be slow and 'red tape' can be a problem.
Operates on a large scale.	Problems of being too large.
Easy to raise finance from banks.	Employees and shareholders distanced from one another.
Employs specialists.	Affairs are public.

Figure 2.2 The Stock Exchange. (*Source:* Bank Information Service)

become larger than the other forms of private business organization. They are allowed to raise capital through the Stock Exchange, which quotes their share prices.

Only two persons are needed to form a public company and there is no stated maximum of shareholders. The process of becoming a public company is in many ways similar to that for a private company. A memorandum of association and articles of association, as well as a variety of other legal documents, have to be approved by the Registrar of Companies, who will issue a Certificate of Incorporation as evidence that the company is registered. The public company will then have to issue a *prospectus*, which is an advertisement or invitation to the public to buy shares in the company. The issuing of shares then takes place and the Registrar of Companies issues a Trading Certificate. Business can then start and share prices will be quoted on the stock market.

Table 2.4 outlines some of the advantages and disadvantages of this form of business ownership.

Shares may be issued when a new company is formed, when a nationalized industry is privatized, when a public limited company wishes to raise additional capital and when a private limited company wishes to become a public limited company.

Without the Stock Market, public companies could not operate on the scale that they do and the selling of a variety of securities helps both industry and the government. Fig. 2.3, on page 18, shows types of shares and securities sold on the stock market.

Shareholders receive dividends as a return on their shareholding. These are provided at a set percentage of the original sale price of the share. If a share was sold for £1 (par value) and the dividend is 10 per cent, the shareholder will receive 10p for each share he or she holds.

However, if the market value of that share rises to £2 and the dividend is 10 per cent, the shareholder will receive 10p per share which is only a 5 per cent return on his or her capital. This would be a low yield and shareholders would have to consider alternatives unless they expected the market price of the share to rise and/or expected a higher dividend in future years.

On 27 October 1986 changes

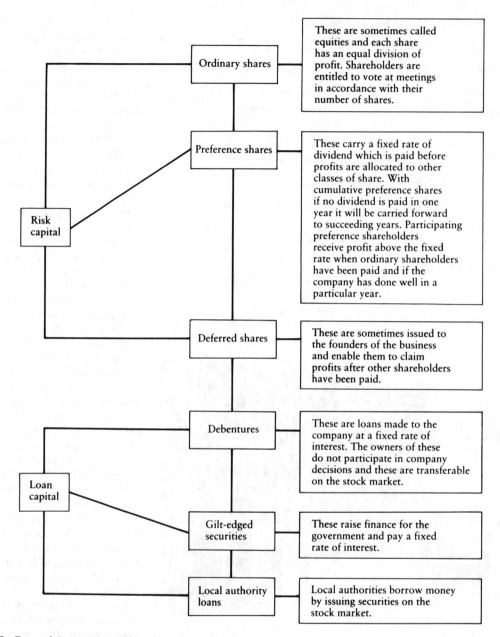

Figure 2.3 Types of shares and securities sold on the stock market.

which became known as the Big Bang took place, bringing fundamental alteration to the role of the Stock Exchange. They abolished the separation of 'brokers' and 'jobbers' (a jobber was a wholesaler in shares who did not meet the public), and also did away with minimum commission so that brokers can charge as little as they like. A broker is a person who buys or sells something for someone else. A stockbroker buys or sells shares for a member of the public.

Some giant public companies such as Shell, Tate & Lyle, and Marks & Spencer have manufacturing and sales outlets in many countries. These business units are sometimes called 'multinationals' and have greater powers to control and change prices because of their size and because they can switch their operations between countries. Because they employ so many people they can sometimes influence national policy decisions.

Cooperative

The cooperative movement began with the Rochdale Pioneers in 1844 with the aim of benefiting customers by buying goods in bulk and ploughing back the profits. Customers own the business and receive dividends in relation to their purchases.

In recent years the term 'workers' cooperative' has become widely known. This term has been applied to factories where the workers have attempted to keep the business operating by taking on the responsibility of management, organization and ownership.

The producers' cooperative has become quite popular as a form of organization for small businesses in Britain in the 1980s. In the 1970s producers' cooperative often came about as a result of workers taking over firms which were already in financial difficulty. As a result they were faced with many difficulties and many collapsed. Today the cooperative structure is more often being chosen by new businesses, particularly in the clothing industry, by small modern engineering firms and in road haulage, and these cooperatives are more successful.

Producers' cooperatives are run in the interests of the workers rather than for shareholders. Workers run the cooperative and make the decisions. They are thus working for themselves. A problem for such an organization will be finding capital. Thus cooperatives are often set up in industries where only a little capital is needed.

Another problem is that workers may not have the necessary management expertise. However, some modern cooperatives are made up of groups with considerable managerial expertise. Members of the cooperative must decide on the hours to be worked, the products to be produced, methods of production and marketing, how profits are to be shared out and all the other business issues. As a result they normally establish some form of management structure.

Franchising

A recent development in the UK which will continue to grow in the 1990s is franchising. A franchising company such as Thornton's toffee company sells the franchise, i.e. the sole right of selling its product, to private individuals. The person taking out the franchise puts up the capital but is usually supplied with equipment, training, merchandise and a well-known name to trade under.

Building societies

The organization of building societies is somewhat different from that of other businesses. They do not set out to make a profit and are supervised by the Registrar of Friendly Societies rather than the Registrar of Companies. In the late 1980s the trend is for there to be fewer and fewer building societies as the smaller ones are swallowed up by merger with larger societies. Today the banks and building societies are competing vigorously to take over business from each other. In the past building societies tended to act as a middle body taking money from savers and re-lending it to individuals and firms that wanted to buy property. The building society would lend by means of a mortgage, which is a long-term loan often repayable over a period of 20 or 25 years usually to purchase a house. The building society would then hold the deeds of the property until such time as the mortgage had been repaid. If the borrower ran into financial problems the building society could then resell the house.

The building societies charge interest to borrowers of money and pay out interest to people who save money in the building society.

Nowadays all the main banks also offer mortgages and so there is some healthy competition in this field. In their turn the major building societies are offering many bank services such as cheques, cash-dispensing machines and standing-order services. It is likely that in future building-society accounts and bank accounts will become increasingly similar.

Public enterprise

Public corporations

In the UK the government still owns a number of industries and businesses on behalf of the people. Most of these take the form of public corporations.

A public corporation is set up by an Act of Parliament. Examples of public corporations include British Rail, British Coal and the Bank of England. Once a public corporation has been set up, the government appoints a chairperson to be responsible for the day-to-day running of the industry.

There are a number of reasons why public corporations have been set up:

1. To avoid wasteful duplication. In the nineteenth century, for example, there were three railway lines between Leeds and Harrogate. This is wasteful competition. Imagine the problems caused by having three electricity companies operating in your street.
2. To set up and run services which might not be profitable. Would a private company supply post, electricity, gas and water to a small remote village if a lot of capital is needed to set up services which may not make a profit?
3. To gain the benefits of large-scale production. It may be more effi-

cient to have one big firm producing lots of output than to have several smaller firms. When there is only one firm the government as owner might be less inclined to charge high prices than a private firm.

4. To protect employment. The government might take into consideration the need to create and keep jobs rather than just considering profits.
5. To control industries which are important to the country such as coal, steel and the railways.

During the 1980s a number of public corporations have been privatized. This means that they have been sold to shareholders. There are a number of reasons for this, including the following:

1. Some people argue that state-run firms are not efficient because they do not have any real competition and do not have the threat of going bankrupt because the government will always pay off their debts.
2. It is argued that in a modern society as many people as possible should have shares in businesses. The idea is that everyone—not just the very rich—should become shareholders and therefore people have been encouraged to buy just a few hundred pounds' worth of shares in enterprises like British Telecom and British Gas.

When a public corporation is set up, an independent body is also formed to protect consumers' interests. Consumers can take their complaints to this body; for example, the Post Office Users' National Council will take up complaints made by users of the Post Office such as those about the late delivery of letters.

The government keeps the power to make major decisions about how public corporations should run such

as the decision to close down large sections of the railway network and whether to build new power stations. However, the chairperson and managers will decide on day-to-day issues such as wages and prices, time-tables and industrial relations. The government does sometimes interfere even in these areas, leading to public argument and debate.

Whereas a limited company has to make an annual report to its shareholders, a public corporation must present its annual report to the appropriate government minister, who makes a verbal report to Parliament, and at this time Members of Parliament will make criticisms or voice support for the way the corporation is running. A committee of MPs has the job of studying the running of each public corporation and of reporting on its operation. For example, there is a select committee of MPs acting as a watchdog over British Coal.

Municipal undertakings/local government

In the UK certain services in local areas are supervised by locally elected councils. These councils usually run some forms of business organizations such as the municipal car-parks, swimming-baths, sports centres, bus services, toilets, etc. Local councils receive money from two main sources: a grant given to them by central government, and a local tax. Local councils often subsidize loss-making activities such as local parks which provide a real benefit to the community.

CASE STUDY—A PRIVATE COMPANY

Tessier Printed Circuits Ltd is a private company situated in Langley on the outskirts of Slough. The company was set up in 1942.

Nowadays it has two main shareholders who are both active in the running of the company. In a private company shares can only be sold with the permission of the board of directors. In total there are five shareholders but the bulk of the shares are held by Mr Pugsley (the chairperson) and Mr Taylor— (the managing director).

Because there are only two main shareholders, not only are they the major owners of the business, but they also control it. They make the major decisions and they can make them quickly. They both draw healthy salaries from the company, and should the company run into financial difficulty the maximum amount they could lose would be the value of their shareholding because they have limited liability.

The company manufactures *printed circuit boards* which go into the back of radios, videos, televisions and other electrical equipment. Tessier Ltd is a classic case of a private company operating in a market which is best suited to small firms which can change their technology quickly as the market changes. In the UK there are over 400 companies in the printed-circuit market. The business is subject to frequent changes in demand and companies need to be sharp in winning orders in a very competitive market.

Questions

1. Who owns Tessier Ltd?
2. What is meant by 'limited liability'?
3. Why can Tessier Ltd make quick decisions?
4. From reading the case study, make a list of the advantages and disadvantages of being a private company.

CASE STUDY— FRANCHISING

Mary Watson had worked for a local builder as a contract plumber for several years. She worked long hours and the work was irregular. In September 1984 she saw an advertisement in a national newspaper inviting people to buy franchises for £20 000 from a franchising company called National-Rod.

Using her savings and a loan from the bank she was able to buy a franchise. National-Rod provided her with training and equipment (an electric plumbing device that quickly unblocks drains and pipes, and a van). She was also given the monopoly of selling her services within a 10 mile radius and the right to trade under a nationally advertised name.

In return, Mary had to hand over 5 per cent of her profits to National-Rod.

Mary described the advantages: 'At last I am working for myself. I work hard but I know nearly all the profits are my own. I work my own hours and there is nobody to tell me what to do.'

Questions

1. Make a list of what you consider to be the advantages and disadvantages for an individual taking out a franchise.
2. Make a list of what you consider to be the main advantages and disadvantages for the company granting a franchise.
3. In what lines of business is the franchise system operated in the UK?

CASE STUDY—MARKS & SPENCER plc.

Michael Marks arrived in the north of England in 1881 from Russia as a Jewish immigrant. He started off as a hawker (a person who sells from door to door), going around the mining villages selling buttons, needles, ribbons and other small items. He adopted a slogan which he tied on his tray: it said, 'Don't ask the price, it's a penny'. He had this slogan to avoid complications as he could not speak much English.

After he had become quite successful he hired a stall at Leeds market, and as this brought in profits, he started to hire stalls at different markets. He decided that to become more successful he would have to find a partner. In 1894 he became partners with Tom Spencer. Spencer put in £300 to become a partner.

Soon they had 24 stalls at markets and 12 shops. They each began to specialize in specific jobs. Spencer would mainly work at the warehouse and organize administration, whereas Marks specialized in buying goods and looking for new places from which to sell. Their shops were all 'penny bazaars'.

Unfortunately, Spencer became an alcoholic and less reliable. They decided to open up the company into a private company with Marks and Spencer being the major shareholders. Michael Marks remained with the business whereas Spencer retired and left to run a chicken farm. Marks was, therefore, an executive director and ran the company while Spencer was willing to sit back and be a non-executive director.

Michael Marks and Tom Spencer died and Simon Marks (Michael's son) began to develop an important role in the running of the company. His boyhood friend Israel Sieff also began to play an important part. Simon married Israel's sister, and Israel married Simon's sister.

In the early 1920s, Simon Marks went to America to learn about retailing. When he returned he decided that he wanted to change the image of Marks & Spencer, giving it a more up-market image. He decided to expand into a whole chain of stores, and start buying from manufacturers in bulk, so getting a discount, as opposed to buying from wholesalers.

To get the capital for doing this, the company decided to become a public company and sell shares on the Stock Exchange. From here, Marks & Spencer grew to the size it is today and developed the image and quality that it has today. There are now a large number of shareholders and it is controlled by a board of directors.

The four stages in the growth of Marks & Spencer are summarized in Fig. 2.4.

Type of business	Ownership	Control
One-person business	Michael Marks	Michael Marks
Partnership	Michael Marks and Tom Spencer	Michael Marks and Tom Spencer
Private company	Marks and Spencer and other shareholders	Michael Marks and other executive directors
Public company	Shareholders	Directors, including Sieff family

Figure 2.4 The development of Marks & Spencer.

Questions

1. List the four stages in the growth of Marks & Spencer.
2. Explain why Marks & Spencer went through these four stages of growth.
3. Explain why ownership and control are not always in the same hands in a public company.

CASE STUDY—HOW SHARE BUYING WORKS

A member of the public can buy or sell shares by asking his or her bank manager to approach a broker/dealer on his or her behalf or by going direct to a broker/dealer in person. The broker/dealer will be a member of a firm that operates at the Stock Exchange. Nowadays much of the work involving share dealing is done through computer terminals. If Jane Smith asks her broker/dealer to buy shares in Shell then the broker/dealer will consult a visual display unit showing the prices at which other broker/dealers will be prepared to sell shares. Firms that are prepared to deal in stocks and shares are known as market-makers. As Jane Smith wants to buy Shell shares her broker/dealer will look for the name at the top of the display screen showing firms offering Shell shares. The name at the top of the screen will be the market-maker selling Shell shares for the lowest price. The price of the shares will be shown in pence. There will always be at least 2 market-makers for a share but there may be as many as 20.

If Adrian Manley wishes to sell ICI shares then he will ask his broker/dealer to sell them for him. The broker/dealer in this case would consult another visual display unit. The market-maker offer-ing the highest price for ICI shares would now appear at the top of this screen. Broker/dealers earn a commission for dealing in shares. The system whereby market-makers make deals by computer link-up is known as the Stock Exchange Automated Quotation System (SEAQ system) and the visual display units are known as SEAQ screens.

On the day the deal is struck a contract note will be sent to the investor.

Questions

1. What is an investor?
2. What does a broker/dealer on the Stock Exchange do?
3. What does a market-maker do?
4. Explain how market-makers compete.
5. Explain how SEAQ screens make Stock Exchange trading possible.
6. Why do you think that members of the public cannot go direct to the Stock Exchange to buy stocks and shares?

CASE STUDY— MULTINATIONALS

The Indies Sugar Company was set up in the nineteenth century by two families, the Taylors and the Jones, with sugar plantations in the West Indies and South America. Between the Wars it went public with a very large issue of shares and attracted many small shareholders although the bulk of the shares remained with the families.

After the Second World War, the firm bought its own fleet of merchant ships, a wholesaling chain, and a soft-drinks manufacturing plant. It became one of the world's major multinationals in the sugar business, establishing pro-cessing plants and distribution networks in five continents. In total it employed 32 000 people throughout the world.

In 1970, it closed down production plants in several African countries because of civil unrest, and in 1972 it closed down a plant in France because of industrial action. At the same time it opened up a major refinery and European base in Spain where wages were cheaper and taxation was lower.

In the late 1970s it moved its head office to Spain and sold off its soft-drinks plant to another multinational.

Questions

1. Why can the Indies Sugar Company be described as a multinational?
2. What advantages and disadvantages are there to being a multinational?
3. Why do multinationals switch their operations between countries?
4. List five other multinational companies.
5. In which country would you expect to find the head office of the greatest number of multinationals?

CASE STUDY—RETAIL COOPERATIVES

Nowadays, people tend to think of the Co-op as just another supermarket chain. This is not the case. Co-ops place far greater emphasis on serving the community. The first co-op was set up by a group of weavers in Toad Lane in Rochdale in 1844. At that time, workers were paid low wages partly made up of tokens which could only be exchanged in the company shop where prices were high.

Twenty-eight weavers, known

as the Rochdale Pioneers, pooled money to buy foodstuffs at wholesale prices which were then sold cheaply to members. Profits were shared out amongst members in the form of a dividend depending on how much each had bought. Since then Co-ops have spread and there are many retail Co-ops in Britain.

To become a shareholder in a Co-op you need only buy a £1 share and this entitles you to a vote at meetings to chose the president and other officers of the local Co-op society.

Co-ops now give stamps to shoppers. These stamps can be collected and stuck in books which can be used in payment for goods. This is the new way of distributing the Co-ops' dividend. In the 1980s, the Co-ops feel that they should plough some of their profits into the local community. The idea is to give a 'social dividend'—i.e. profits of local Co-ops should be ploughed into projects like building local sports centres and homes for old people.

Some Co-ops don't just provide supermarket services; they also have their own bank, milk delivery service, funeral service and libraries and provide other benefits such as community-life education courses.

In the later part of the nineteenth century the Co-ops flourished and societies sprang up all over Britain. It was the Co-ops that brought in the first supermarkets. However, the multiples like Tesco have been much too competitive for the Co-ops. The Co-ops were organized into too many small societies and did not really benefit from bulk buying. They employed inexperienced managers and generally were not as slick as the new multiples.

The Co-ops have continued to suffer with the development of the new hypermarkets. To fight back, small societies have merged together, small shops have been closed and in the 1980s the Co-ops have started to build their own hypermarkets. The Co-ops are now beginning to employ specialist managers with good qualifications and retailing experience.

Questions

1. How do you become a member of a retail cooperative?
2. How has the way in which the Co-ops distribute their dividend changed over the years?
3. What is meant by a 'social dividend'?
4. What is the main difference between retail cooperatives and other private retailers?

CASE STUDY—BRITISH COAL

British Coal (which used to be called the National Coal Board) was nationalized in 1947 by Act of Parliament. It is a public corporation and general policy is supervised by a government industry minister. However, like all public corporations, the day-to-day running of the industry is in the hands of a chairperson and board of managers. Since the Second World War the profitability of the industry has depended very much on the price of competing fuels. With the oil price rises of the 1970s, the coal industry was fairly prosperous. However, many pits became out of date. Many pits were small, coal seams were fractured and coal was sometimes miles underground. Coal production was expensive in terms of labour and other costs. This compares unfavourably with coal min-

ing in countries like Australia and the United States, where coal lies at the land surface, and far less labour is required and modern cutting machinery is easily employed.

In the 1980s, British Coal has been cutting back the labour force dramatically. In 1984, British Coal experienced widespread industrial action as a result of its pit-closure plans. Negotiations between management and trade union were heated. In the meantime, the government stood back saying that negotiation was in the hands of the day-to-day managers.

Questions

1. How is a public corporation set up?
2. Who owns a public corporation?
3. Who is responsible for the general policy of a public corporation?
4. Who is responsible for its day-to-day running?
5. How are coal consumers interests protected?
6. Should the number of workers employed by British Coal be cut?

QUESTIONS

1. Complete the following sentences using the words below.

Producers' cooperative
Sole trader
Partnership
Private company
Public companies
Nationalization
Public corporations
Privatization
Franchising
Multinational company
Limited liability

(a) The process through which the government takes control over industries from the private sector is known as ....

(b) When workers set up a business organization which they run themselves they are said to have formed a ....

(c) A .... normally has to have between 2 and 20 owners.

(d) A .... produces and distributes goods in many countries.

(e) The process whereby the State sells off State industries to shareholders is known as ....

(f) Shareholders in companies can only lose the value of their shareholding. They are said to have ....

(g) A typical form of business ownership for an ice-cream seller or a decorator would be as a ....

(h) In the UK most nationalized industries take the form of ....

(i) .... is a system whereby you can buy the local monopoly to sell a product or service which is nationally advertised.

(j) In a .... shareholders can only sell shares with the permission of the board of directors.

(k) Secondhand shares in .... can be traded on the Stock Exchange.

2. Which of the following are in the private sector and which in the public sector?
   (a) British Coal
   (b) Private companies
   (c) Partnerships
   (d) Municipal enterprises
   (e) Public corporations
   (f) The Bank of England
   (g) Virgin Atlantic plc
   (h) Public companies
   (i) British Rail
   (j) A producers' cooperative

3. Which of the following might be reasons for privatization and which arguments for nationalization?
   (a) To reduce government control over the economy
   (b) To give consumers greater choice
   (c) To control industries of strategic importance
   (d) To create wider share ownership
   (e) To provide a social service
   (f) To control dangerous competition

4. Fig. 2.5 shows 14 town-centre business premises. List the three partnerships, the three

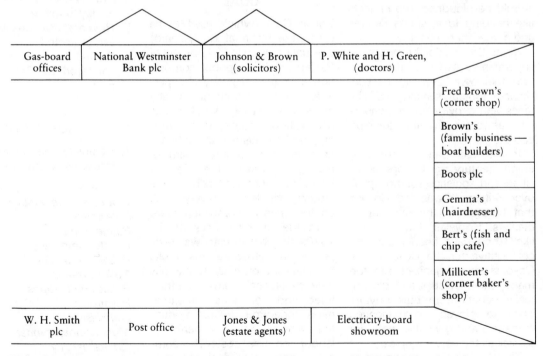

Gas-board offices	National Westminster Bank plc	Johnson & Brown (solicitors)	P. White and H. Green, (doctors)	
				Fred Brown's (corner shop)
				Brown's (family business — boat builders)
				Boots plc
				Gemma's (hairdresser)
				Bert's (fish and chip cafe)
				Millicent's (corner baker's shop)
W. H. Smith plc	Post office	Jones & Jones (estate agents)	Electricity-board showroom	

Figure 2.5 Fourteen businesses in a town centre.

public limited companies, the one private company, the four sole traders, the two government-owned nationalized industries, and the industry that has been privatized.

5. British Gas is an industry which benefits from economies of scale. Local bus services can be run on quite a small scale. Does this make the case for privatization stronger in the latter example?

6. Anna Neidzwiedzka wants to start up a small business producing tee shirts. She is not sure whether she has sufficient capital to start up on her own. Advise her on the advantages and pitfalls of taking on a partner.

7. Three men who have been unemployed for several years have been repairing bicycles at the local unemployment centre. The local council offers them a grant to set up a business of their own. They decide to set up a workers' cooperative. Why do you think they chose that form of organization?

8. Why do you think that large cutbacks are made in public corporations in the run-up to privatization?

COURSEWORK

This section on business units is a very fertile ground for coursework. Coursework assignments can either be broken down into group assignments or done by individuals.

Examples of groupwork

A study of a local firm or industry
This is another possibility for coursework and would be a useful class exercise or something for you to do during work experience. Work experience provides an excellent opportunity for coursework. This type of work, if presented as final coursework, needs to be kept tightly within the framework of the business-studies syllabus (i.e. be careful not to give merely descriptions).

The focus of the work should be an investigation of the firm. Working in a group, you should suggest possible questions.

- What does the firm produce?
- Who owns the firm?
- What factors of production are employed?
- How are these factors combined?
- How much do factors cost?
- How is production organized?
- How is value added to the product?
- What investment projects are there in operation?
- How are investment decisions made?
- How are the company's receipts distributed?
- What competition does the firm have?
- How does this affect pricing?

Having looked at the range of possible questions, you can split up into groups and choose a set of related questions which would enable you to establish a theme question for a piece of coursework.

Individual work

1. Interview a typical sole trader, e.g. a window cleaner, corner-shop owner, decorator or hot-dog seller. Pose your assignment as a question, e.g. 'What are the advantages of being a sole trader?' or 'What type of market is served by the sole trader?'

2. Similar exercises can be done with local partnerships and private companies. It is useful to make comparisons between different forms of organization. A suitable question might be, 'How is a partnership set up?' or 'How does a partnership operate?'

3. Nowadays you will often find examples of producers' co-operative in your local area. A suitable question could be, 'Why was the XYZ co-operative set up?'

4. Franchising is also a growing field of business. A suitable question might be, 'What are the advantages of the franchise system in the fast-food business?'

5. An interesting piece of coursework might be to study how a company goes public. This could be done through the newspapers and by writing off for a prospectus. The privatization of a public corporation could be handled in a similar way.

3 Influences on business activity

Business activity takes place against a background of many competing interests. These influences include:

1. Consumers
2. Suppliers
3. Other producers
4. Central government
5. Local government
6. Trade unions
7. Local residents

The effect of each of these influences is examined in other chapters but it is worth looking at them as a combined problem here. We will look first at the influences on an individual business person.

Francesco owns his own hairdressing business employing three full-time members of staff. He runs his own town-centre hairdressing salon (see Fig. 3.1) and over the years has built up a steady group of customers. However, he is aware that unless he charges competitive prices and offers a good, friendly service, customers will go elsewhere. His suppliers provide him with materials and equipment. If they raise their prices he will have to pass on the increases to his own customers. He usually buys his equipment on credit and so depends on the goodwill of his suppliers.

In the town centre there are three other salons offering similar facilities to Francesco's. It is important to keep an eye on their methods and any improvements that they make.

The way that Francesco runs his business is controlled by certain Acts of Parliament. He can only work six days a week and he must look closely at health and safety at work. He pays value added tax on the value added by his business and income tax on his own earnings.

Figure 3.1 Francesco and his hair salon. (*Source:* Kim Hooper, Reading)

The local council also exercises control over his activities in that he had to apply for planning permission to extend his business, he must be careful how he disposes of waste, and he also pays rates to the council.

Francesco's employees do not belong to a trade union but he is aware that if he does not offer acceptable conditions, he will find it hard to recruit the right sort of labour.

The business is located in a largely non-residential part of town. Francesco did, however, have a complaint from a neighbouring shop because Francesco's customers were parking their cars across the shop's loading bay.

Demand from consumers

The demand for a product means the actual amount that will be bought at a given price. Common sense tells us that more of a product will be bought at a cheaper than at a higher price. For example, market research on the number of people who would use a new swimming-pool produced the following results:

Price for adults	Demand to use the facility per week
£4	100
£3	150
£2	250
£1	800
75p	1200
50p	1400
40p	1500
30p	1600

Apart from price, other main influences on demand include the following:

Tastes

As time moves on, new products become more fashionable and popu-

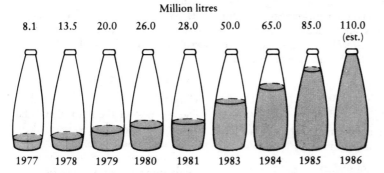

UK BOTTLED WATER CONSUMPTION

Million litres

| 8.1 | 13.5 | 20.0 | 26.0 | 28.0 | 50.0 | 65.0 | 85.0 | 110.0 (est.) |

| 1977 | 1978 | 1979 | 1980 | 1981 | 1983 | 1984 | 1985 | 1986 |

Source: Ashbourne Water

Figure 3.2   The consumption of bottled water in the UK between 1977 and 1986.

lar whilst others go into decline. In recent years, for instance, there has been a steady increase in the demand for mineral water (see Fig. 3.2). A number of reasons have been put forward for the current popularity of mineral water: the fashion for foodstuffs with no additives; the distaste for tap water, which for the Londoner has on average already passed through eight other Londoners beforehand; increased foreign travel, which has introduced more people to mineral water; the use of mineral water as a mixer with other drinks; and increased eating out.

Income

The more money people have, the easier it is for them to buy products. The amount of income people have to spend on goods is known as their disposable income and is their pay minus taxes and other deductions.

The price of substitute products

The demand for products which have close substitutes will often be strongly influenced by the price of the substitutes. This would be the case, for example, with tinned tomatoes and tinned fruit because there are many different brands of these products.

The price of complementary products

Some products are used together so that the demand for one is linked to the price of another. An example of this might be typewriters and typewriter ribbons. In a college it might be cheaper to train students in keyboarding skills by using manual rather than electronic trypewriters because the ribbons on electronic typewriters are far more expensive and have much shorter lifespans.

Suppliers

Most firms are part of a chain of production. Many producers are therefore influenced by what goes on at the previous stage. In the 1970s and 1980s this has been an important fact of life, particularly in the way that oil price changes have changed costs of production for all producers. In 1973 and 1979 there were dramatic rises in oil prices when oil exporters joined together to raise prices. Because fuel costs are a basic cost of production for most products, this led to price rises for thousands of products. This in turn led to wage increases for millions of workers to keep up living standards. Because wages are a cost

to producers, prices had to be raised again, leading to a period of instability.

Competition from other producers

This is a major influence on business behaviour. A firm's prices and many other policies will be influenced by the level of competition it faces. A business that does not face direct competition is said to have a monopoly. It does not have outside pressure on it to compete. We must be careful, however, not to assume that monopolies are inefficient. Monopolies will often put a lot of money into product development and research in order to keep up a long-term competitive edge.

Many markets in Britain have only a few producers or sellers in them.

> A **market** is a situation in which buyers and sellers come into contact.

Other markets are dominated by just a few firms. Examples of products made and sold in markets with few firms are:

– National newspapers
– Petrol
– Breakfast cereal
– Beer
– Biscuits
– Chocolates and sweets
– Disposable nappies
– Washing powder

These markets can be highly competitive and firms only keep up their profits by making very high sales.

Central government

The central authorities set up a legal framework within which businesses operate. As we shall see later, there is a wide range of laws that constrain the activities of businesses. The government establishes the rules of the game. An example of this is the way that the government has implemented anti-monopoly legislation to encourage competition between firms.

> **Monopoly legislation.** For over 40 years the UK government has tried to prevent companies and traders from holding too large a share of the production or sale of a good or service. As a result, some mergers between companies have been stopped and the activities of a number of companies have been enquired into by a government committee.

The Monopolies Commission is a body which has been set up to investigate cases involving monopoly situations referred to it by the government.

Local government

A small local business or a plant of a larger business must take into account local by-laws and rules. The local authorities are responsible for looking after the interests of local residents. Business activity is thus constrained by a wide range of local influences, including the protection of the local environment and planning-permission specifications. An example of this might be when a redevelopment project can only take place if it fits in with the style of the existing architecture.

Trade unions

These can be looked on as both an internal and an external influence on the business. The local branch of a trade union can be seen as part of a larger national movement. Bargaining may take place between a group of employers and trade-union representatives. Trade unions are dealt with in depth in Chapter 11.

Local residents

Local people may interact with a firm in a number of ways:

1. As consumers
2. As workers
3. As shareholders
4. As neighbours

In each of these situations the firm will have to take account of their interests.

The location of the business

One of the earliest decisions any entrepreneur has to make is where to locate his or her business. In order to do this, he or she has to make a careful assessment of costs. The ideal location would be the one where costs are minimized. The entrepreneur would need to look at the benefits which each area had to offer as well as any government help which might be available. (See Fig. 3.3.)

Factors affecting location

Market
The nearness of the market and the cost of delivering the goods are likely to be important factors. Centres of population tend to attract consumer-goods industries and many of these are likely to be *bulk-increasing industries*. These are industries where the output is more expensive to transport than the raw materials; so, in order to minimize transport costs, the businesses are located near to the market (see Fig. 3.4).

Raw materials
If the raw materials are bulky and expensive to transport it will clearly be in the entrepreneur's interest to locate near to them (see Fig. 3.5). These industries are known as *bulk-decreasing industries* as their output

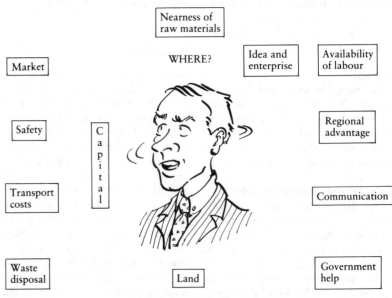

Figure 3.3 Factors affecting the location of a business.

Figure 3.4 Bulk-increasing industries are better placed near their market.

Figure 3.5 Bulk-decreasing industries are better placed near their source of raw materials.

is substantially cheaper to transport than their input.

Transport costs
The two major influences are the pull of the market and the pull of the raw materials and these are determined by whether or not the industry is bulk-increasing or bulk-decreasing.

Land
Land costs vary considerably nationally and some firms, e.g. wholesalers, might need a large square-footage. They might, therefore, be influenced by the cheaper rents and property prices found in some areas.

Labour
The availability of labour might well attract firms to an area, particularly if that labour force has the skills they require. If a firm moves to an area with a limited availability of labour, it might have to offer inducements to entice workers away from elsewhere. It could also be saddled with relocation expenses and the cost of training. This lack of availability of labour would increase costs.

Safety
Some industries have to locate their premises well away from high-density population levels and their choice of location is limited. These would include nuclear power stations, munitions factories and some chemical plants.

Waste disposal
Certain industries produce considerable waste and the costs associated with the disposal of this might affect their location.

Communications
The accessibility of motorways, ports and airports has become an increasingly important locational factor over recent years. A sound infrastructure creates the opportunity to trade with ease and this is reflected by the number of head offices in the South East.

Regional advantages
A number of facilities for certain industries might be concentrated in particular regions. A concentration of similar industries and subsidiary industries could well attract a firm, as could skilled labour, local research facilities and commercial markets.

Government
One of the aims of any government is to seek balanced economic growth. However, unemployment rates vary considerably between the regions. Governments attempts to create a balance and reduce this disparity in unemployment rates. Successive governments have attempted to provide locational inducements and thus influence the location of industry. Over the years, areas have been designated as Intermediate Areas, Development Area, Special Development Areas and Enterprise Zones, according to needs. Government help in these areas is offered in the form of grants for approved expenditure on buildings, removal grants, loans at favourable rates, factories to rent on favourable terms and help in transferring key workers.

Enterprise zones. Decaying inner-city areas have many problems including high unemployment. The old industries in these areas went into decline and new industry was not keen to set up in these areas. The government has created Enterprise Zones in many British cities, such as parts of Clydebank, London (Isle of Dogs) and Liverpool (Speke). A major encouragement for firms to move to these areas has been relief from local rates until 1991 and from certain other taxes as ·well. Some of these areas have had a lot of success, e.g. the Dockland Scheme in London. However, a criticism of such schemes is that they make the problems worse in neighbouring areas and that the new industries are not very labour-intensive.

Economies of scale

Every entrepreneur must aim for the scale of production which suits the business best. This level of production is achieved when unit costs are lowest for the output produced.

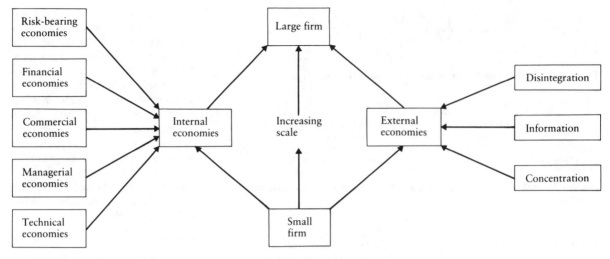

Figure 3.6 The economies of scale that come into play as a small firm becomes a large one.

Many businesses thrive more the larger they get and the advantages they gain are known as economies of scale.

Most advantages of being large are internal economies enjoyed by the firm as it benefits from becoming larger and makes the most of its situation. However, external economies outside the direct control of the firm can be enjoyed within its locality and market. (See Fig. 3.6.)

Internal economies of scale
Technical economies
Techniques and equipment can often be employed in large-scale production which cannot be adopted by small-scale producers. For example, a firm might have two machines which produce 1000 units per week; as the firm gets larger these machines might be able to be replaced by one machine which is technologically more advanced and produces 2500 units per week at lower unit costs. (See Fig. 3.7.)

Managerial economies
A large firm will employ specialist managers, such as cost and manage-ment accountants, marketing managers, etc. These well-qualified administrators will increase effi-ciency.

Commercial economies
As production is on a large scale, raw materials will have to be purchased in bulk, and bulk discounts from sup-pliers will reduce the unit cost. Larger firms may be able to organize their retail outlets or have a financial stake in their suppliers and thus collect profit at other stages. Market re-

Figure 3.7 Mass-production techniques allow low-cost production. (*Source:* Ford Picture Library)

30

search and advertising can be scientifically approached and rent can be spread over a larger output.

Financial economies

Large firms tend to be a secure investment and they find it easier to borrow money. Their reputation can often gain them loans at preferential interest rates.

Risk-bearing economies

Large-scale producers can benefit from spreading the risks both in the supply of raw materials and in changing customer demand. For example, a large-scale producer can invest in research and development and produce a wide range of products, thus covering itself against any reduction in business in any of its product areas.

External economies of scale
Concentration

As firms within an industry grow larger in a locality (e.g. steel in Sheffield), a concentration of special services develops. This might include local college courses, a skilled work force and a reputation.

Information

Larger industries can set up special information services to benefit producers, e.g. the *Building Trade Journal*, the Motor Industry Research Association.

Disintegration

Firms producing components might well be attracted to areas of specialized industries as well as firms able to help with maintenance and processes, e.g. software houses for the large computer companies in the Thames Valley.

Integration

In order to become large quickly and gain from specialization, many firms

Figure 3.8 Example of horizontal integration.

will look to merge with or take over others. Amalgamation increases size and enables companies to benefit from the economies of large-scale production. Works managers will prefer expansion with little variety in the size or colour of output, whereas sales managers will look for a wider variety to attract customers. Any decision to merge will be aimed either towards increasing the benefits of specialization or towards diversifying in order to minimize the risks.

Horizontal integration

This type of merger is where one company takes over another which produces goods of a similar type and which is involved at the same level of production. Companies will benefit from increasing economies such as having only one head office and this will also reduce competition but could ultimately lead to monopoly. (See Fig. 3.8.)

Vertical integration

Products are made in stages and often stages are carried out by separate

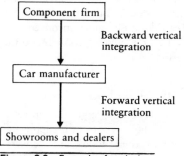

Figure 3.9 Example of vertical integration.

firms. This type of merger is where a firm either takes over a supplier or an outlet for its products which are involved at different levels of production. A backward vertical integration would be the take-over of a supplier and a forward vertical integration would be the take-over of an outlet. (See Fig. 3.9.)

Lateral integration

This is where two businesses merge that produce similar products which are not perfect substitutes. These types of mergers maximize risk-bearing economies. (See Fig. 3.10.)

Conglomerate integration

Another way of maximizing risk-bearing economies is for a firm to acquire businesses which are not connected in any way with its present activities. A conglomerate integration provides a perfect form of diversification. (See Fig. 3.11 on page 32.)

Holding/parent company

This type of company owns the majority of shares in another company and is thus able to control the other company's operations. A holding company creates the advantages of large-scale production whilst allowing subsidiaries to retain their independence.

Multinationals

Large companies will seek to expand their markets overseas and this often leads to opportunities to manufacture or assemble goods abroad. In many cases they will develop by

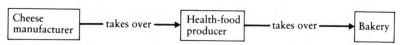

Figure 3.10 Example of lateral integration.

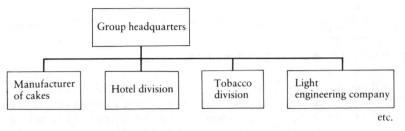

Figure 3.11 Example of conglomerate integration.

taking over companies in other countries. It is estimated that exports from the United States are only equivalent to about a quarter to a sixth of the goods produced by factories located overseas by their multinationals.

Diseconomies of scale

Despite the enormous advantages associated with large-scale production, the majority of business units in the UK tend to be small. Small companies often supply large companies with components and have the ability to provide specialist goods at low overheads. Small firms are also important in areas such as haulage, agriculture, retailing, building and professional services. In these areas it is possible to start with a relatively small amount of capital, make rapid decisions, compete with firms of similar size and provide for the personal requirements of customers. Large organizations are more difficult to manage and these inefficiencies are known as diseconomies of scale. These disadvantages of large-scale production are a predominant factor in many businesses wishing to remain relatively small.

Human relations
Large numbers of workers are always likely to be difficult to organize. Personal contact between senior staff and shop-floor workers will be reduced and this can often lead to problems of industrial relations. Larger firms tend to be involved in more industrial disputes than smaller firms.

Decisions and coordination
The sheer scale of production may limit the management's ability to respond to change and exploit the market. The improvement of products may involve considerable delays and cost while a production line is being fitted. Decisions may be discussed by a number of areas in a firm and this could involve considerable paperwork, large numbers of meetings and therefore wasted time. It is difficult for large organizations to provide a personal interest in satisfying customer demands.

External diseconomies
Public displeasure with a particular industry can turn into action which can affect output. For example, some large stores refuse to stock South African goods and the Campaign for Real Ale caused much inconvenience to the large brewing combines in the 1970s.

Competition

As firms become larger they increase their ability to control the supply and price of their goods and services. They are developing monopoly power. However, absolute monopolies, with total control over the supplies of goods and services in a particular field, are rare and in the UK tend to be state-controlled.

A technological monopoly exists in situations where only large firms can afford the vast amounts of capital needed to mass-produce certain products. Natural monopolies exist where one country has an almost exclusive supply of one type of mineral. Cartels exist where groups of firms in a particular industry meet to reduce competition between themselves, e.g. to change prices or to limit quotas.

Governments tend to be suspicious of all types of monopolies and are aware that these firms might not always operate in the interests of consumers. Since 1948, there has been a variety of legislation relating to monopolies and restrictive practices so that activities which are against the public's interest can be referred to Parliament. Activities which might be looked at include the removal of competitors, preventing entry into an industry, the making of abnormal profits and the fixing of prices by collusion.

CASE STUDY—A BUSINESS IN ITS ENVIRONMENT

Deborah Gomez (see Fig. 3.12) is the owner of the Waverley Gap Service Station which is located on a stretch of motorway on which there are no exits for 27 miles, giving her considerable *monopoly powers*. She is able to charge prices which are 15 per cent higher than the national average for petrol sales. However, weighed against this, she has to pay higher-than-average wages to attract staff. She is able to operate the firm on a 24 hour a day basis, but must keep a daily check on sales figures because the *turnover* is so high.

She buys in her supplies of fuel from a well-known *multinational* oil company. Because her demand for petrol and accessories is so high, she is able to negotiate a sizeable *trade discount*. However, she

Figure 3.12 Deborah Gomez and her service station. (*Source:* Kim Hooper, Reading)

finds that prices tend to fluctuate because of frequent price wars between the giant companies.

Because of the importance of the product, Deborah is not affected by regulations restricting Sunday trading. However, her pumps are regularly checked by the local *trading standards department* and her cashiers are only allowed to work the regulation number of hours in the day. She is also bound by local by-laws to keep her premises tidy and safe.

Questions

1. (a) Explain the following terms found in the case study:
    - (i) Monopoly powers
    - (ii) Turnover
    - (iii) Multinational
    - (iv) Trade discount
    - (v) Trading standards department
    (b) Explain one advantage and one disadvantage of the location.
2. Explain four different groups which might have an external influence on the activities of the garage.
3. (a) What do you learn from this case study about the following?
    - (i) The demand for petrol
    - (ii) The supply of petrol
    (b) Explain at least four ways in which Deborah could increase the sale of her petrol.
    (c) Why is she able to gain a trade discount?
4. (a) Why might the multinational consider buying up the Waverley Service Station?
    (b) What advantage does the Waverley have as a result of being owned by a sole trader?
5. Explain how you think Deborah's activities are influenced by having to take account of external influences?

CASE STUDY—LOCATING A TIN-BOX FACTORY

Firms belonging to a particular in-dustry need to take many factors into consideration when deciding upon the location of a plant or factory. Important factors are:

1. The cost of transporting the finished product to the market
2. The cost of transporting raw materials to the plant or factory
3. The cost of labour travelling to work

The firm will locate its plant where these costs, taken together, are minimized. We assume that production costs within the factory are constant wherever the factory is located. In the following simulation exercise, a tin-box manufacturer is comparing the advantage of locating nearer to its labour supply, to its markets and to the source of its raw materials. The purpose of the simulation exercise is that you should compare the transport costs involved and then provide a recommendation. This is done by calculating the transport costs in producing tin boxes at each of the four possible places, A, B, C and D (see Fig. 3.13 on page 34), and choosing the two with the lowest cost.

To simplify the task, it has been assumed that a market exists for the tin boxes only at B, C and D but workers would have to commute from B if the factory was to be located at A. A labour force is therefore only available at B, C and D.

For each thousand tin boxes produced:

1. It costs 10p per mile to trans-port the required labour from B to A.
2. Transporting oil from the refi-nery at A costs £12 per mile by road and 20p per mile by canal.
3. The cost of transporting tin boxes is £6 per mile by road and 20p per mile by canal.

33

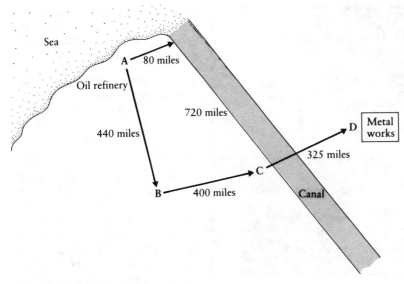

Figure 3.13 A, B, C and D are the four possible locations for the tin-box factory.

4. Transporting metal from the metal works at D costs £9 per mile by road and 30p by water.

Work out the transporting costs of locating the factory at either A, B, C or D by filling in Table 3.1.

Table 3.1 Table for working out the costs in the different locations.

	A	B	C	D
Labour transport costs				
Oil transport costs				
Metal transport costs				
Market costs				
Total				

Some parts of the table will be blank. For example, there will be no costs for transporting metal to D.

Questions

1. Which is the location with lowest cost?
2. Which is the location with the next lowest cost? Would the business necessarily locate at the site with the lowest cost?

CASE STUDY—FALLING DEMAND

Firms operate against a background of what is happening to other firms and to the economy in general. In business studies we talk about a multiplier effect of upturns and downturns in business activity. In Aberdeen, in the mid-1980s, there was a downward multiplier effect.

The **multiplier effect** occurs when an original change in demand goes on to create further changes in demand in a given area. If the government spends £50 million in the North East and workers who receive this income re-spend some of it in the North East, this will help to create further income and jobs in the area. If, in the end, total spending in the area rose by £100 million, the multiplier would be two.

Because oil prices fell dramatically, the oil-drilling boom came to an end. Industries related to oil were the first to suffer. Work almost came to a standstill in firms producing oil-rigs and components for drilling. The fall in incomes and earnings spilt over into a wide range of other businesses from beer to engineering. Unemployment rose and at a time when house prices throughout Britain were rising, many houses in Aberdeen could not find buyers at the asking prices and house prices tumbled.

Questions

1. What sorts of factors would cause an upward multiplier?
2. What do you think is meant by the term 'regional multiplier'?
3. Make a list of the industries that you would expect to have suffered a slump in sales in Aberdeen.
4. If you were the manager of a retailing firm in a slump, how would you react to this change?
5. What has caused the Aberdeen downturn?
6. Would anyone in Aberdeen benefit from the recession?

CASE STUDY—THE GROWTH OF A FIRM

HODGSON BUYS FUNERAL FIRMS

Hodgson Holdings, a firm of funeral directors, is shortly to join the Stock Exchange unlisted securities market.

It has recently taken over two more businesses, J. Stone and Wm. Ham, both in Cardiff. This will add an extra 500 funerals a year to the group's total.

Hodgson expects shortly to be handling 5600 funerals a year. Recently Hodgson's has taken over seven firms.

Figure 3.14 Newspaper cutting about two take-overs by Hodgson Holdings.

Questions

1. What type of integration is taking place at Hodgson Holdings?
2. What do you think are the motives behind the integration?
3. Find out what the unlisted securities market is.
4. What do you think will be the advantages of the take-overs?
5. In what ways might the public benefit and how might they lose out from the growth of Hodgson Holdings?

QUESTIONS

1. Complete the following sentences using the words below.

Bulk-increasing industry
Bulk-decreasing industry
Technical economy
Financial economy
Risk-spreading economy
Merger
Take-over
Demand
Supply
Industrial inertia
External economy
Monopoly

   (a) A .... occurs when one firm buys at least 51 per cent of the shares of another.
   (b) Furniture manufacture is an example of a....................
   (c) .... is the quantity of a product that consumers are prepared to buy at a given price.
   (d) A .... exists when one firm controls the production or sale of a good.
   (e) An example of a .... of scale would include the division of labour.
   (f) An example of a .... of scale would be diversification of output.
   (g) An example of a .... of scale would be the ability of a large firm to borrow money at a lower interest rate.
   (h) The .... of a good is the quantity that producers are prepared to sell at given prices.
   (i) .... occurs if firms do not change location after their original locating factors have disappeared.
   (j) An example of an .... of scale is the development of a technical college in a city.
   (k) The manufacture of matches is an example of a ....
   (l) A .... occurs when two firms voluntarily join together.

2. In the late 1980s the Welsh Development Agency ran an advert on television to the tune of 'Cwm Rhondda':

   'Dunlop. G Plan. Revlon. Berlei ... British Airways. Hotpoint. Kraft. Kelloggs. Esso. Hoover. Sony ... Metal Box. Ferranti. Ford.
   Made in Wales. Made in Wales. And there's room for many more (many more). And there's room for many more.'

   (a) Put the firms from the jingle into a table using the headings shown below. (The details for Sony have been filled in to start you off.)

Name of company	Products made	Country of company's head office
Sony	Tape recorders, televisions, electrical equipment	Japan

   (b) What questions would a firm producing motor cars want answering before it decided whether or not to set up in Wales?
3. Which of the following are examples of (i) horizontal integration, (ii) vertical integration, (iii) lateral integration and (iv) conglomerate integration?
   (a) Coca Cola buys up a firm that produces equipment which takes the salt out of sea-water.
   (b) Two cat-food manufacturers combine.
   (c) A holding company buys up several unrelated businesses.
   (d) An oil company buys a chain of petrol stations.
   (e) An examination board buys up a paper manufacturer.
   (f) A bank buys up a factoring company.
   (g) Two cigarette giants combine.
   (h) A Japanese car manufacturer buys up a British car manufacturer.
   (i) A brewery takes over a distillery.
   (j) An exporting agency buys a small shipping company.
   (k) An insurance firm buys up several estate agents.
   (l) Two banks combine.
   (m) A biscuit firm buys up a tin-box manufacturer.
4. The local council has given a property-development company permission to develop a new shopping facility which

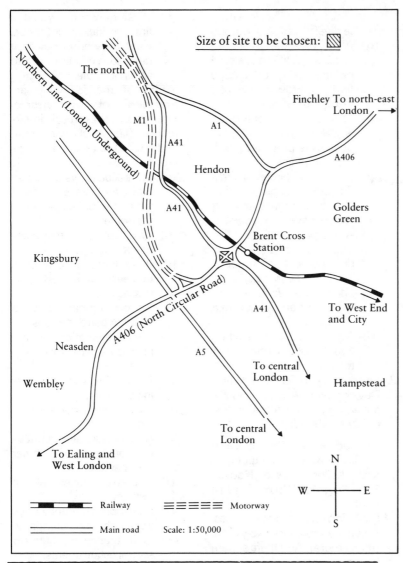

Size of site to be chosen: ▨

The north

Northern Line (London Underground)

M1

A41

A1

Hendon

Finchley To north-east London →

A406

Golders Green

A41

Brent Cross Station

Kingsbury

A406 (North Circular Road)

A41

To West End and City

Neasden

A5

To central London

Hampstead

Wembley

To central London

To Ealing and West London

N
W — E
S

▬▬▬ Railway   ═════ Motorway

▬▬▬ Main road   Scale: 1:50,000

Figure 3.15   Where should the shopping centre be built?

will be the largest in Western Europe. Choose a location on the map in Fig. 3.15. Explain why you have chosen this location.

5. Outline the factors affecting the location of industry and explain why the government intervenes in this process.

6. Small firms continue to exist despite pressures from larger units. In what fields do small firms predominate and why are they so successful in these areas?

7. What benefits do firms derive from large-scale production?

8. Using recent examples where possible, outline the various types of integration and merger.

9. Examine the dangers of too many firms being too large.

COURSEWORK

1. Where should you locate your business?

   For this exercise the class needs to work in three groups. You are the directors of a small, modern, light industry. The exact type of firm will be selected by the teacher. One group of students will research the case for locating the firm in Winchester in Hampshire (see Fig. 3.16). A second group will research the case for locating the firm in Corby in Northamptonshire (see Fig. 3.17 on page 38). Both groups will produce a business report.

   The third group will research the locational requirements of the firm. When the background work has been completed, the first two groups will present a verbal report at a meeting and the third group will select a location from the two alternatives.

   (Alternatively the teacher might decide to compare locating in Corby with locating in your own locality as the basis for the exercise.)

2. How do local businesses compete?

   A group of students set out to study how firms in different lines of business compete with each other. Some of them looked at how souvenir shops in Windsor competed with each other, others looked at the competition between taxi firms, and a third group studied jewellery shops. They then pooled their results to look at the nature of competition. The

Figure 3.16 Advertisement designed to attract businesses to Hampshire and the Isle of Wight.

group looking at souvenir shops found that location was the most important factor giving a business a competitive edge. A souvenir shop needed to be on the main tourist route close to Windsor Castle. Other important elements of the competition mix were window display, cleanliness of the shop, variety of items sold, opening hours and service. The students were able to glean their information by preparing a questionnaire and interviewing shop-owners and customers.

The group was surprised to find that price was only a minor factor in competition because tourists were not really aware of price differences for items such as postcards.

The group looking at taxi firms found that price was more important, particularly for regular users of taxis. Reliability was also important, as well as the location because taxi firms needed to be close to their calls. Other important factors included the telephone number (5555, for example, is easy to remember), the presentation of the cab, and the politeness of the driver.

The group studying jewellery stores found price to be particularly important in terms of value for money; window display, opening hours and the timing of sales were also important.

From doing this particular piece of coursework students were able to discover a lot about the nature of competition. In order to answer their main question, 'How do firms compete?' the students had to think out carefully the questions they were to ask in order to collect a lot of good information.

Do your own piece of coursework looking at price and non-price competition between a set of businesses in your area, e.g. hotels, coach companies, video shops, etc. In order to do this exercise well you must carefully construct the subset of questions that enable you to answer the title question.

3. Are big schools efficient?
   Interview your head-teacher, economics teacher, other teachers, parents and pupils to answer the above question.

Development areas: nowhere else comes within miles of Corby

If you're planning to develop your business you need look no further than Corby.

Corby is a **Development Area** so your business gets the help of Development Area benefits. For most companies this means the better deal for them of either 15% grants on plant, machinery and equipment or £3000 per job created. There is also selective assistance for some job creating projects.

Corby is also a **Steel Opportunity Area**, and this means even more incentives.

Corby is **England's first Enterprise Zone.** There are factories off the peg, from 500 sq. ft. to 50,000 sq. ft., some of which are rates free until 1991. You can also choose from offices, warehouses, and high tech buildings.

Corby has **EEC aid for small businesses.** £1m is now available to aid efficiency.

Above all, Corby is right in the heart of England. Within 80 miles of London. 50 miles from Birmingham. Strategically placed for any business that needs fast, inexpensive, easy access to the big South East and Midland population centres.

However far you look, you will find that, as a total package for the success of your business, nowhere else comes within miles of Corby.

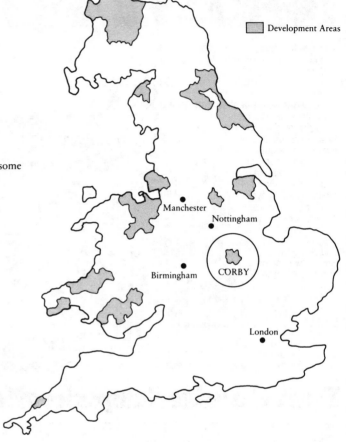

Figure 3.17 Advertisement designed to attract businesses to Corby.

You should first review your notes on economies and diseconomies of scale. See how the various economies of scale relate to the topic.

What is the optimum size of a school? What is the optimum size of class for different subjects?

What inefficiencies—technical, managerial, financial, risk-spreading, etc.—begin to set in as the size of the school increases? Highlight inefficiencies in school organization.

4 Work and pay

There are many different types of jobs and there are many reasons why people receive different wages. These reasons include differences in levels of education, training and skill. Fig. 4.1 shows part of an advertisement for a highly paid job requiring a high level of skills and experience.

Managing Director

Fast-growing manufacturing company
c£30,000 + Car + Bonus   Nottingham

Figure 4.1   The managing director of a company is paid more than those in jobs for which fewer skills are needed.

Calculating pay

The amount paid for a normal working week is referred to as a 'basic' wage or salary. Many workers receive other benefits in addition to their basic wage, in either a money or a non-money form. Not all workers receive a wage or salary. Workers such as some types of salespeople are paid on a commission basis. They are paid according to their success in selling.

The main ways of calculating pay are outlined below. Sometimes elements of these methods are combined.

Flat rate
This is a set rate of weekly or monthly pay, based on a set number of hours. This system is easy to calculate and administer but it does not provide an incentive to work harder.

Time rate
Under this scheme, the worker receives a set rate per hour. Any hours worked above a set number are paid at an 'overtime' rate.

Piece rate
This system is sometimes used in the textile and electronics industries amongst others. Payment is made for each item produced which meets a given quality standard. The advantage of such a scheme is that it encourages effort. However, it is not suitable for jobs which require time and care. Also, the output of many jobs such as service occupations is impossible to measure.

Bonus
A bonus is paid as an additional encouragement to employees. It can be paid out of additional profits earned by the employer as a result of the employees' effort and hard work. Bonuses may also be used as an incentive to workers at times when they might be inclined to slacken effort, e.g. at Christmas and summer-holiday times..

Commission
This is a payment made as a percentage of the sales a salesperson has made.

Attendance records

In order to make up pay packets, it is essential to keep an accurate record of how much work is being done. Nowadays, most wages for large employers are paid by bank multiple giro. Large firms can now make out giro payments through computer discs.

Multiple giro. The wages department of a firm has a record of the bank and bank-account number of each of its employees. A wages clerk then simply fills in a multiple giro form authorizing the firm's bank to make payments to its employees' bank accounts.

There are several ways in which a record can be kept of attendance at work:

Clock-cards
Large firms will often have a clocking system so that the employee 'clocks on' and 'clocks off'. Each employee picks up his or her card on arriving at work and punches it into the clocking device. Employees may have to clock off and on again when they take a lunch-break, and then off again when they finish work.

At the end of the week, the wages department will have a clear picture of how much to pay individual workers.

Time books
Smaller firms may keep a time book. Employees simply sign in and out of the book.

Time-sheets
This method is often used when workers do not always work in the same location, e.g. contract workers, such as painters and decorators, film crews, road builders, etc. The sheet is filled in each day and is signed by the supervisor to prove accuracy.

Flexitime

Flexible working time (FWT) is increasingly used in modern work. At 'peak' times, all members of staff will be at work. Outside these 'core' hours, there is more flexibility and staff have a certain amount of choice about when they work, provided they work a minimum number of hours.

The firm's working day is divided into three sections:

1. *Band time*. This is the total period for which the business is open, e.g. 8 a.m. to 8 p.m.
2. *Core time*. This is the period in which all the members of the firm are expected to be working, e.g. 10 a.m. to 12.30 p.m.
3. *Flexible time*. This is the period of time in which workers can select the hours they work, e.g. 8 a.m. to 10 a.m. and 2 p.m. to 8 p.m.

If, for example, workers are expected to work 36 hours in a five-day working week and they work 20 hours of core time, then they choose the other 16 hours in which they work. Some workers may prefer to work more in the morning, others in the afternoons. Other workers may vary their hours.

The advantages of flexitime are as follows:

1. It gives workers more control of when they work. Workers may enjoy this type of freedom. Flexibility also enables them to fit in private engagements such as hair and dental appointments.
2. At least for the basic core time, all the work-force is operating together.

Staff may be responsible for keeping their own record of the hours they have worked, or they may 'clock in' and 'clock out' (see Fig. 4.2).

Shift work

In a number of business enterprises, it is essential to have machinery working continuously in order to use it most effectively. This is true of industries such as textiles, chemicals, steel, coal-mining and even confectionery.

There are a number of ways of organizing this. In some textile businesses in West Yorkshire, for example, there are distinct day and night shifts, with workers working exclusively on one or the other. In the North Sea oil industry, production workers may work on a rig for two weeks and then take a two-week break. In the chemical industry, workers sometimes work the day shift for one week, followed by a week on the night shift.

Workers will be paid higher rewards to work unsocial hours.

Gross and net pay

> **Gross pay** is the total amount earned by an employee before any deductions have been taken off. It includes the basic pay, plus any additional payments such as bonuses and overtime.

> **Net pay** is the total amount received by an employee after any deductions have been taken off. This figure represents take-home pay.
> Net pay =
> gross pay − deductions

A typical pay slip illustrates the difference well. Fig. 4.3 shows one belonging to Mr A. L. Patel who works in the accounts department of Modern Electronics plc. We can look at it a column at a time.

Column 1
1. The name of the company.
2. The employee's basic month's pay.

Figure 4.2 Clocking in on a flexi-meter. (*Source:* Kim Hooper, Reading)

Column 1	Column 2	Column 3	Column 4

Pay Advice (1) MODERN ELECTRONICS PLC	Name (5) AL PATEL	Ref. no. (Quote on any query) 27 2687 2017	27 NOV 86 MODERN ELECTRONICS PLC
BASIC PAY/ADDITIONS	DEDUCTIONS	PAY CUMULATIVES	

(2) BASIC PAY   1052.25
(3) OVERTIME   40.50
	(6) TAX CODE 0365H 209.96
	(7) NAT. INS 78.41
	(8) SUPERANNUATION 63.13
	(9) UNION 4.00
		THIS YEAR	YOUR NET PAY HAS BEEN CREDITED TO
			YOUR ACCOUNT AS STATED BELOW:
			(17) BANK NAT. WESTMINSTER
			    SORTING CODE 06 17 25
			    ACCOUNT NUMBER 76256905

	(10) NAT. INSURANCE NO.
	    YT82034B
	(11) DATE OF PAYMENT 28 NOV 86
	(12) INCOME TAX YEAR 1986/87
	(13) PAY PERIOD 08
	(14) ENTER 'X' IF FINAL PAY
	    PERIOD IN TAX YEAR
	    ☐
			MR AL PATEL

(4) TOTAL PAY ADDITIONS £1092.75	(15) TOTAL DEDUCTIONS £355.50	(16) NET PAY /£737.25	

Figure 4.3 Typical pay slip. (The numbers in brackets refer to the explanatory notes.)

3. Mr Patel has worked some overtime.
4. If we add (2) and (3) we get Mr Patel's gross pay.

Column 2

5. The employee's name.
6. Mr Patel is a married man with a mortgage and is entitled to a tax allowance of £3650 a year. He is having to pay £209.96 in income tax each month which is at the rate of 29p in the pound (1986) for every pound he earns over his tax allowance.
7. As well as income tax, employees have to pay a compulsory National Insurance contribution to the government. This money goes towards providing benefits like pensions and unemployment benefit.
8. Mr Patel also contributed £63.13 towards his company's pension scheme.
9. Mr Patel is also a member of a trade union to which he pays a monthly subscription.
10. Mr Patel's National Insurance number.
11. The date on which money will be transferred to Mr Patel's bank account.
12. The tax year runs from 1 April 1986 to 31 March 1987.
13. The pay period is for the eighth month, i.e. November.
14. An 'X' would appear in this box in March.
15. The total amount of deductions.

Column 3

16. Net pay, i.e. gross pay minus deductions.

Column 4

17. A statement of the fact that the money is being paid by multiple giro into Mr Patel's bank.

In addition to the above details, the pay slip would typically show the overall amount of gross pay, tax, superannuation and National Insurance paid in the financial year up to that date. For instance, the November pay slip might show the following for Mr Patel:

Gross pay up to November	£8500
Income tax paid up to November	£1500
Superannuation paid up to November	£500
National Insurance paid up to November	£500

This would have meant that during the first eight months of the year his total net pay would have been £6000.

Statutory deductions from pay

These are some compulsory deductions from pay.

Income tax

This is paid through the pay-as-you-earn system (PAYE). People of working age in the UK are sent a tax form to fill in. They have to state the name of their employer from whom the tax office will get the details of their salary. Many people also get additional money from doing extra work for other employers, or in the form of interest and dividends on savings and shares. All this information must be filled in on the tax form. People whose work involves expenses can make claims for these to be allowed against tax so that they do not pay so much.

The amount of income tax paid depends on:

1. Income
2. Allowances

Everyone is given tax allowances depending on their status (including whether they are married or single, the size of their mortgage, whether they have dependent relatives at home, etc.). Each employee is given a tax code by the Inland Revenue. By looking at the 'free-pay' table issued by the Inland Revenue, the firm's wages department knows how much tax to deduct.

Rates of income tax in this country are progressive and go up in bands.

A **progressive tax** is one where the more income a person earns, the greater the percentage of this income he or she pays in tax.

The amount of allowances and the tax bands change as time goes on, so it is best to illustrate the way in which income tax works by using a simple example based on imaginary figures.

Let us assume that single people are given a tax allowance of £2000. The next £10 000 earned above this is taxed at 30p in the pound (30 per cent). The next £2000 above this is taxed at 35 per cent, and for each extra £2000 earned tax goes up 5p in the pound until it reaches a top rate of 60p in the pound.

Now let us assume that Mary Forbes earns £10 000 a year and Sarah Lewis earns £18 000. The tax paid by Mary Forbes is as follows:

£2000 at zero tax	0
£8000 at 30p in £	£2400
Total tax	£2400
Pay after tax	£5600

The tax paid by Sarah Lewis is as follows:

£2000 at zero tax	0
£10 000 at 30p in £	£3000
£2000 at 35p in £	£700
£2000 at 40p in £	£800
£2000 at 45p in £	£900
Total tax	£5400
Pay after tax	£12 600

We can see that the effect of this tax system is to reduce the difference in pay between Forbes and Lewis. Before tax, Lewis earned £8000 more than Forbes. After tax, Lewis earned only £7000 more than Forbes.

When a worker leaves his or her job, the employer completes Form P45. The P45 must then be given to the new employer who can then continue tax deductions with no complications.

At the end of the tax year an employee receives Form P60 which is a summary of gross and net pay during the year. It must be kept safely as a record because an employee may want to apply for a mortgage on the basis of earnings, or claim sickness or unemployment pay in the coming year, and these benefits are earnings-related.

A person taking up work for the first time will probably not have a tax code or P45. Such people are normally taxed on an emergency code. If they are over-taxed, they will be entitled to a tax rebate.

National Insurance contributions

These are paid jointly by the employer and the employee, to the government. Contributions from National Insurance go into the National Insurance Fund, the National Health Service and the Redundancy Fund. These contributions pay for sickness and unemployment benefit, old age pensions and the National Health Service. The wages department of a firm deducts National Insurance as a percentage of the worker's wage. The employer's contribution makes up the greater part of the overall contribution. Contributions are not made by the unemployed or when an employee is claiming sickness benefit, provided a doctor's certificate is obtained.

The National Insurance scheme was introduced as part of the overall scheme of the Welfare State. National Insurance provides a safety net for citizens who fall on hard times.

Voluntary deductions from pay

Many employees also voluntarily pay over some of their wages for other purposes.

1. *Superannuation/private pension schemes.* Many employees nowadays pay money into a private pension scheme to supplement their state pension. For some workers, this is a necessary condition of taking employment with a firm. The pension paid then depends on how much the employee contributes to the fund over the years.
2. *Savings.* Some workers contract to pay a certain amount each month into a fund such as the govern-

ment's Save-as-You-Earn scheme (SAYE). By saving regular sums, the worker is entitled to a lump sum with interest after a given period of time.

3. *Trade-union contributions.* These can also be paid directly from wages.
4. *Private-medical-scheme contributions.* An increasing number of people contract to make payments into a private medical scheme.
5. *Contributions to the company social club.*
6. *Contractual contributions to charity.*

Statutory sick pay

The government has now made businesses largely responsible for paying sick pay to employees. This is called statutory sick pay (SSP). These payments are made if a worker is sick on normal working days.

Computerization of wages

In large firms, much of the work on wages is done by computers. This involves the calculation of wages, the printing of wage slips, and the production of payment instructions to the bank. Data relating to the time an employee works is picked up by computer from magnetic tape, enabling the continuous recording of wages. Computers are able to handle a lot of work quickly and accurately.

One danger of using computers to calculate and record wages is the risk of losing information if something should happen to the wages program or disk. Therefore, firms will normally keep at least two 'back-up' copies of a disk which will be continually updated.

Making up a payroll

In order to make up a payroll, a firm must prepare a total outline of the work-force and the pay it is entitled to each week. Nowadays, firms encourage employees to open bank accounts because this simplifies the whole process of paying wages. When some employees are paid in cash, the wages department will make up a cash payroll. To do this, it has to calculate the amounts of bank notes and coins needed to make up the wage packets. The firm will make out a wage cash analysis in which it will use the minimum number of notes and coins to make up the wages (see Fig. 4.4).

We can see that by making out a clear wage cash analysis, we get an accurate representation of how much needs to be paid out. The process of making up the wage packets is made very simple.

WAGE CASH ANALYSIS FOR RJP ELECTRONICS LTD

CLOCK No.	NAME	WAGE	£10	£5	£1	50p	20p	10p	5p	2p	1p
001	D. BYRNE	120.00	12								
005	J. DAVIDSON	100.53	10			1				1	1
006	C. DRAVSKY	134.26	13		4		1		1		1
007	D. GREEN	107.32	10	1	2		1	1		1	
009	B. MULLEN	82.32	8		2		1	1		1	
010	S. MULLEN	136.62	13	1	1	1		1		1	
012	J. PATEL	115.00	11		1						
017	D. THOMAS	137.21	13	1	2		1				1
036	P. WHEELAN	95.18	9	1					1	1	3
038	G. WEST	82.32	8		2		1	1		1	
	TOTAL	1,110.76	107	5	13	2	5	5	2	5	6

SUMMARY OF CASH REQUIRED FROM BANK TO MAKE THE ABOVE PAYMENTS

```
                    £     p
107 @ £10    =   1070    00
  5 @ £5     =     25    00
 13 @ £1     =     13    00
  2 @ 50p    =      1    00
  5 @ 20p    =      1    00
  5 @ 10p    =            50
  2 @  5p    =            10
  5 @  2p    =            10
  6 @  1p    =             6
                 ————————————
                 1110    76
                 ————————————
```

Figure 4.4 Example of a wage cash analysis.

Fringe benefits

When considering a job, an employee will not only take into account the money rewards but also all the other positive and negative aspects of a job. Among the positive advantages will be the non-monetary benefits of a job known as 'fringe benefits'. These include:

1. Loans at a low rate of interest to purchase a house
2. The use of a company car and other subsidized travel
3. Help with payment of medical expenses and school fees
4. Free or subsidized meals including luncheon vouchers
5. Subsidized private telephone and other bills
6. Free or subsidized company products
7. Subsidized holidays

CASE STUDY—WAGES AT SMITH'S ENGINEERING

Smith's Engineering is a small firm producing lamiplate (plastic-coated metal items) for the motor-vehicle industry. An example of its product is interior car panels. The firm employs a production-line team of 42 manual workers, 5 supervisory and inspection workers, an office staff of 3 and a management team consisting of the managing director, who also handles personnel, a sales manager and a production manager. The company pays an outside accountant to supervise the books which are kept on a daily basis by the office. The office also manages wages.

The manual work-force must clock in to work in the morning between 8.30 a.m. and 8.45 a.m. Workers lose pay if they clock in after 8.45 a.m. They are entitled to a 15 minute break in the morning and afternoon at set times. The lunch-break is taken between 12.30 p.m. and 1.45 p.m. in two shifts. The afternoon session ends at 4.15 p.m.

Wage packets are handed out to workers on Friday afternoons. Workers have to work a 'week in hand', which means that the wages they receive are not for the current week but for the previous week. The company also runs a bonus scheme, setting production targets for work. The bonus scheme sets three levels of bonus. The first is fairly easy for the work-force to achieve; the second is quite difficult; and the highest level of bonus has only been achieved once.

If orders for the firm's products are high, it will offer overtime to some workers. Overtime pay is one and a third times the normal rate. If workers work on Saturdays, they will get one and a half times the normal rate.

The supervisors, inspection and office workers sign in rather than clock in. The supervisory workers must sign in between 8.15 a.m. and 8.30 a.m. The office workers do not have to report for work until 9 a.m. Office workers are entitled to a fixed rate of salary. Supervisory and white-collar workers are not entitled to a bonus but their rate of pay is higher than that of the manual workers. Overtime is paid at time and a half. The office workers' day ends at 4 p.m.

The managerial staff have no fixed hours or method of recording hours worked. The managerial staff also get fringe benefits in the form of a petrol allowance for mileage on company business. They can also include other expenses and their telephone bills are paid by the company.

Fringe benefits for all employees include a subsidized canteen, and subsidized drinks and confectionary machines.

Questions

1. What method of checking hours worked is used for each of the following?

(a) Manual workers
(b) Office staff
(c) Management

2. Why do you think different methods of checking are used for these groups?
3. Who works longer hours—office workers or production staff? Explain your answer.
4. Do you think that it is fair that different groups of employees at Smith's are paid in different ways? Explain your answer. What alternatives could you suggest?
5. Explain how the company bonus system works. Why do you think that it is structured in this way?
6. What is a 'fringe benefit'? List the different benefits received by different groups in the case study.
7. Explain what is meant by working a 'week in hand'.
8. Why is overtime pay higher than basic pay?

QUESTIONS

1. Complete the following sentences using the words below.

Gross pay
Net pay
Commission
Band time
Core time
Flexitime
Clock cards
Time-sheets
Wage cash analysis
Statutory sick pay
National Insurance
Piece rate
Time rate

(a) Salespeople often earn .... on the basis of the sales they make.

(b) When workers travel from one job site to another, the supervisor will sign their ....

(c) Total pay before deductions are taken away is known as ....

(d) .... is the total working time of a business.

(e) The hours a worker can choose whether to work or not are known as ....

(f) The compulsory hours employees must work are known as ....

(g) The wages department will make up a .... when workers are paid in cash.

(h) .... is total pay minus deductions.

(i) An example of a statutory deduction from pay is ....

(j) .... are used by firms to check the number of hours employees work.

(k) One method of paying workers by results is by a ....

(l) One method of paying regular wages per hour is by a ....

(m) The employer has now taken over a major role in paying .... from the Department of Health and Social Security.

2. Read the pay slip in Fig. 4.5.

(a) How much is J. Summers's gross pay?

(b) How much is J. Summers's net pay?

(c) Explain the difference between gross and net pay.

BASIC PAY		DEDUCTIONS	
Basic pay	800.00	Tax	150.00
Overtime	100.00	Nat. Insurance	70.00
		Superannuation	50.00
		Union	5.00

PAY ADVICE: J. Summers
SOUTHERN CHEMICALS

Figure 4.5 Pay slip of J. Summers.

3. Make out a wage cash analysis for Summerfield Confectionery, following the pattern in Fig. 4.4. The employees and their wages are as shown below.

Name	Wage
J. Arthur	£117.12
B. Brown	£32.14
C. Condery	£15.86
D. Davis	£12.31
S. Egerton	£48.92
T. Fish	£112.19
R. Grist	£135.73
S. Haralambos	£86.32

4. The card in Fig. 4.6 appeared in a jobcentre in Reading.

JOB CENTRE

JOB: Apprentice tool-maker

AREA: Woodley

WAGES: Starting at £85 per week. Fringe benefits

HOURS: 38 hour week including flexitime

DETAILS: School-leaver required with GCSEs in technical subjects.

Card no: 112

Figure 4.6 Jobcentre advertisement for an apprentice tool-maker.

(a) What is a jobcentre?

(b) Who funds the jobcentres?

(c) Why is it important for the jobcentre to make clear the location of the job?

(d) Name a fringe benefit that may go with the job.

(e) Explain what is meant by flexitime as advertised on the card.

(f) What sort of training would you expect to go with the job?

5. Mullen Enterprise operates a bonus scheme to discourage absenteeism from work. The scheme covers the 7000 manual workers in three plants at Dunstable, Southampton and Liverpool. The firm agreed to pay a weekly bonus if plant absenteeism fell below 12 per cent on the following scale:

Rate of absenteeism (%).	Bonus
11–12	£0.50
10–11	£1.35
9–10	£2.25
8–9	£3.40
7–8	£4.25
6–7	£5.10
5–6	£6.00

(a) What per cent bonus would workers at a plant receive if the rate of absenteeism was 6.5%?

(b) Julia Nash works at the Dunstable plant and earns £150 a week regularly. How much would her gross pay be in a week in which absenteeism was 9.5 per cent?

(c) From the employer's point

of view, what would be the advantage of operating the above scheme?

(d) At what times of the year would the scheme be particularly effective?

6. Below are some figures showing the extent to which the times at which employees start and finish work are formally checked. (*Source:* Workplace Industrial Relations Survey.)

	%
Manual workers checked in some way	54
Non-manual workers checked in some way	13

Methods of checking

Clocked:	
Manual	32
Non-manual	2

Checked in:	
Manual	13
Non-manual	6

Sign in:	
Manual	10
Non-manual	5

(a) What percentage of manual workers are *not* checked in at work?

(b) What percentage of non-manual workers are *not* checked in at work?

(c) Give an example of a manual worker.

(d) Give an example of a non-manual worker.

(e) What is the most common way of checking in manual workers? Explain how this system operates.

(f) Under what circumstances is signing in a suitable way of checking on workers?

7. (a) Compare time and piece rates as methods of payment.

(b) Explain how statutory sick pay operates.

(c) Describe in detail statutory and voluntary deductions from pay.

COURSEWORK

1. Why do wage rates vary for different jobs?

   Collect some job advertisements from a newspaper and investigate why these differences exist. The best way of doing this is to deal with firms directly to find out why they are prepared to offer the salary they do.

2. This class assignment on wages should be tackled in conjunction with the personnel department of a local firm. A class discussion should determine the range of suitable questions, for example:

   1. What wages system does the firm operate (piece, time, etc.)?
   2. How are the wages calculated?
   3. When are the wages paid?
   4. How are the wages negotiated?
   5. What system does the firm use to measure work?

   Working in groups, the class should establish sets of related questions for tackling the assignment as groupwork.

3. How is a wage cash analysis done?

   Make up an imaginary wage cash analysis for your class assuming that students with surnames starting with the letters A–J are paid £33.32 and those with K–Z names £40.

4. What are the main deductions from gross pay?

   Design an imaginary pay slip for a job advertised in the local paper, analysing the items as you go through it.

5. What is the purpose of shift-work? Compare and contrast the shift-work patterns of local firms.

6. What is flexitime? Examine the flexitime arrangements of a local firm.

5 Production

This chapter is concerned with the production process and concentrates mainly on manufacturing (see Fig. 5.1). This is in many ways a distortion of what goes on in the UK because today much of production has a service-industry base. A large insurance company, for example, will employ thousands of workers in the production of the service of insurance. The company will have line managers and supervisors with offices concentrating on accounts, underwriting, life policies and other areas. It will use warehouses to store its supplies of paper and stationery and modern automated computer technology for records and calculations, and it will exercise quality control through its checking procedures.

In looking at this chapter the student needs to be constantly aware that similar processes and changes are taking place in all forms of production whilst at the same time appreciating that every individual unit of production will have its own special features that make it different from other units.

Research and development

A considerable amount of planning must take place before a product is released. This planning has to involve knowledge of the market and its constantly changing tastes as well as research and development. Setting up a production process or a new line can involve considerable cost, and careful work in the early stages will help to ensure that profits are made.

Product researchers and marketing managers attempt to answer all the questions indicated in Fig. 5.2, on page 48, before a decision is made to produce a product. After receiving marketing information, researchers attempt to develop a product and choose a suitable design. The design must be attractive to consumers, functional and efficient. The researchers must also consider production costs, ease of manufacture and selling prices. A company might be reluctant to change an earlier design, particularly if it provides status, e.g. the radiator grill on a BMW car. A designer must bear in mind the type of treatment a product may receive; for example, toys have to be particularly durable. They may also build into the design planned obsolescence so that the product will need replacing after a particular period; many cars, for example, are only built to last a limited number of years.

Once a design has been developed the researchers will build a prototype which can then be tested. Many prototypes will be tried and then discarded while others may be modified and improved. Once a product has been tested and proved to be successful, and all the marketing and production questions have been answered, the firm will patent the product and will then consider 'tooling up' its production line.

What is production?

Production is the process whereby manufacturing resources are used to buy in raw materials and then trans-

Figure 5.1 Producing the Model T Ford. (*Source:* Ford Picture Library)

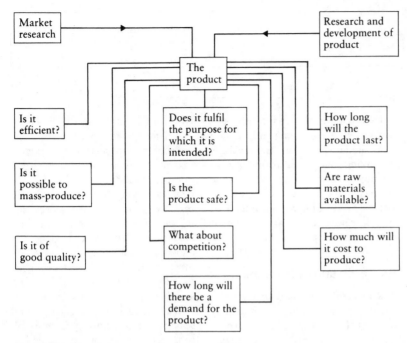

Figure 5.2 Planning a new product.

form them through a variety of processes and stages into finished products which can then be distributed to the market (see Fig. 5.3). Production must reflect needs and tastes discovered through marketing as well as new technology created by research and development.

All manufacturing businesses will operate some sort of chain of command dealing with production. Fig. 5.4 shows one form this might take.

The *purchasing manager* and purchasing department are not only concerned with the buying-in of raw materials but will also buy in goods, to enable the production process to take place, e.g. machinery, tools and equipment. Many components for the finished product may be made within the company while others will have to be bought in. For example, motor manufacturers tend to buy in components such as lamps, batteries, tyres, etc.

Quality controllers ensure that finished products match the design specifications so that they will satisfy customers. *Inspectors* look carefully at samples at various stages of production so as to evaluate the quality of production as a whole. If defects are spotted quickly production faults can be 'ironed out' and this may save on replacement under the product's guarantee at a later stage.

Engineers are important at all stages in the productive process. Production engineers work with drawing-office staff to ensure that the design is easy to manufacture. They then become involved with developing the stages, techniques and equipment needed to manufacture the product. Maintenance engineers ensure that production machinery is serviced and functions, and deal with day-to-day hiccups on the production line.

Planning production

In any industry, production is a 'pressure area'. Targets have to be met and standards have to be kept up. A failure to meet orders or to maintain efficiency can often cost a company sales and future orders. Firms will use a production schedule which will list types and quantities of products to be produced within the following 12 months. Each product will have its processes mapped out on a process planning sheet. Documents are issued to production supervisors to tell them what to produce. At all times there is liaison with the sales department to ensure that orders can be filled and to ensure that stockpiling is not taking place.

Obviously all the areas of a company depend on production running

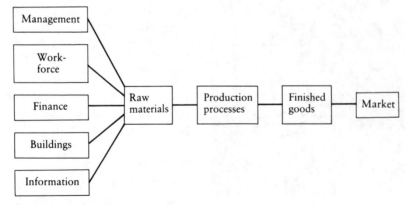

Figure 5.3 The production process.

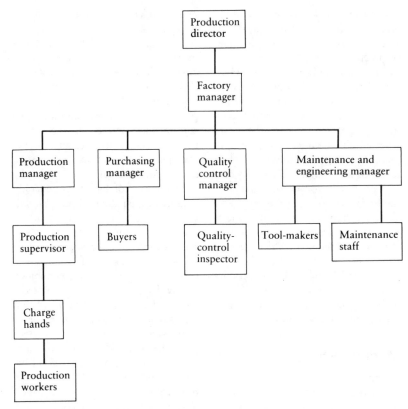

Figure 5.4 A possible chain of command for production.

managers can assess whether or not the production of particular goods is meeting the profit objectives and market forecasts. If a particular product shows a small contribution it could be a loss leader used to entice customers to buy other goods. A loss leader is an item sold for less than the cost of producing and selling it in order to attract customers to buy from that firm. Of course the bulk of a firm's products will not be loss leaders.

Types of production

Job production

This is concerned with the production of single individual items, e.g. the Humber Bridge or a frigate for the Navy. A firm might be producing several different jobs at the same time. The danger of this type of production is that when a particular job is finished, other orders may not be forthcoming, and workers may be laid off and resources become idle. This is a major problem in the ship-building industry.

Batch production

With this type of production batches of similar products are made when orders are received. This type of production often takes place when a range of different products is being produced.

Flow production

With this type of production parts are passed on from one production process to another in a regular sequence and in an uninterrupted flow. Each stage adds a little more to the finished product.

Mass-production and standardization

This is the production of goods in large volumes and need not be flow production if a product can be made in one stage. The major benefits of

smoothly and efficiently and that any decisions taken must not harm this production process. Many companies employ a production controller to keep an overall eye on production.

Costing methods

The management accountant will be involved in production decisions. He or she will look carefully at the costs of production and compare them with the revenues by using break-even analysis. Costs will be broken into two distinct areas: fixed costs, which do not vary in the short run as output changes, e.g. rates, rent, salaries, etc; and variable costs, which change directly in proportion to output, e.g. wages, raw materials, etc.

Break-even analysis will show the sales necessary to cover both sets of costs and will allow profit projections based upon production targets to take place. This is essential because it tells the production department how much must be produced for the product to be profitable.

The production manager will wish to see the break-even analysis but will also want further information. He or she will wish to know the profitability of different departments and products within his or her control. A company might produce three or four products. The production manager might wish to know which of these products is more profitable. In order to do this costs must be separated and apportioned to each product. From this information

mass-production arise from increasing economies of scale. Standardization can take place. However, if a firm places too much emphasis on this they might limit their variety of goods in a market and their market share could be affected. There is often a dilemma between a sales manager who wants a wide choice to appeal to a market and production manager who wants further standardization to ease manufacture.

Ergonomics

This is a form of study used by many manufacturers to ensure that resources are being used efficiently. It is an investigation of the efficiency of each worker and the tools that he or she is using. This investigation often takes place in the form of a *time and motion study* which will observe a job being done, and often suggest new and more efficient methods of operation so that a product can be produced more quickly, with greater ease, to a better standard, etc. (see Fig. 5.5). This study might look at types of machines, production-team relationships, noise, working en-

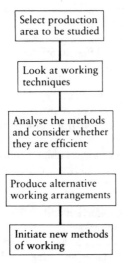

Figure 5.5 The stages of a time and motion study.

50

vironment, workload, etc. A study might be broken into a variety of stages to ensure that a job is being completed efficiently.

Time and motion study has often led to industrial-relations difficulties. Workers often perform slowly and with exactitude under tested conditions particularly if they are worried about targets going up and piece rates going down if their methods are changed. They may also be prepared to argue that the methods they use are the most efficient and that they are used to them. However, managers may argue that studies provide them with detailed information which enables them to operate efficiently and that product and plant design will be less effective if they do not consider workers and their techniques of working.

Modern technology

Technology is the process of applying knowledge to the development of tools, products and processes for human purposes. For example, we might want to improve the production of chocolate bars so that one chocolate bar tastes like another with a given recipe. A technologist might work out a solution to this problem—machinery that provides a consistent taste.

A technique of production is concerned with the way in which labour, equipment and other means of production are combined to make a finished product. Therefore we can change the technique of production by altering the way we combine factors; for example, if we made a cake using an electric mixer rather than a spoon we would have changed the technique of production.

Technological change is concerned with adding new techniques of production to those already known. Today we live in a world in which technological change is very rapid,

and in which some industries are described as 'high-tech'.

How high is the 'high' in high-tech? This is a difficult question to answer. Most people when asked to define modern technology will mention things like microchips, computers and telecommunications equipment. High technology products generally involve an 'above-average' concentration of scientific and engineering skills.

Definitions of high-tech generally concentrate on the number of scientists and engineers involved in an industry or the amount of money spent on research and development in a particular industry. If we take a broader view of modern technology as involving rapid changes in techniques of production we can see that this would apply to a wide range of businesses. Obvious areas of modern technology would include information processing in banking and insurance and the automation of production lines in many factories. Today even the small corner shop might employ a small business computer with an accounts package and also use a telephone answering machine.

Automation
Mechanization involves the use of machinery. The machine is, however, controlled directly by the operator.

Automation, on the other hand, involves the creation of a control unit to control the machine. Instructions are fed into the control unit which then controls operations.

Machines are at work in our homes. Examples of machines controlled directly by the operator include a food mixer, a hair dryer or a vacuum cleaner. Automatic machines, however, are under automatic control. These machines are able to control themselves once they have been fed the instructions. Examples would include a washing

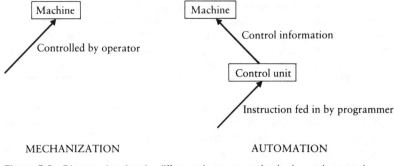

| MECHANIZATION | AUTOMATION |

Figure 5.6 Diagram showing the difference between mechanization and automation.

machine, the central-heating system or a video recorder. (See Fig. 5.6.)

An automatic machine needs to have some method of controlling itself. It must be able to sense and measure when and when not to take action. An example of the way this operates is the central-heating system in a house. Generally this system will be triggered off by one of two mechanisms: the timer and the thermostat. The system can be programmed to switch on and off at set times, or to come on whenever the temperature in a building falls below a certain level.

Industrial robots

Most of the automated machines used by businesses are dedicated to a particular task. A dedicated word processor, for instance, is a machine that can only be used for word processing. A dedicated production-line part is only able to do one specific task on the production line.

Robots are multi-purpose machines that can be programmed and reprogrammed. An industrial robot in a car factory may be able to be programmed to paint, and reprogrammed to weld pieces together, or to assemble parts. We can thus see that robots have the following advantages over human labour in doing simple repetitive tasks:

1. They can work longer hours.
2. They will not get bored.
3. They can often operate faster.
4. They may be able to work more accurately.
5. They are usually cheaper to run.

Robots in industry are now being fitted with vision recognition systems. This makes it possible for them to recognize objects by their shape and size and to fit items like car windscreens by measuring up and centring the screen.

Computer-aided design

Computer-aided design has improved the reliability and speed with which the design of complex structures such as aeroplanes, cars and bridges can take place. The system couples the electronic drawing board of a powerful computer system with a magnetic pen. The designer is able to use the computer to draw automatically sections of a car or whatever he or she is working on. The computer will also make mathematical calculations and thus the designer is saved thousands of hours of background work.

CASE STUDY—USING NEW PROCESSES

When Teresa Dawson set up her advertising agency she had a photocopier that could produce one sheet of copied material at a time. Within months a new model had come on to the market which would run off 100 copies of an item at a time. Most recently Teresa has been able to purchase a model which prints in colour and allows printing on both sides of the paper.

Questions

1. How has the technique of photocopying altered over time?
2. What is the existing state of technology in photocopying?
3. How could technology develop still further in photocopying?
4. At this stage it is worth writing down on a piece of paper what you understand by modern technology. This involves two processes:
   (a) Try to describe what you mean by modern technology.
   (b) List some examples of what you consider to be modern technology.

CASE STUDY— AUTOMATION IN A MODERN BREWERY

In the UK today the beer and lager market is dominated by a few large breweries. These firms are able to produce high outputs at a low average cost per unit. The brewing process is controlled by a central computer which checks that the mixing of ingredients has taken place correctly and takes regular readings on temperatures and fermentation.

Bottles returned from public houses and other outlets will be returned on palettes containing several crates of bottles. The crates will be lifted off the palette automatically and a machine will pick up the bottles and they will pass down a line into a washing

51

machine. The bottles will then be checked for faults by an electronic device that looks at the structure of the bottle. The bottles will be automatically filled and an electronic eye will check that the contents reach a certain level in the bottle. The machine line will then label and cap the bottles. They will be placed in crates and a number of crates will automatically be placed on a palette which is automatically stacked on an out-going lorry. The whole process has been pre-designed to eliminate the need for labour in the main line of production. Labour will only be required to supervise the computer, and maintain the machinery and keep an eye on it in case it breaks down.

Questions

1. Why is the beer and lager market suitable for mass-production?
2. What other production lines can you think of that are suitable for automated production?
3. What types of production would be unsuitable for mass-production?
4. Who benefits from automation?
5. Who loses out as a result of automation?

CASE STUDY—PRODUCING TIN BOXES AT HUNTLEY, BOORNE & STEVENS

The first stage of making a tin box is to find a customer. This is done by a salesperson who finds out exactly what the customer wants: the size, the materials required, the colours, and a basic idea for a design. The salesperson then goes back to the designer who designs the tin box. They make up a model of the box in stiff cardboard. This model is then taken back to the customer and if it is acceptable and they can agree on a price the factory will go into production.

The purchasing department orders the tin plate and the ink, which is in four colours: red, blue, yellow and black. It also buys the extra parts that the production department needs to put on the machines the firm already has so they can do the required job. The next stage is to paint the design on to the tin plate. The tin box is usually made up of a number of components. A square tin has three separate parts: the bottom, top and sides. A number of the same components are printed on one sheet of tin plate. The bottom is not always printed. The printing method used is offset lithography. The printing is not done straight on to the tin but on to a rubber blanket. The colours are printed as thousands of tiny dots; the closer they are together the darker the colour. The print is transferred from the rubber roller to the tin plate.

The first colour to be printed is blue, then yellow, followed by red, and finally black which gives an outline to the other colours. When the pieces have all been printed they are cut into individual bodies. The lids are pressed into shape by putting them in a power press. The sides of the box are folded into the right shape on a body former; the sharp edges are all folded in under the seams and rolled and pressed tightly. The bottom is placed with the body and the edges of both components are rolled up together. The lid is then put on and the box is finished. Different types of boxes are made in slightly different ways, but the process is basically the same. The machines are fitted differently for making each type of box.

Questions

1. Where does the process of manufacturing a tin box begin?
2. Identify six different occupations involved with the manufacture of a tin box.
3. How does the division of labour come into tin-box manufacture?
4. How is specialization of machinery (rather than specialization of labour) involved at Huntley, Boorne & Stevens?
5. What is the most important stage in the production of a tin box?
6. From what you have read, would you say that Huntley, Boorne & Stevens use a job, batch or flow method of production?
7. In what way can the firm be said to be employing a technique of production?
8. In what ways might tin-box manufacture be subject to technological change?
9. Would computer-aided design be helpful to the firm? If so, why might it not be prepared to use it?
10. Why would Huntley, Boorne & Stevens use quality-control inspection?

Questions

1. Complete the following sentences using the words below.

Research and development
Planned obsolescence
Prototypes
Purchasing manager
Quality control
Drawing office
Production supervisors
Break-even analysis
Ergonomics
Automation

(a) Before going into production it is common to test several .... of a product.

(b) .... is essential to ensure that finished products meet the required standard.

(c) The .... has the responsibility of buying in the parts required for production.

(d) The .... is a place where manufacturing drawings are produced.

(e) Documents are issued to .... to tell them what to produce.

(f) Manufacturers employ a process known as .... to check that resources are being used efficiently.

(g) .... involves setting up a control unit so that machines can run themselves.

(h) Many manufacturers build .... into their products so that consumers will have to replace them after a period.

(i) High-technology industries involve a lot of ....

(j) .... highlights the amount of sales required to cover costs.

2. An advert for an office messenger appeared in a national newspaper. It said: 'Must be willing to work 24 hours a day, 7 days a week. No breaks, pay or conditions.'

What do you think that this advert was trying to sell and what was the argument it was putting over?

3. Which of the following are examples of productive employment?

(a) Machine-minder
(b) Farmer
(c) Boxer
(d) Ballet dancer
(e) Factory supervisor
(f) Author
(g) Teacher
(h) Tool-maker

4. Would you classify each of the following as an example of job, batch or flow production?

(a) Mars bars
(b) Portrait photographs
(c) A commemorative issue of tin boxes
(d) An ocean liner
(e) Tinned cat food
(f) Insurance policies for households
(g) Haircuts
(h) A play
(i) Electronic circuit boards
(j) Cars
(k) Wallpaper

5. Below are listed some countries and the number of industrial robots each had in early 1985.

Japan	67 500
United States	14 500
West Germany	6 600
France	3 400
United Kingdom	2 700

What does the list tell you about industrial production in these countries? What further information would you like?

6. The advert in Fig. 5.7, on page 54, was produced for the Burton Group plc.

(a) What questions would you want to know the answers to before deciding to produce the outfits below?

(i) Set out a market-research questionnaire to find out such things as whether there would be a demand for the outfits and what prices people would be prepared to pay for them.

(ii) Draw up a list of questions which the production department would want answering before production takes place.

(b) What does the advert (which was produced in 1987) tell you about the market for clothes?

7. In the second half of the 1980s the top ten high-tech sectors of the American economy in terms of money spent on research and development were:

- Missiles and spacecraft
- Electronics and telecommunications
- Aircraft and parts
- Office automation
- Ordnance and accessories
- Drugs and medicines
- Inorganic chemicals
- Professional and scientific instruments
- Engines, turbines and parts
- Plastics, rubber and synthetic fibres

Try to divide the following 10 products into the above sectors:

(a) Vaccines
(b) Generators
(c) Satellites
(d) Non-military arms
(e) Helicopters
(f) Desk calculators
(g) Telephone apparatus
(h) Nitrogen
(i) Optical instruments
(j) Synthetic resins

8. Outline the considerations a manufacturer has to take into

The secret of successful retailing is giving the market what it wants.

Figure 5.7 Advertisement produced for the Burton Group plc.

account before making a decision to produce a product. Describe the problems of research and development.

9. Explain what is meant by 'production' and describe the roles of some of the personnel involved with this process.

10. Why is costing important to the production process? Illustrate your answer with references to the basic techniques used.

COURSEWORK

Why is different technology used in different circumstances?

The sealing of cans is the process of closing one end of the can with a lid. This process can be done by using two different methods of production technology.

The first way is to use a semi-automatic machine that makes one can at a time. Not much skill is required to operate the machine, but the quality is poor, and 5 per cent of the cans are rejected by quality control. As a result it is necessary to have a supervising officer at every fourth machine.

The second method is to use an automatic machine that seals four cans at a time. There is very little manual work involved except the control of the machine. The workers need to be skilled in operating the machine. The quality of the work is very high and there is less need for quality inspection.

Southworld, a multi-national company, has canning factories in many countries throughout the world. All these canning plants were set up at the same time but in some countries the firm installed the semi-automatic machines and in others the automatic machines. As a group, discuss the reasons why the firm may have chosen to use different technology in different countries. You should then go on to ask the question whether advanced technology is most suitable in all circumstances.

Questions

1. How is production organized in a local manufacturing or service business?
2. Contrast the production constraints in a service and a manufacturing business. How and why do they differ?
3. Pick a local firm and say why it has employed automated technology.
4. What is the purpose of work study?

6 Marketing

A market is a situation in which goods can be bought, sold or exchanged. The essential requirements are buyers, sellers, goods and money. Any form of transaction will involve a 'market process' of some description. The marketing function of an organization is to link the flow of goods and services from the producer to the wishes of the consumer. Consumers' tastes constantly change and so marketing must be a dynamic area aimed at moving an organization forward. It is the information extracted by the marketing department which determines the products a company makes and how it allocates its resources to various departments. For this reason the marketing process is closely connected to the research and development function in the development of new products. (See Fig. 6.1.)

Though marketing might involve considerable expense which could be reflected in the selling price, the process provides management with a degree of safety. Management will know, on the basis of the marketing information and advice, that it can go ahead with the development of a product which will ultimately provide the firm with returns.

An important feature in marketing is the consideration of a product's life cycle. When a product is introduced, its sales are likely to be low and promotion will be expensive. If the product is successful, sales will increase until they reach their peak. Eventually new products will come on to the market and the sales of existing products will decline. When we look at the curve in Fig. 6.2 we must bear in mind that the time period for dif-

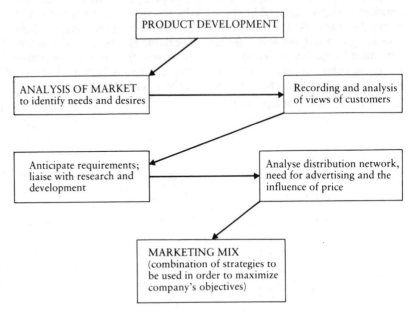

Figure 6.1 The functions of the marketing department.

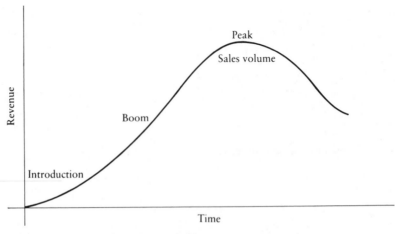

Figure 6.2 A product only has a certain lifespan.

ferent products will vary a lot. For example, the sales of Mars bars are still, after many years, only somewhere between boom and peak. Other products such as fashion clothes and products that only catch the public imagination for a short while have much shorter product lives.

An understanding of the lifespan of a product will enable the marketing manager to plan his or her activities.

The term 'marketing mix' refers to a number of areas which might require detailed analysis in relation to each other in order to maximize profits. Elements of the 'marketing mix' might include details about:

1. The product
2. Its price
3. Its promotion
4. The market-place

The correct combination of such elements will enable a company to fulfil its role. Elements of the mix will vary in emphasis from one product to another. Fig. 6.3 compares the marketing mix for two different products.

Market-research information must be obtained and then analysed so that all the options are revealed. (See Fig. 6.4.)

Data collected can be either primary data or secondary data. Primary data is gathered first-hand for the current investigation while secondary data is the use of data already gathered by somebody else.

Primary data is usually gathered by doing a survey in which information is obtained by interviewing a sample of the population being investigated. It is usual to use a questionnaire, which should be made with care. The questions should be clear and simple, should not be open-ended and thus difficult to analyse, and wherever possible should be pre-tested.

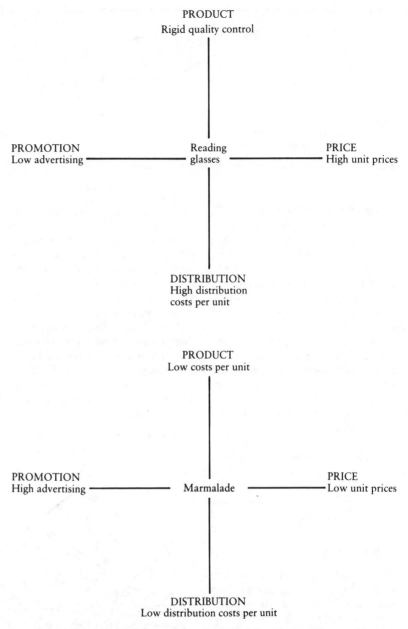

Figure 6.3 The marketing mix for reading glasses and marmalade—different products need different elements of the mix to be emphasized.

Information may be gathered in the following ways:
1. By personal interviews with an experienced interviewer
2. By post, though postal surveys tend to lead to slow results and the response rate is low
3. By telephone, which is speedy and easy to administer particularly for industrial markets

57

Areas of market research

CLIMATE FOR SELLING
Incomes, population statistics, business activity, political factors

CONSUMERS' WISHES
Desires, needs, uses

PRODUCT
Features, price, acceptability

MARKET
Competition, prices of competitors, trends in sales, opportunities for the future

SELLING
Costs, strategy, markets

Figure 6.4 Market research considers many different factors.

Sampling might be random, with each member of the population having an equal chance of being picked; or it could be systematic, including, for example, every tenth member of the population; or an interviewer may have selected people to interview (e.g. the 100 best dressed people in Grantham).

Data must be processed and organized into an easily understood format so that trends or patterns can be detected (see the notes on presenting information in Chapter 1). Information may be represented in the form of pie charts, bar charts and pictures, and statistical analysis may take place. Once the data has been analysed, a series of plans will be required and marketing managers will provide both short-term and long-term objectives.

Advertising

Most people understand advertising to be sellers publicizing their goods to customers. In fact, any type of publicity is advertising. In the UK, the body that spends most money on advertising is the government, which has all sorts of messages to put over to the public (see Fig. 6.5).

The government rarely tries to sell things to people. More often it tries to inform them of their rights. This passing-on of information is a very important part of advertising.

Most adverts, however, are not just there to inform the public—you do not see a soap-powder advert that simply gives information about the powder. The advert goes further and contains a persuasive message. Most firms that try to sell goods will use *persuasive advertising.*

A persuasive selling message is one that promises to the people to whom it is addressed a desirable and believable benefit.

There are many different types of advert that can be used to persuade, including the following:

1. Adverts showing a famous personality using the product

2. Adverts comparing one product with other products

3. Adverts using sex appeal

Many firms aim to develop strong brand images for their products. A brand is the name of a company's product, such as 'Frosties', 'Marathon', and 'Fairy Liquid'. If people associate a brand name with a product then a firm will make large sales and attract a loyalty to the brand. The creation of a good brand image

Figure 6.5 An example of the sort of message that the government may try to put over through advertising.

depends on developing a good marketing mixture including producing quality products at competitive prices coupled with careful advertising.

Advertising agencies

If you were advertising the village dance you could simply make out some posters and place them around the village where they would attract most attention. However, firms risking a lot of money on an advertising campaign must make sure that their advertising is in safe hands. Generally firms will therefore employ an advertising agency to carry out the campaign.

For advertising to be successful it must do the following:

1. Reach the right audience
2. Be attractive and appealing
3. Cost little in relation to the extra sales made

Reaching the right audience

An advertising agency will know how best to reach the right audience. It will have several media available to it, depending on the size of the audience that it wants to reach. (See Fig. 6.6.)

The advertising agency will be in a good position to advise on the best media to use. Perhaps if a firm wants to produce a new biscuit or bar of chocolate it will be advised to use television advertising. People in Britain watch a lot of television, and firms showing their adverts during popular programmes like *Brookside* can reach millions of people.

Recently, television advertising has been somewhat threatened by television gadgetry. More and more families have push-button remote-control units for their televisions, allowing them to switch over during the adverts without leaving their seats. In America, people have automatic switch over controls to their televisions so that when the adverts

Figure 6.6 Advertising must be directed at the right audience.

come on, the television switches over to a pop or other station until the adverts are over.

Obviously, if a firm is selling a specialized product like expensive fur coats then the advertising agency will

suggest that it uses a specialist medium like an exclusive women's magazine.

Attractive and appealing advertising
The advertising agency will have

59

wide experience in planning the lay-out of advertising campaigns. Sometimes the firm selling the goods will have a big say in what goes into the advert, and sometimes the advertising agency will decide alone how the advertising should be done.

Sometimes the advertising agency will hire another specialist firm to come up with a name for the product.

Market research will be carried out to find out what potential customers want. For example, when a new biscuit is introduced on to the market, members of the public might be tested to find out what they think of the presentation of the product. For instance, several differently coloured labels might be designed for the product. A selected audience of people might then be asked to watch a television screen whilst the labels are flashed in front of them. They will then be asked to fill in a questionnaire saying which labels they remember and which they liked the best.

Cost in relation to the extra sales made

The extra sales made as a result of an advertising campaign are expected to bring in far more money than the cost of the advertising. This is a difficult problem for the advertising agency because it may be able to design a very attractive set of adverts but this will be of little use unless the adverts attract far more sales.

Sometimes when a new product is being marketed it will be given a trial run in a selected area of the country. Usually this will be in a particular Independent Television (ITV) region. For example, a crisp company brings out a new star-shaped crisp. Its advertising agency might then advertise the crisp in the Southern television region. The product will first be marketed purely in the south of England and if it proves popular it will then be

advertised and sold in the rest of the country.

By carrying out a cheap pilot scheme in one part of the UK, the company will not lose a lot of money if the campaign is a flop in that one area.

Advertising agencies will also 'cost' an advertising campaign. They will work out the cost of the advertising campaign and calculate the extra profits from the campaign to see if it will be worth while.

Control over advertising in the United Kingdom

Advertisers can't say anything they like when preparing an advert.

1. They must keep within the law. For instance, the Trades' Description Act lays down that goods put up for sale must be as they are described (e.g. a waterproof watch must be waterproof).
2. The advertising industry has its own code of practice which advertisers must obey.

The British code of advertising practice

This is a voluntary agreement by firms in the advertising industry to keep their adverts within certain standards. For instance, when advertising slimming products like slimming pills and biscuits, the advertiser must say that these should be taken in addition to a balanced diet. In other words, the advertiser should not suggest that a person can slim simply by eating slimming biscuits—this would obviously be dangerous to health. The British Code of Advertising Practice covers newspapers, magazines, cinema adverts, leaflets, brochures, posters, and commercials on video tape, but not TV and radio adverts.

The advertising standards authority (ASA)

The ASA is responsible for supervis-

Figure 6.7 The Advertising Standards Authority uses advertisements like this one to put its own message across.

ing the British Code of Advertising Practice except for Independent Television. You might have seen an advert that appears in national newspapers and magazines part of which looks like Fig. 6.7. The advert goes on to say that if you have any complaints about adverts in the paper you should write to the ASA, which will take up your complaint. Of course, some of the complaints received by the ASA are frivolous like the man that complained that he had poured Heineken on his pot plant and it had died.

However, if the ASA feels that an advert is indecent or untrue it will ask the advertising agency that produced the advert to change it.

The advertising agency will then change the advert because they know the ASA can ask the media to stop printing adverts by that agency.

The Independent Broadcasting Authority (IBA)

The IBA controls radio and television advertising. Examples of some of the rules involved are that products which appear in a programme cannot be shown in advertisements immediately before or after the programme and that newsreaders cannot appear in adverts.

Pricing

Pricing is an important part of the marketing mix

Businesses will have different pricing policies depending on what their objectives are.

Maximizing profits

It is possible that some firms will set a price that will enable them to maximize profits. Although this may be the objective of some firms there are many others that set their prices to meet other objectives.

Cost plus pricing

Some firms set a target of how much profit they would like to make over what their costs are, e.g. costs + 10%. The firm would then work out their expected costs and add 10% for profits.

Competitive pricing

Pricing decisions might be based on following what competitors charge.

Maximizing sales

Some firms may be more interested in increasing sales in order to take a large share of the market than in maximizing profits.

Short term pricing objectives

In the short term a business may also have other pricing policies. For example it may sell new promotional items at a low price in order to introduce them to the market. A firm might also adopt a low price policy in order to destroy the market share of rivals or to prevent new firms from entering the market.

After-sales service

After-sales service usually applies to durable goods such as washing machines, central heating system, electric cookers and other items of equipment. A business must decide whether it is going to offer its services for a period of time after the sale has been made. The advantages of running an after-sales service are that once you have managed to create confidence in the consumer then you are likely to maintain their loyalty. Groups like the electricity board work on the principle that a customer is a customer for life and therefore selling an appliance is only the start of a business relationship. Another aspect of after-sales service is the handling of enquiries and complaints from customers. Some firms will actually send out circulars encouraging customer comment whereas others will respond to customers as and when required.

Offers of after-sales service may be an important part of the promotion of a product. An example of this would be where a car sales firm offers a free service after a given number of miles.

Sales

This is an area of great importance to the success of the business. Selling involves getting customers to purchase a company's products. The salesforce must have a good understanding of the product it is selling and must know the market well enough to know the customer's desires. A salesperson's job requires persistence and energy and can be one of the most difficult in industry. Salespeople's salaries are often linked to commission.

Any salesforce must cover as many areas of a market as possible and often sales representatives are each allocated a territory which comes under the supervision of an area sales manager. Salespeople can provide a close link with customers and often establish such a good relationship that repeat orders are made. They are often involved with the promotion of new products, providing displays and demonstrations as well as helping at exhibitions. Sales relate directly to profits and of course break-even forecasts, and sales targets may be set for the salesforce. Export orders are often fundamental to the success of a business and well-qualified representatives are involved with overseas promotion.

Distribution

The *channel of distribution* is the route which products follow from the manufacturer to the consumer. Market research will often reveal channels of distribution used by competitors.

The traditional way of distributing goods from a manufacturer to a market is through a small number of wholesalers who then sell the goods to a larger number of retailers (see Fig. 6.8 on page 62).

In this way a wholesaler is a go-between who buys in bulk from manufacturers and break the bulk down into small units for retailers. Wholesalers often provide a variety of services which benefit both manufacturers and retailers, such as warehousing, credit, transport and packaging. However, the existence of wholesalers adds to the selling price and wholesalers cannot be expected to concentrate on any one manufacturer's goods.

If a manufacturer sells to a retailer directly it can exert firmer control over its sales and the manufacturer and retailer can work together on sales-promotion schemes. Selling direct to retailers involves a larger salesforce and increased transport charges when sending smaller consignments. If circumstances allow, it can be possible for manufacturers to sell directly to consumers, particularly if the product is a high-cost one and has a good reputation within the market. (See Fig. 6.9 on page 62.)

The manufacturer has to think carefully about choices for distribu-

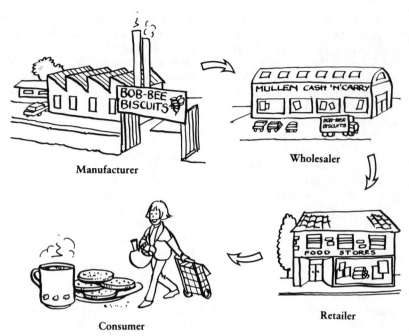

Figure 6.8 The traditional route from manufacturer to consumer—via a wholesaler and a retailer.

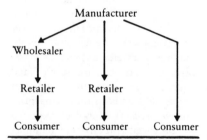

Figure 6.9 Sometimes a manufacturer will sell direct to a retailer, missing out the wholesaler; and sometimes even the retailer will be missed out, when a manufacturer sells direct to the consumer.

tion and aim to minimize selling costs and maximize sales.

Retailers are in direct contact with consumers and are therefore in the best position to understand individual consumers' desires. An efficient system of retailing is essential if the types of commodities made by producers are to relate closely to consumers' desires. A retailer is the outlet through which goods are sold to the consumers and may exist in a variety of different forms.

Transport

The location of a firm will influence its costs. Most organizations employ a transport manager whose responsibility is not just to provide transport for raw materials and finished goods but also to provide a fleet of vehicles for sales representatives and senior staff. A transport manager's knowledge is of particular importance when goods are dispatched overseas. A fundamental decision is whether to purchase a fleet of vehicles for the company, to use private carriers or to lease vehicles. If a company runs its own fleet the transport manager must choose the right size and type of vehicle, arrange maintenance and staffing, and be responsible for company policy relating to vehicles. The transport department will be concerned with documentation such as delivery schedules and loading sheets to ensure the vehicles cover authorized routes with the correct loads. Often return loads can be picked up so that vehicles do not run back empty.

Major forms of transport
Road
Such large volumes of goods are transported by road that congestion is now a major problem. The development of motorways and ring roads has improved journey times but these are costly. The major benefit of road transport is that it can provide a door-to-door service and thus it cuts out intermediate handling—and reduces the possibility of theft, loss, or damage. Specialized vehicles have been developed for particular types of loads and this method of transport is fast over short distances.

Rail
The use of containers which can be transhipped from road to rail developed in the late 1960s and still exists today but it has never really lived up to expectations. Undoubtedly railways keep a certain amount of traffic away from roads and their major benefit is for bulky goods needing to be transported over long distances. Bad weather has little effect on journey times—but a strike can paralyse the network.

Sea
Shipping often provides the most suitable form of transport for low-value bulky goods (in bulk carriers) and for containers (in container ships) as well as for a wide variety of other loads.

Air
Though this form of transport is expensive and can only take loads of a certain size, it has developed rapidly over recent years. The major advant-

age of air transport is its speed, and it tends to be used for cargoes which are expensive in relation to their weight; for items which are needed urgently; and for items which have a short shelf-life, e.g. newspapers, fresh exotic flowers, etc.

CASE STUDY—NOT JUST SELLING NEWSPAPERS BUT SELLING CLASSIFIED ADVERTISEMENTS

A major source of revenue for newspapers is their classified columns. These are particularly important for bringing in money to regional and local newspapers.

In February 1987 the *London Daily News* was launched to compete with the *London Evening Standard* for the massive London market. There are very few areas of business life as competitive as selling newspapers. One of the most favoured newspaper ploys for competing with rivals is the 'spoil-up'. One newspaper finds out what a rival paper plans to do next and then does it before the rival, or spoils whatever the rival is going to do by some other means.

The *London Daily News* referred to its classified columns as the breadbasket of the operation. The *News* started off by undercutting what the *Standard* was charging per line of classified advertising: in February 1987 the *Standard* was charging £7 per line, whilst the *News* was charging £5.50 per line.

The *Standard* had got in first, however, by advertising the size of its readership and the number of job advertisements it carried.

(The student may be interested to note that the *Daily News* went out of business in the summer of 1987.)

Questions

1. Find out the difference between *display* and *classified* advertisements.
2. What are the various elements of the marketing mix involved in selling newspapers?
3. Why was the *News* taking a risk in undercutting the rate charged by the *Standard*?
4. If you were marketing the classified columns in a new London newspaper what strategy would you use?
5. What is the charge per line of classified advertising in the following?
   (a) Your local paper
   (b) Your local free paper
6. What is the circulation of your local papers?
7. How important do you think the classified advertisements are to these papers?
8. What sorts of businesses advertise in them and for what purposes?

CASE STUDY—MARKETING A PHOTOGRAPHER

Jane Rodgers (see Fig. 6.10) is a very talented photographer. She is in her late twenties and has won several artistic awards for her photography. Up to now she has concentrated on the art side of her work and has been happy to make a steady living. She now concentrates on photographing children at playgroups and nurseries. She wants to organize her business in

Figure 6.10 Jane Rodgers and her photographic business. (*Source:* Kim Hooper, Reading)

a slightly more structured fashion in order to increase turnover. She has never advertised her work or done any deliberate marketing. She approaches her local business advice centre for help with marketing. Assuming that you represent the business centre, what advice would you give her?

CASE STUDY—SELLING BRITISH GAS SHARES

The advert in Fig. 6.11 was part of one of the most successful *advertising campaigns* ever launched in the UK. The aim of the campaign was to encourage people who would not normally think of buying shares to do so. The campaign started with a gradual build-up of television adverts introducing the idea of gas as a major British industry. It then developed into a joky campaign in which members of the public where invited to find a fictitious character called Sid and tell him to buy British Gas shares. The notion of finding Sid captured the public imagination. The campaign was run in the *tabloids*, and on the sides of bus shelters—anywhere where it would catch the attention of the citizen on the street.

Questions

1. What is meant by the following terms?
   (a) Advertising campaigns
   (b) Tabloids
2. What was the target market of the advertising campaign?
3. Why do you think the government wanted to sell shares to a wider group?
4. Why do you think the campaign reached such a wide audience?
5. What would your target market be if you wanted to sell the following?
   (a) Grain silos
   (b) Riding equipment
   (c) Cassette tape recorders
   (d) Wallpaper
   (e) Soft drinks
   (f) Margarine
   (g) Bulldozers
   List two advertising media you would use in each case.

QUESTIONS

1. Complete the following sentences using the list of words below and in the next column.

Direct mailing
Mass media
Advertising agency
Informative advert
Trade journal
Persuasive advert
Market research

(a) An advert just giving the plain 'hard facts' about an item for sale would be an example of an ....

(b) An advert which tries to entice somebody into buying an item through subtle techniques is an example of a ....

(c) A firm specializing in helping people to advertise their products is called an ....

(d) National newspapers, television, the radio and cinema are collectively called the ....

(e) A magazine providing specialist information about a particular line of business is called a ....

(f) Before firms market a product, they will normally carry out .... to estimate demand for it.

(g) Advertising by posting leaflets direct to potential customers is known as ....

UP AGAINST TIME by Jeanne Willis and Trevor Melvin

Figure 6.11 Advertisement for British Gas shares.

2. Design (a) an informative and (b) a persuasive advert to illustrate the difference.
3. Explain what is meant by 'market research'. How would you carry out a market-research campaign for a new type of crisp?
4. Ramesh Gehlot (see Fig. 6.12) has just opened up a new greengrocer's business and decides to spend £500 launching the business by advertising.
   (a) Suggest four ways in which this advertising budget could be spent.
   (b) Explain three motives to which the advertising could appeal.
   (c) Describe two ways, other than advertising, in which Ramesh could promote his sales.
   (d) Which of the methods of sales promotion you have given in answer to (c) would you expect to be the most effective?
   (e) Explain with reasons whether you think it is worth promoting a new greengrocer's business.
5. You are the marketing manager for sporting equipment with a well-known national supplier. In recent months your rivals have started marketing inferior imitations of your football boots. The managing director has called you into her office and told you that you can have an extra sum of advertising money to win back customers. What methods of marketing would you employ?
6. Explain how the marketing mix will vary for the following products:
   (a) Chocolate
   (b) Chicken food
   (c) Newspapers
   (d) Electric blankets
   (e) Tablecloths.
   It might be worth writing to some local firms to find out what marketing mix they employ.
7. Compare the marketing mix of manufacturing firms and service industries.
8. Study the adverts in a teenage magazine. Which products would you expect to have long life cycles and which ones short life cycles?
9. What is the function of the wholesaler in the chain of distribution? In what situations is the wholesaler eliminated from distribution?
10. Sylvia Whitbread, who owns a manufacturing business, decides to acquire her own fleet of delivery vehicles instead of using road-haulage contractors. Why do you think she might have chosen to acquire her own vehicles?

COURSEWORK

1. Margaret Greaves was going to open up a dress agency in Castlegate, Grantham. The dress agency was to deal in good-quality nearly new clothes. She had learnt on a business-studies course that the Post Office provides a free service of up to 1000 first-class mail shots for any business just starting up. She decided that this would be the best way of telling the sort of people she wanted to come to her shop how to find her and what she had to offer. She thought that any other form of advertising would not be sufficient because it would not target the right audience. The letter that Margaret prepared for her mail shot is shown in Fig. 6.13 on page 66.
   (a) Put yourself in Margaret's position—you have 1000 mail shots to send out. How are you going to decide who to send the mail shots to and how will you go about the task?
   (b) The dress agency was going to open on Monday, 7 April. Margaret decided to send out a small poster on an A4 sheet of paper just giving the important details about the opening and the business on it. She decided to have the picture of the carousel in the centre of the poster. Draw the poster putting in the details which you would regard as important.
   (c) Why do you think that the Post Office is prepared to

Figure 6.12 Ramesh Gehlot and his greengrocer's business. (*Source:* Kim Hooper, Reading)

CAROUSEL

Dress Agency

Prop: M. Greaves

13 Castlegate
Grantham
Lincs
NG31 6SL

Telephone: (0476) 79983

Dear

On Monday 7th April the "Carousel" Dress Agency will open
at 13 Castlegate, Grantham.

I am approaching a very select clientele who have good dress
sense and taste, in the hope that we may be of help to one
another.

In your wardrobe you possibly have a range of good clothes which
you may simply have tired of, dislike, or which represent a
mistake (which of us hasn't!). My service may help to recoup
some of the considerable outlay of those purchases.

Carousel will sell for you ladies' and childrens' clothing on a
commission basis of 60% to the client and 40% to Agency, plus a
10p per item handling charge (maximum 50p). Naturally all items
must be in excellent condition and seasonal.

It is my intention that the Agency will provide quality
merchandise, personal service and the guarantee of a confidential
relationship with my clients.

In addition I will stock some select new clothing - hand
knitteds, fashions made exclusively for Carousel, and a range of
inexpensive, pretty gifts.

I look forward to hearing from you on either my business or home
telephone number (Grantham 79391).

Sincerely yours,

M. Greaves

Figure 6.13   Letter produced by Margaret Greaves for her mail shot.

offer new businesses a free mail shot of 1000 letters?

(d) Once the business was under way would Margaret need to carry out any follow-up marketing? Explain your answer.

2. How do mail-order firms advertise? This would be a suitable coursework topic for all students.

3. A high-street bank is considering the development of a new cash-dispensing machine. How would it go about carrying out this decision? You should try to think up suitable questions to investigate. The class could then be split into groups each of which is to investigate a particular topic area. Possible questions might be:

(a) What type of market research should be carried out?

(b) What questions should be asked in the market research?

(c) Who will be the bank's competitors?

(d) What should be the design of the cash dispenser?

(e) What should the service be called?

(f) How much would it cost to produce and install?

(g) How could the dispenser be promoted?

(h) How should charges be made for using the service?

(i) How will the scheme be financed?

(j) Who will organize the project?

(k) How will the bank decide whether the scheme is a success?

7 Communication

Communication is the passing-on of ideas and information. In business we need good, clear communications. The contact may be between people, organizations or places and can be in a number of forms such as speech, writing, actions and gestures.

Try out the following exercise:

1. Select a volunteer from the group.
2. Give him or her the pattern sheet (Fig. 7.1). The volunteer must now describe the patterns to the rest of the group.
3. The rest of the class should try to draw the shapes described by the person with the pattern sheet. See how clearly you can understand the instructions given. Why is it easier to draw some of the shapes than the others?

The aim of this exercise is to show how difficult it is to communicate even simple shapes.

Communications problems arise when one of the following is the case:

1. The language used is not fully understood.
2. The means of passing the message is poor.
3. There are too many steps in the communication of the message.

What other barriers to communication can you think of?

The passage of information can be seen as a flow from the sender to the receiver (see Fig. 7.2).

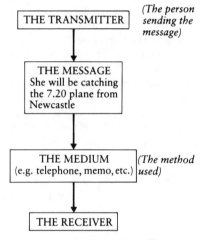

Figure 7.2 The flow of information from sender to receiver.

Basic communication inside a business

The most frequent type of communication within a business will be spoken communication as a result of face-to-face contact.

The most frequently used form of written communication will be the internal memorandum (memo). Memos should be brief and straightforward (see Fig. 7.3 on page 68).

Figure 7.1 Shapes for the describing exercise.

```
MEMO from the Safety Officer

   To: all staff  .......

Please make sure that cars are not
parked across the fire exit.
```

Figure 7.3 Example of a brief, straightforward memo.

Reports are another common form of internal communication and will frequently be used as a basis for discussion. When writing a report, put a clear heading at the top. List all the people to whom the report is to be circulated. Then break up the report into numbered sections under clear subheadings (see Fig. 7.4).

Perhaps the most important part of report writing is making clear your recommendations and conclusions. The point of a report should be clear and precise so that it builds up to some forceful recommendations or conclusions, e.g., 'I would strongly suggest that if (a) all staff wear protective headgear, (b) regular safety checks are carried out and (c) safety notices are displayed in prominent places, *then there will be fewer factory accidents.*'

Notices are another common form of business communication and will be placed in prominent places. The telephone and intercom can be used as a quick way of communicating with people in the same building.

Business meetings

Within a business a meeting will be the situation in which much of the formal communication takes place. The aims of a meeting may be to do any of the following:

1. Make plans
2. Pass on information
3. Discuss issues
4. Iron out problems
5. Motivate people

The agenda

Meetings in most organizations follow a standard pattern. Before the meeting takes place, an agenda will be circulated to the people taking part. A meeting usually takes the following form:

1. *Apologies.* A list of the people who are not able to attend is read out.
2. *Minutes.* The notes from the last meeting are read out. Sometimes people might question the accuracy of these minutes.
3. *Matters arising* (from the minutes). This will be a discussion of decisions made at the last meeting and their follow-up.
4. *Correspondence.* This will be a discussion of relevant letters received since the last meeting.
5. *Reports.* Some members may have been asked to make a report for the meeting. These reports will be read and discussed.
6. *The meeting itself.* This involves a discussion of issues which might require a vote to be taken on policy.
7. *Planning the next meeting.* A date, place and time are chosen for the next meeting.
8. *Any other business.* If there is still time it may be possible to raise issues not on the original agenda.

Who runs the meeting?

The *chairperson* runs the meeting and all remarks must be made 'through the chair' (see Fig. 7.5). The *secretary* sets out the agenda for the meeting, informs members of this agenda and takes the notes (minutes). The *treasurer* will sometimes make a statement on the finance of the business.

Types of meeting

General meetings are open to all members of an organization. They are held on a regular basis, e.g. the *annual general meeting* (AGM) of a club or business, but an *extraordinary general meeting* can be called to deal with a special event. An example of this would be if the shareholders were not happy with the way a business was being run.

A *committee meeting* is made up

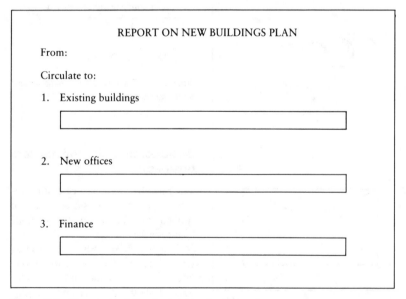

Figure 7.4 Reports should be clearly laid out, with headings.

Figure 7.5 Chairperson Anne Macdonald runs the meeting. (*Source:* Kim Hooper, Reading)

of only a small group of members of an organization who are chosen for this purpose.

The electronic office

The office lies at the heart of a business organization. Modern businesses have benefited greatly from the development of office technology.

Computers have become a very important method of communicating and storing information within a firm. Modern electronic computers are able to process words, numbers, pictures and even sound—any kind of information which needs to be stored, transmitted, analysed or reproduced.

The three main types of computers are:

1. *Mainframe computers.* These are large units, housed in special rooms with air-conditioning, specially trained staff, etc. They are extremely expensive, and are used or owned mainly by very large companies. They can handle very large and complex tasks very quickly, and are usually connected to the users through local terminals. The system used in, for example, your local electricity-board offices or travel agent is almost certainly of this type.

2. *Minicomputers.* These are slightly smaller in both size and cost, and reflect the advantages of modern technology in that they have the latest development built into their design.

3. *Microcomputer.* The 'desktop', 'personal', or 'home' computer which is seen advertised everywhere. Costing between £100 and several thousand pounds these computers can be used on their own or linked together with other computers to form a network which can exchange information or facilities.

Storing, retrieving and using information

All offices keep records of information. The more records a firm has, the more storage space they take up. Not only do traditional paper records take up space, but they also take time to sift through and sort out. To replace these large amounts of paper, information can now be stored in very little space, on magnetic tapes, floppy disks or hard disks. Files can be changed in just a few seconds. An example of this might be if a firm's employees got a 3 per cent pay increase. Instead of every single record in a filing cabinet having to be altered, the records could be altered electronically.

Writing letters/memos

Instead of writing letters and memos and posting them or delivering them by some sort of internal mail, a business can now use a system of 'electronic mail'.

The 'mail-box' is a computer terminal linked to the telephone network; it can put messages into the system and store messages that have been sent through the system. Every user has a 'password' to allow him or her to use the system. A message can be sent to several mail-boxes at once, and so the system can be used for internal memos in a company with several branches. The message will be stored in a terminal's memory until the mail-box is 'opened'.

Telex

This is a commonly used method of communicating between firms although today it is being replaced by more versatile services such as facsimile machines (see page 70).

The main disadvantage of using a telephone for business purposes is that the message is not presented in a printed form. Sometimes it is essential to have a printed record of a message, particularly when dealing with figures and other detailed pieces of information. The telex system is operated by British Telecom, and subscribers to the service rent a machine called a teleprinter and have

69

their telex number listed in the telex directory which is the equivalent of the phone book. Firms can contact each other simply by dialling the right telex number for national and international calls. The telex operator types the message into the teleprinter and the message is transmitted immediately to the receiving machine. Telex machines can be left unattended and operate 24 hours a day. They are particularly useful for sending international messages which may need translation, and because the telex can be left unattended messages can be sent to other countries where the time is different. The following is an example of the presentation of a telex message:

126841   TRAVELQUICK G

284123   Thompsons

Thompson Holidays.   Please

confirm booking for Carolyn

Coombs March 25th

Facsimile and Bureaufax

Many paper communications involve diagrams, pictures and documents. These can be sent electronically by using facsimile ('fax') machines. With the Bureaufax service, copies of diagrams can be sent overseas electronically.

Confravision

This service makes it possible for conferences to be arranged in sound and pictures from British Telecom studios in London, Birmingham, Bristol, Glasgow and Manchester. Meetings can take place as if the people involved were in the same room. We are all familiar with this type of situation from when television presenters link studios in different parts of the country. Businesses

using this service arrange for their staff to visit the nearest Confravision studio. This can save a lot of time and money (hotel bills, air fares, etc). This service is most frequently used when meetings are arranged for highly paid employees and when large distances are involved.

Prestel and teletext

These are services whereby at the press of a button a great range of useful and up-to-date information can be called up, such as share prices, travel information, exchange rates and business law. Prestel links up an adapted television screen with the telephone service and gives users access to a great range of computer-held information. The information is set out in 'pages'. A page is a screenfull of information and the pages are organized into groups.

As well as getting information from the Prestel service business people can input their own information and use the service for sending messages. Prestel can be used to make hotel reservations and for holiday bookings. Orders can be fed into

the system and company personnel can use the system to keep in touch with their offices.

Whilst many of the pages of Prestel are accessible to all users it is possible for a firm to arrange to use private pages only available to members of the firm.

Word processing

A skilled typist can produce 60–70 words a minute working at speed. However, in their everyday work, typists will produce under 20 words a minute. This is because of mistakes, and changes that need to be made, and because it takes longer to type items such as tables. Typing also involves a considerable amount of repetition. For example, the Prudent Insurance Company want to interview the following people:

1. Mr Alberts at 9 a.m.
2. Ms Anees at 10 a.m.
3. Mr Cook at 11 a.m.
4. Ms Davis at 12 noon

The letters inviting them to the interview will be identical except for the names and times. The idea behind word processing (see Fig. 7.6) is that

Figure 7.6   Word processing. (*Source:* Kim Hooper, Reading)

a letter only needs to be typed once and then all the standard sentences and paragraphs will be typed automatically.

Text can easily be corrected or changed on the word-processor screen, and can be proof-read there before being printed out.

Letters can then be stored on a floppy disk and retrieved at a later date for further use.

A word processor is made up of:

1. The *keyboard* for typing in material and instructions
2. A *visual display unit* which displays the material on a screen
3. A *disk storage* unit
4. The *printer* for finished copy

Databases

A database is a store of facts that can be called upon to provide up-to-date information. It may be used, for instance, in a bank or building society to store information on the state of all the accounts. Data (information) is fed into the base in a clear form. For instance, a firm could store information about the firms it supplies credit to. For example, it might have a record for the account of Johnson's Stores. It would store the information in a number of *fields*, such as address, value of goods bought, payments, and balance on the account. If Mr Johnson rings up asking for the state of his account the firm can simply order the computer to find the balance on Johnson's account.

Under the provisions of the Data Protection Act, companies wishing to store personal information on a computer system must register with the (government-appointed) Data Protection Officer, and indicate the type of data they are storing, and the use they make of it. Any individual has the right to request (on payment of a small fee) details of any information held about them by any firm, and to require any mistakes to be corrected.

	JAN	FEB	MAR	APR	MAY	JUN	JUL	AUG	SEP	OCT	NOV	DEC
REVENUE	200	200	300	400	400	400	500	500	500	500	500	500
COSTS												
Heat	20	20	20	20	20	20	20	20	20	20	20	20
Fuel	20	20	20	20	20	20	20	20	20	20	20	20
Labour	50	50	60	70	70	70	80	80	80	80	80	80
Materials	50	50	60	70	70	70	80	80	80	80	80	80
TOTAL COSTS	140	140	160	180	180	180	200	200	200	200	200	200
PROFIT	60	60	140	220	220	220	300	300	300	300	300	300

TOTAL PROFITS: 2720

Figure 7.7 Spreadsheet of a firm's forecast income and outgoings for a year.

Spreadsheets

A spreadsheet is a table of numbers which can be organized and altered on a computer. A spreadsheet is used for making forecasts and calculations—the computer does the work for you. Spreadsheets will often be used in financial forecasting. For instance, a firm will make a forecast of all the money that will come in and go out of the firm over a 12 month period (see Fig. 7.7).

The person using the spreadsheet can then alter the inputs, to calculate, for example, the effect of lowering the heating bill by a certain amount each month. The computer will automatically recalculate the columns to change the heating figures, total cost figures and profits for each month. It will also recalculate the total-profit figure.

The managing director, accountant or any other user of a spreadsheet can quickly carry out business calculations such as working out the effect of a 3 per cent wage increase or the cost of meeting a new order.

Datel

This is a telecommunications system whereby a computer in a firm can communicate with computers on sites in other parts of the country, and in many overseas countries.

Teletex

This is a means of communicating a message by means of a word processor or adapted typewriter. The text can automatically be transmitted in seconds over an ordinary telephone line to a receiving word processor or typewriter where the text will appear.

Microfilm

In a modern office, microfilm may be used as an alternative way to store information. A lot of information can be stored in a small space. Office space is wasted by using traditional filing cabinets. It is often a legal requirement for a firm to store information for a certain length of time before it is destroyed. These records can be stored away on microfilm. Computer data can now easily be transferred to microfilm. Data can be rapidly retrieved from a microfilm and viewed in an enlarged form. Printed copies can be obtained quickly and duplicates of these copies can be made. The records are durable and it is a safe way of storing information.

Microfilm is a sheet of film which can be used to store a complete set of material such as this book.

Communications outside the business

The business also communicates with individuals and groups outside itself.

> **Internal/external.** It is important that you learn the meaning of these words as they come up quite often. Internal means inside something. External means outside something.

The business communicates externally with its suppliers, its customers and other groups.

It will use a wide range of methods including:

1. Postal communications
2. Telecommunications
3. Advertising and the media
4. Transport systems

CASE STUDY— COMMUNICATIONS

Patricia Perry was appointed office manager of a small engineering firm in Derby that was going through a phase of reorganization and modernization. Pat was instructed to bring the office into the twenty-first century. The firm employed 250 manual operatives, a salesforce of 6, 10 office workers, and 3 management staff. The office staff worked with manual typewriters and there was one switchboard operator using old-fashioned equipment. Pat's brief was to prepare a report which could be presented at the next board meeting in which she should set out a list of priorities for modernization, and cost the changes required, bearing in mind that the firm was keen to spend anything up to £100 000 on the venture.

Question

Imagine that you are Pat and set out the report you would present.

QUESTIONS

1. Complete the following sentences using the words below. In each case give what you consider to be the best answer.

   Memo
   Agenda
   Minutes
   Fax
   Confravision
   Telex
   Teletex
   Floppy disk
   Database
   Word processor

   (a) .... makes it possible to link up, visually, people in different parts of the country.
   (b) Word-processed information can be stored on a ....
   (c) The .... of a meeting sets out the matters to be discussed.
   (d) The .... system allows for word processors to be hired from the Post Office and for them to be connected through the telecommunications network.
   (e) A .... speeds up the process of preparing information.
   (f) A .... can be used to store information.
   (g) An internal .... is an effective way of communicating within a firm.
   (h) A .... is a special electronic typewriter terminal.
   (i) A .... machine enables the electronic communication of maps and diagrams.
   (j) The .... of a meeting record the main points discussed.

2. In the mid-1980s the number of electronic-mail users was doubling each year. In the last quarter of 1986, twice as many fax machines were sold as in the same period in 1985. In contrast the number of telex terminals was growing at only 5 per cent a year.

   What reasons would you give to explain the above figures?

3. What sort of office tasks can be performed on a microcomputer?

4. What sorts of telecommunication methods could be used for the following?

   (a) Sending an internal memo within a building
   (b) Sending a sketch plan overnight to a firm overseas
   (c) Sending a typed report from London to Newcastle
   (d) Finding out the time of the trains from London to Aberdeen
   (e) Visually linking up Penzance and Dover
   (f) Storing records of employees' absences
   (g) Typing out a standard legal letter

5. What do the following stand for?
   (a) VDU
   (b) AGM
   (c) AOB
   (d) RSVP
   (e) ASAP
   (f) CPU

6. Write a business report on health and safety conditions

in your school or college canteen to form the basis of a class discussion.

7. Argue the case for the electronic office.

8. What are the advantages of storing information on microfilm?

9. Argue the case for recording votes at a meeting by secret ballot rather than by a show of hands.

10. How would you set up a database recording the following?
    (a) The particulars of members of a firm
    (b) The different methods of telecommunication

11. Try to finish exercise in two minutes.
    (a) Read all the instructions carefully.
    (b) Pick up your pen in your hand.
    (c) Write your name at the top of the paper.
    (d) Underline your name.
    (e) Rule a margin on the left-hand side of page.
    (f) Number the next 20 lines 1–20.
    (g) Starting on the top line, drawn an arrow going to the right side of the page, but stopping half an inch short of it.
    (h) Now draw a diagonal line going to the bottom left-hand side of the page.
    (i) Draw a box in the left-hand corner of your page, half an inch high and six inches long.
    (j) Write in it: 'I must read instructions carefully.'
    (k) Do none of the above.
    From doing this exercise you should be able to appreciate the need to read carefully instructions communicated to you.

COURSEWORK

1. Should a large firm run a crèche so that the skills of people with small children to look after are not wasted?

    This is the only item on the agenda of a class meeting. The discussion will take place in class and every student must keep minutes of the meeting. When the minutes are copied up they should be compared in order to find the most efficient way of making minutes. (Frequently the minute-taker at a meeting will also participate in discussion.)

2. How should a business letter be set out?

    Study the letter layout in Fig. 7.8. Now write a business letter, using the same layout, to the bank asking for an appointment to discuss a loan to build an office extension. (You represent Financial Services plc, Church Street, Grantham.)

    If you think that the layout given in Fig. 7.8 is a bit old-fashioned what alternative layout would you use?

3. Pick a local firm and say what methods of internal communication it uses.

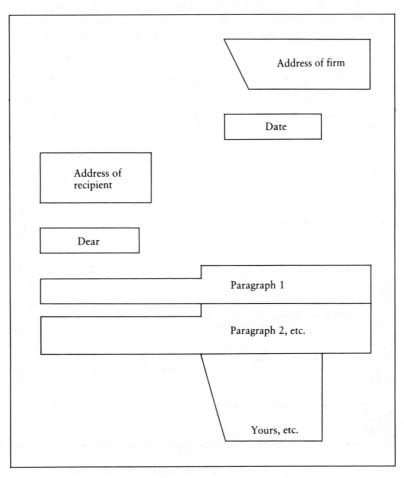

Figure 7.8 Possible layout of a business letter.

8 Business documentation

There are many different types of business document and each type has a specific purpose. Documents are necessary as proof of business activity, as a check against goods ordered and for bookkeeping purposes. The vast majority of transactions today are on credit and documents can show who owes what and to whom. (See Fig. 8.1.)

It is possible for all the documents in Fig. 8.1 to relate to a single transaction though this would be unusual.

Trading documents are normally headed with the name of the organization and tend to differ in style. Large organizations often use continuous stationery, keep their records on computer and have the documents properly printed.

Letter of enquiry

Enquiries will often be sent to several suppliers before goods are ordered. The buyer or buyer's representative may wish to acquaint him- or herself with a variety of information before deciding who to buy from. The information he or she requires may include:

1. Prices
2. Specifications of the goods available
3. Catalogues/price lists
4. Delivery dates
5. Discounts
6. Details of carriage

The enquiry may be a short letter or on a specially printed form (see Fig. 8.2).

Quotation, price list and catalogue

The purchasing officer will receive several quotations (see Fig. 8.3 on page 76) and a variety of information from potential suppliers. A decision will then be made based upon prices, terms, delivery dates and the suitability of the goods.

The next stage in the business transaction is for the buyer to send the seller an order (see Fig. 8.4 on page 77). A member of the purchasing department will sign the order. The order is numbered so that it can be traced easily and it is also dated. Upon receipt of the official order the seller will check the details on it such as prices and delivery. In some instances an acknowledgement of order is sent to indicate that the details on the order can be met.

Advice note and dispatch note

Before sending the goods the seller will send an advice note to indicate

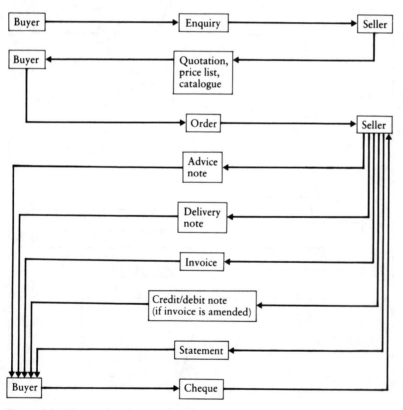

Figure 8.1 Diagram showing the documents that may be needed for a business transaction.

74

```
                        WOODFIELD COSMETICS

                          12 Hall Street
                              Hull
                        North Humberside
                            HU12 3JT


Tel:  0482 516783                                3 March 19__



ENQUIRY FORM


To:   Natural.Products.Ltd..
      5.Neath.Avenue........
      Darlington............
      DN4.25R...............


Dear Sir/Madam

Could you send me details of the following:  Welhair.Shampoo.for.normal/dry/...

greasy hair, bath salts, luxury soap..............................................

..................................................................................


Your reply should include prices, delivery period, carriage and terms.

Yours faithfully

Woodfield Cosmetics




R Ramsden
Purchasing Officer
```

Figure 8.2 Example of an enquiry form.

that the goods are being sent and that their arrival should be expected within a few days (see Fig. 8.5 on page 78). If the goods do not arrive within a reasonable time the buyer can then contact the seller to inform him or her that the goods have not arrived so that the delay can be investigated.

Delivery note

A delivery note is often sent with the goods (see Fig. 8.6 on page 79). It lists the items in the parcels and enables the buyer to check that all the goods listed on the note have arrived. If a company has used its own vehicles to deliver the goods the driver will receive two copies of the note. One copy is given to the *goods received section* on delivery and the other one is signed by the person(s) receiving the goods and is used as proof of the receipt of the goods. The goods received section of the company will prepare a goods received note to in-form internal departments of the arrival of their order.

Invoice

This document (see Fig. 8.7 on page 80) is essential in any credit business transaction. It outlines the relevant details of the deal and includes the amount charged and the terms. The following could be found on the invoice:

1. *Order number.* This enables the

NATURAL PRODUCTS LTD

5 Neath Avenue
Darlington
DN4 25R

Tel: 0273 514001

7 March 19__

QUOTATION

To: ..Woodfield.Cosmetics.

 ..12.Hall.St..........

 ..Hull..............

 ..HU12.3JT..........

Dear Sir/Madam

Following your enquiry of 3 March 19__, we are able to quote you the following:

Description	Catalogue Number	Price
Welhair Shampoo: normal	Q3421	£3.20 per doz
dry	Q3210	£3.05 per doz
greasy	Q3321	£3.10 per doz
Bath Salts	A4628	£2.18 per doz
Luxury Soap	F8933	£1.88 per doz

Delivery: carriage paid 10 days from receipt of order:

Terms: $2\frac{1}{2}$%   30 days

R Thomas
Sales Manager

Figure 8.3 Example of a quotation.

buyer to check that the goods on the invoice match the goods on the order.

2. *Terms.* This refers to how much time buyers have to pay for their goods and the cash discount which is given to buyers if they pay quickly. For example, '$2\frac{1}{2}$% 30 days' means that if buyers pay within 30 days they can allow $2\frac{1}{2}$ per cent off the invoice price.

3. *Carriage.* This refers to the cost of transporting the goods to the buyer. 'Carriage paid' is where the cost of transportation is met by the seller. 'Carriage forward' means that the cost of transport must be met by the buyer.

76

WOODFIELD COSMETICS

12 Hall Street
HULL
North Humberside
HU12 3JT

Tel: 0482 516783   9th March 1987

ORDER   No 87651

To: Natural Products Ltd
     5 Neath Avenue
     Darlington
     DN4 25R

Catalogue Number	Quantity	Description	£	p
Q3421	1 doz	Welhair Shampoo - normal hair	3	20
Q3321	2 doz	Welhair Shampoo - greasy hair	6	20
A4628	3 doz	Bath Salts	6	54
		Total	15	94

Terms: 2½% 30 days
Delivery: carriage paid 10 days from receipt of order

Signed R. Ramsden

Figure 8.4 Example of an order.

4. *E & OE.* Sometimes these letters appear on the invoice; they stand for 'errors and omissions excepted'. This enables the seller to correct any mistake on the invoice at a later date.
5. *Trade discount.* This is often given to regular customers in the same line of business and reduces the invoice price.
6. *VAT.* Value added tax is added to the amount appearing on the invoice.
7. *Invoice number.* This enables the accounts departments of both the buyer and the seller to identify the invoice quickly.
8. *VAT registration number.* Most

businesses print their VAT registration number on their invoices, for tax purposes.

There are several copies made of an invoice on different coloured paper. One copy is normally packed with the goods.

If the seller has not done any business with the buyer before or the buyer has been late with payments in the past, the seller might send the buyer a pro forma invoice. This document avoids a credit transaction. It is sent to the buyer before the goods are delivered and charges for the goods in advance. After the payment is made the goods are delivered.

Credit note and debit note

These are sent by the seller and alter the amount appearing on the invoice.

A credit note (see Fig. 8.8 on page 81) reduces the invoice price. This could be for any of these reasons:

1. A mistake on the invoice.
2. Goods have been returned either because they are faulty or because the wrong goods have been delivered.
3. Fewer goods have been sent than appear on the invoice.

A credit note is often printed in red.

A debit note will increase the invoice price. This could be for the following reasons:

1. A mistake on the invoice.
2. Too many goods have been sent.

Statement of account

The seller sends all regular customers a statement of account at the end of every month (see Fig. 8.9 on page 82). This is a copy of the customer's account in the sales ledger and usually contains a record of all transactions with the customer during the month. The debit column shows the sales by the seller to the buyer and includes anything which increases the debt such as a debit note, while the credit column shows any credit notes or payments and anything which reduces the debt.

Computerized systems

Computers provide a fast and accurate method for firms to keep a record of transactions; indeed accounts is an area of business life particularly helped by computers.

When a firm's sales department receives an order, an employee will type the details in on a keyboard and these then appear on a visual display unit. Every customer is given an

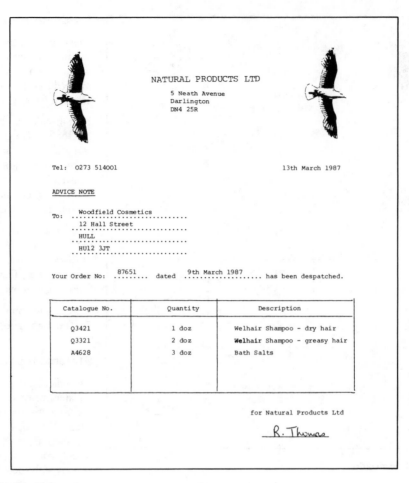

NATURAL PRODUCTS LTD

5 Neath Avenue
Darlington
DN4 25R

Tel: 0273 514001   13th March 1987

ADVICE NOTE

To: Woodfield Cosmetics
    ....
    12 Hall Street
    ....
    HULL
    ....
    HU12 3JT
    ....

Your Order No: 87651 .... dated 9th March 1987 .... has been despatched.

Catalogue No.	Quantity	Description
Q3421	1 doz	Welhair Shampoo - dry hair
Q3321	2 doz	Welhair Shampoo - greasy hair
A4628	3 doz	Bath Salts

for Natural Products Ltd

R. Thomas

Figure 8.5 Example of an advice note.

index number and when the operator types in this number the customer's records and details appear on the screen. The operator can then add the details of the new order—item numbers, prices, terms offered, etc. The computer then carries out a number of operations:

1. It prepares a packing note for the packaging department, requesting the packaging department to make up the order.
2. It checks off the items ordered against stock records. If items are running low it prepares a reorder for fresh supplies, or instructs the production department (in the case of a manufacturer) to make more of the items.
3. It prepares invoices for the customers in relation to goods supplied.
4. At the end of the month it makes up a statement for that month's transactions.

Credit control

There are certain dangers in credit transactions. Many customers may take too long to pay their bills and some may not pay their bills at all. The latter eventually become bad debts. Cash discounts are designed to encourage customers to pay promptly but they do not always work.

Large firms employ credit controllers whose job it is to ensure that a regular review is made of all customers, that credit limits are not exceeded and that payments are prompt. Letters and phone calls are used to remind customers about payment and, in some circumstances, legal action has to be taken.

Businesses can also sell their debts to a factoring company. This procedure simply involves selling off

```
                    NATURAL PRODUCTS LTD

                        5 Neath Avenue
                        Darlington
                        DN4 25R


     Tel: 0273 514001                        16th March 1987

     DELIVERY NOTE                    Your Order No: 87651

            Woodfield Cosmetics
     To:    ...............................
            12 Hall Street
            ...............................
            HULL
            .........................
            HU12 3JT
            ...............................


     Please receive:
```

Quantity	Description	
1 doz	Welhair Shampoo - normal hair	)
2 doz	Welhair Shampoo - greasy hair	) one
3 doz	Bath Salts	) crate

```
                        Received by: R. Ramsden
```

Figure 8.6 Example of a delivery note.

debts to a third party for less than they are worth. Many small businesses need cash to keep the business ticking over. Financially, it makes sense to sell off debts for less than their face value in order to make more money by producing goods. Banks in Britain offer a wide range of factoring services for good-quality debts.

During the 1980s many companies have been slow in paying debts. This makes life difficult for other firms that have supplied goods on credit. The government is considering passing a law to limit the amount of time a firm can hold back payment.

Firms can take out bad-debts insurance with an insurance company to cover themselves against non-payment. The disadvantage, of course, is the cost of the insurance premium.

Before granting credit a firm will usually ask for a trade or bank reference.

A **trade reference** is given by a supplier who has previously given credit to a business vouching for the reliability of the business.

Before giving credit the firm could also make enquiries with a credit reference agency which is a firm specializing in keeping lists of people who have defaulted on payments. For a fee it will verify whether a particular firm has ever had problems or whether it has a clean bill of reliability.

Stock control

A certain amount of documentation is associated with stock control. This is so that records can be related to physical stock checks and pilfering

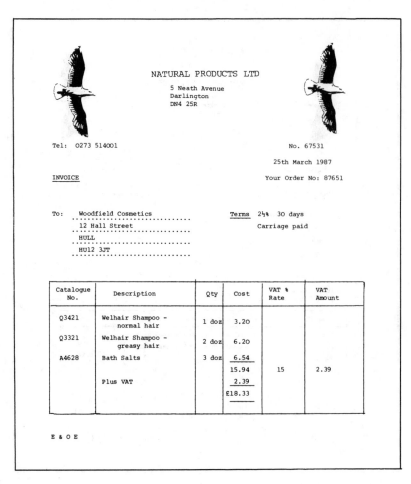

Figure 8.7 Example of an invoice.

can be detected. It also enables the business to calculate its stocks at any time and so facilitates accounting processes as well as reordering.

A stock-control card (see Fig. 8.10 on page 82) is kept for each item held and it contains maximum and minimum figures. When the stock level is at or near the minimum figure, the stock-control clerk advises that further quantities should be ordered. A minimum-stock figure stops the company from running out of parts which might be used in a productive process or parts which could lose the company business if they were not available. Maximum stock figures are given to stop the company from tying up too much of its capital in stock which could be wasting space and squandering liquid capital. Requisitions are used by internal departments to obtain stock from the stores.

QUESTIONS

1. Complete the following sentences using the words listed below and in the next column.

E & OE
Pro forma invoice
Advice note
Quotation
Order form
Invoice
VAT registration number
Statement
Payment
Enquiry

(a) A buyer wishing to find out details from a seller will start off by sending a letter of ....
(b) When the seller has made up the order he or she will send the buyer an .... to give

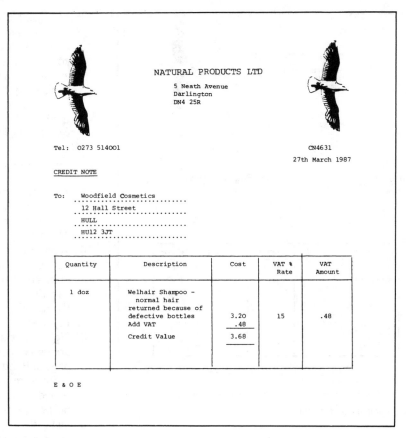

NATURAL PRODUCTS LTD

5 Neath Avenue
Darlington
DN4 25R

Tel: 0273 514001

CN4631

27th March 1987

CREDIT NOTE

To: Woodfield Cosmetics
     12 Hall Street
     HULL
     HU12 3JT

Quantity	Description	Cost	VAT % Rate	VAT Amount
1 doz	Welhair Shampoo - normal hair returned because of defective bottles	3.20	15	.48
	Add VAT	.48		
	Credit Value	3.68		

E & O E

Figure 8.8 Example of a credit note.

details of when and how delivery will be made.

(c) For tax purposes a .... will be printed on an invoice.

(d) A seller will send a buyer a .... indicating the types of goods, and the prices and terms under which he would be prepared to supply.

(e) A .... would be sent by a seller dealing with a buyer for the first time.

(f) The letters .... printed on an invoice give the seller the right to put right an incorrectly filled-in invoice.

(g) .... can be made by cheque.

(h) There are several copies made of an ...., one of which is packed with the goods.

(i) An .... will be used when placing an order for goods.

(j) A .... gives a record of all transactions made within a certain time period.

2. Maureen Coombs, a retail grocer, deals regularly with a wholesale firm, Suppliers Ltd, and one transaction took place as follows:

(a) Coombs ordered food worth £300 from Suppliers Ltd on 14 April 1988, and the goods were delivered by Suppliers Ltd's own van on 20 April. The foods consisted of 100 kilograms of butter at 40p a kilo; assorted cereals with a total cost of £60; 100 tins of fruit salad at 30p a tin, and tinned meat totalling £170.

(b) On 21 April, Coombs found out that the butter delivered in one of the boxes had turned rancid. She informed Suppliers Ltd, who arranged for her to send back the

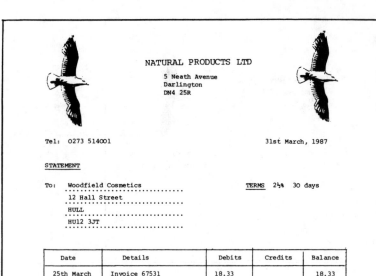

NATURAL PRODUCTS LTD

5 Neath Avenue
Darlington
DN4 25R

Tel: 0273 514001   31st March, 1987

STATEMENT

To: Woodfield Cosmetics   TERMS 2¼% 30 days
      12 Hall Street
      HULL
      HU12 3JT

Date	Details	Debits	Credits	Balance
25th March	Invoice 67531	18.33		18.33
27th March	Credit CN4631		3.68	14.65

Figure 8.9 Example of a statement of account.

STOCK CONTROL CARD

Item:	A5 Bank paper					Maximum	200
Stores Ref:	B3628					Minimum	80
Location:	B3					Unit	Ream

DATE	RECEIPTS			ISSUES			BALANCE IN STOCK
1986	Qty Rcvd.	Invoice No.	Supplier	Qty Issued	Requi-sition No.	Dept.	
Sept. 1							110
Sept. 2				20	361	Accounts	90
Sept. 3				10	392	Personnel	80
Sept. 4	100	45001	Wenhams Ltd.				180

Figure 8.10 Example of stock-control card.

goods, which were valued at £10.

Make out the documents you would expect to be used in the transaction above, explaining how each document is used.

3. Explain the following terms which might appear on an invoice:
   (a) Four per cent cash within one month
   (b) Less trade discount 10 per cent
   (c) Pro forma invoice
   (d) VAT

4. What do the following mean? (Look them up in a dictionary of business terms.)
   (a) COD
   (b) CWO
   (c) Net

5. Fig. 8.11 is an invoice sent to Jones Grocers by A. B. Supplies of Reading.
   How much would Jones Grocers pay if they settled the bill immediately?

6. List the details normally shown on an invoice, omitting the invoice number, the date and the customer's name and address.
   In many firms, several carbon copies of invoices are made. Why is this done and how are the carbon copies used?

7. What is the current rate of VAT?

9. Outline the various stages of a credit business transaction, mentioning each of the documents likely to be used.

9. Outline the differences between the following:
   (a) A quotation and a catalogue
   (b) An advice note and a delivery note
   (c) An invoice and a statement

```
                    INVOICE

               A. B. SUPPLIES
                  READING

Jones Grocers                          5th November 19__
Reading                       VAT No. 24603

┌──────────┬──────────────┬─────────────┬─────────┬──────────────┐
│ Cat. No. │ Description  │ Unit Price  │ Quant.  │ Total Price  │
├──────────┼──────────────┼─────────────┼─────────┼──────────────┤
│  4538    │ size 3 Eggs  │    80p      │ 12 doz. │   £9.60      │
│          │              │             │         │              │
│  4532    │ size 1 Eggs  │    94p      │ 10 doz. │   £9.40      │
│          │ DELIVERY     │             │         │              │
│          │     CHARGE   │             │         │   £1.00      │
├──────────┴──────────────┴─────────────┴─────────┼──────────────┤
│                                                  │   £20.00     │
├──────────────────────────────────────────────────┴─────────────┤
│ E. & O. E.              Terms: 5% one month                     │
└─────────────────────────────────────────────────────────────────┘
```

Figure 8.11   Invoice from A.B. Supplies to Jones Grocers.

(d) Trade discount and cash discount

(e) A credit note and a debit note

10. Explain the purpose of stock control and draw up a stock-control card to show the following information: A4 bond paper; stores reference B6132; location B9; maximum stock 60; minimum stock 21; 21 October balance 58; 22 October requisition number 912 for purchases department, 10 reams; 25 October requisition number 973 for sales, 20 reams.

11. What is a statement of account? What is the significance of the following?
    (a) The debit column
    (b) The credit column
    (c) The balance

COURSEWORK

1. Students could organize themselves into pairs and run through a set of business documents acting as buyer and seller.

2. Collect invoices from local firms. Are they similar to those in the book? Are there any differences?

3. How do firms computerize their business documentation? This would be a particularly useful study coupled with a spell of work experience.

4. What would be a suitable layout for an invoice? Run a competition to design a suitable invoice for a local firm.

9 Finance and financial control

Operating a business involves considerable expenditure. Often machinery has to be bought and overheads have to be paid. Money is needed to pay for these. Prospective entrepreneurs must be prepared to plan their business idea, to exercise careful control over their business activities and to make financial decisions. A *business plan* is important in order to raise funds from possible backers. This is always likely to be necessary unless individuals have private sources of finance.

A business plan is set out to work out the financial needs of the business. It is a detailed examination of the product, the market and the cash flow of the firm.

The business executive must then decide how to raise the required finance.

Sources of finance

1. *Bank loan*. This is a fixed sum lent for a specific purpose over a time period for which interest is paid.
2. *Bank overdraft*. An overdraft limit is agreed with the bank and can provide a flexible form of short-term finance.
3. *Shares*. Private and public limited companies can issue shares in order to raise finance. This creates a larger number of part-owners, and profits have to be divided between more people. Similarly, a sole trader might wish to obtain a partner, and a partnership might wish to take in further partners.
4. *Trade credit*. Delaying the payment of bills can provide short-term funds and ease cash-flow problems but this could ultimately lead to difficulties in obtaining raw materials and to the running down of stocks.
5. *Hire purchase*. Goods can be obtained and paid for in instalments but they remain the property of the lender until the last payment is made.
6. *Credit sales agreement*. Goods bought become the property of the purchaser after the deposit or first instalment.
7. *Leasing*. The goods can be obtained immediately but ownership is never achieved. This enables capital goods to be paid for from revenue expenditure and makes it easier to predict costs.
8. *Venture capital firms*. These are firms which specialize either by area or by industry in providing capital for investment.

Cash flow

Business firms must carefully consider their pattern of spending and whether or not they are able to meet financial commitments as and when they arise. Cash-flow forecasts are statements which enable them to analyse their expenditure and receipts over a period of time and are particularly important for small firms.

A simple cash-flow exercise could be used to demonstrate your own financial needs. Imagine that you have left school and started work. You earn £80 a week and out of this you have certain fixed weekly expenses.

	£
Rent to parents	20
Daily fares	5
Lunches	10
Weekends	12
Records, magazines, etc.	10
Total	57

On 2 January, you receive your wages of £80. You owe your father £40 from December. There are some clothes that you want to buy costing £15 in a sale that ends on 6 January. A deposit of £30 for a holiday must be paid during the second week. This week you are taking three friends to the cinema which will cost you £9, and you have to pay a dry-cleaning bill of £2. There are four weeks in January, and in the third week you will economize and not buy any records and magazines.

A cash-flow forecast will enable you to see if you can do all the things you want to and predict how soon you can pay back your father's loan.

The cash-flow forecast has indicated that you need to borrow from your mother in weeks 1 and 2, but can pay her back in week 3, and that you can pay your father back in the last week of the month.

Cash flow has, therefore, provided the planning necessary to cope with the timing of various financial commitments.

Just as anticipating the flow of funds is important, accountants can produce a statement showing the source and use of funds. This shows where funds were obtained and indicates the uses to which they have been put.

	1	2	3	4
INCOME	80	80	80	80
EXPENSES				
Rent	20	20	20	20
Fares	5	5	5	5
Lunch	10	10	10	10
Weekends	12	12	12	12
Records, magazines, etc.	10	10	—	10
Clothes	15	—	—	—
Cinema	9	—	—	—
Dry cleaning	2	—	—	—
Holiday	—	30	—	—
Total	83	87	47	57
NET	(3)	(7)	33	23
Loan—mother	(3)B	(7)B	(10)R	—
Loan—father	—	—	—	(40)R
	—	—	23	6

(B) = Borrowing
(R) = Repayment

Accounting

This involves the recording and interpretation of business activity. Records are kept of business trans-

Figure 9.1 The accountant has a major role in looking after the company's finances. (*Source:* Kim Hooper, Reading)

actions and full sets of accounts are produced at regular intervals using these records. From a set of accounts it is possible to use ratios and percentages to analyse the behaviour of the firm, detect difficulties and take action to improve efficiency.

There are various accounting bodies in the UK. Some accountants are involved with financial accounting, which produces the information for managers to use. Other accountants are management accountants and they advise managers upon decisions they have to make. (See Fig. 9.1.)

All transactions are recorded by a bookkeeper. Most businesses employ

the double-entry system, whereby with each transaction one account is debited and another account is credited. This means that for every entry on the left-hand side of one account, there is always a corresponding entry on the right-hand side of another account.

Suppose, for example, that our firm sells goods to A. Buyer on credit 1 January. A. Buyer's account is debited because he now owes us money. Our sales account is credited as goods have gone from the business.

All these accounts are kept in a series of ledgers. When the financial accountant visits the business to produce a set of final accounts, the balances of each account are listed in the form of a *trial balance*. As all the debit entries correspond to all the credit entries, the two sides of the trial balance should agree. The accountant will first assess the profitability of the firm by drawing up a *trading account* and a *profit and loss account*, and will then produce a *balance sheet*. These are drawn up using figures obtained from the trial balance.

The trading account

At the end of a trading period, which could perhaps be at the end of every three months, the accountant will copy out, or take a computer print-out of, all the outstanding balances on all the accounts.

A. BUYER ACCOUNT

Debit		Credit
Jan. 1 Sales	100.00	

SALES ACCOUNT

Debit		Credit
	Jan. 1 A. Buyer	100.00

J. SMITH ACCOUNT

Debit			Credit
	Feb. 4 Purchases	200.00	
	Mar. 4 Purchases	200.00	
		————	
		400.00	

This shows that Smith has sold us £400 worth of goods this quarter. Smith is a creditor. Assuming that we only purchase goods from J. Smith our purchases account will show:

PURCHASES ACCOUNT

Debit			Credit
Feb. 4	J. Smith	200.00	
Mar. 4	J. Smith	200.00	
		————	
		400.00	

Our purchases account is in debit. These figures are now put into a trial balance together with the balances on all our other accounts. The trial balance of 31 March will be:

	DEBIT BALANCE	CREDIT BALANCE
Purchases	400.00	
J. Smith		400.00

Etc.

The two sides of our trial balance will be equal because of the way we double-enter our books.

To find out how the company is doing we must now set up a trading account. This account looks at the total value of our sales and the total value of our purchases. The difference is known as *Gross profit*.

> **Gross profit** = sales − purchases

To simplify, let us imagine that our firm buys one pen for 10 pence and sells it for 15 pence. The trading account for the period ended 31 March will appear as follows:

Debit			Credit
Purchases	0.10	Sales	0.15
Gross profit	0.05		
	————		
	(0.15)		

The figure for the gross profit of a firm, however, does not tell us much about how the firm is performing. We also need to take account of the expenses involved in running the business. These might include rent, rates, light and heat, telephone and postage, insurance and other general expenses.

Accounting for expenses— Combining the trading and profit and loss accounts

To arrive at a figure for the *net profit* of a business, we must deduct expenses from our gross-profit figure.

> **Net profit** = gross profit − expenses

This can be illustrated as follows:

The accountant is now able to extract the far more important figure for net profit. In the example above, the firm has made a gross profit of £50 000. Its total expenses amounted to £23 850. As a result, its net profit was £26 150.

Planning ahead

Earlier we saw that a business will try to plan ahead and think out its expected receipts and expenditures in the coming trading period.

Sava Radmilovic is setting up a business trading in imported wine. She has prepared a cash forecast for the coming six months. (In order to simplify we shall assume that Sava does not pay herself a salary.)

She estimates that her purchases will cost £2000 a month and her sales will bring in £3500 a month. Her expenses will amount to £400 a month on average. The problem is that when she first establishes her business, she will have a shortage of cash because the expenses will be high at first.

Trading and profit and loss account of Ben Cribb Ltd for the period ended 31 December 1987

Purchases	100 000	Sales	150 000
Gross profit c/d*	50 000		
	————		————
	150 000		150 000
		Gross profit b/d*	50 000
Rent	2 000		
Rates	800		
Insurance	50		
Salaries	20 000		
Advertising	1 000		
	————		
TOTAL EXPENSES	23 850		
NET PROFIT	26 150		
	————		————
	50 000		50 000

* b/d and c/d mean brought down and carry down.

	Jan.	Feb.	Mar.	Apr.	May	June	
Balance from last month	0	(300)	1 000	2 400	3 800	5 200	TOTAL
SALES	3 500	3 500	3 500	3 500	3 500	3 500	21 000
PURCHASES	2 000	2 000	2 000	2 000	2 000	2 000	12 000
EXPENSES	1 800	200	100	100	100	100	2 400
Balance carried forward to next month	(300)	1 000	2 400	3 800	5 200	6 600	

(Figure in brackets represents an overdrawn balance at bank.)

We can see that Sava will have most expenses to pay in January (£1800). These include her annual insurance premium, rent, rates and some other expenses.

Her purchases and expenses add up to £3800 in January whereas her sales only total £3500. As a result, she will have to borrow £300 from the bank.

In February, her purchases and expenses equal £2200, whilst sales are £3500. As a result, she will be able to pay off her bank overdraft and build up a balance of £1000. She estimates that as time progresses her balance will build up until by the end of June she will have £6600.

However, we must bear in mind that when a business makes a cash forecast it is looking into the future. Problems arise if any of the following happen:

1. Sales are less than expected.
2. Purchases cost more than expected.
3. Expenses are more than expected.

Sava's projections were:

Projected sales	£21 000
Projected purchases	£12 000
Projected expenses	£2 400

In the event, the following happened:

Actual sales	£18 000
Actual purchases	£12 000
Actual expenses	£2 400

Sava had not anticipated the extent of competition from other wine businesses which reduced her own sales.

The profit and loss account

Earlier we saw how to set up a simple trading account when we looked at the sale of a pen.

A more elaborate trading account is given below for John Ashwell Ltd, which has been trading for a few years.

The *opening stock* is effectively a purchase because it will be sold in the current trading period. The *closing stock* must be deducted from purchases because it will be sold next year.

The profit and loss account then carries down the figure for gross profit and deducts the expenses of running the business to arrive at net profit.

The main points we notice about Ashwell's trading year are:

1. His gross profit was £8500.
2. His net profit was £4490.

Making sense of profit figures

The following figures can be extracted from the accounts:

Gross-profit percentage on turnover

> The **turnover** of a business is the total value of its sales.

Gross-profit percentage is:

$$\frac{\text{Gross profit}}{\text{Turnover}} \times 100$$

Trading account of John Ashwell Ltd at 31 December 19—

Opening stock	3 000	Sales		16 000
Add purchases	6 000			
	9 000			
Less closing stock	1 500			
Cost of sales	7 500			
Gross profit c/d	8 500			
	16 000			16 000

Profit and loss account of John Ashwell Ltd at 31 December 19—

Rent	150	Gross profit	8500
Rates	200		
Insurance	35		
Salaries	3200		
Advertising	425		
TOTAL EXPENSES	4010		
NET PROFIT	4490		
	8500		8500

For example, John Ashwell's gross-profit percentage is:

$$\frac{8500}{16\,000} \times 100 = 53\%$$

This is an important figure because if it falls it could indicate theft of stock or cash losses from the till. It could also reflect increases in the cost of raw materials, changes in supervision and changes in efficiency.

Net-profit percentage on turnover

This enables comparisons to be made with previous years and, if the gross-profit percentage has remained the same, could indicate an increase in expenses.

Net-profit percentage is:

$$\frac{\text{Net profit}}{\text{Turnover/sales}} \times 100$$

For example, John Ashwell's net-profit percentage is:

$$\frac{4490}{16\,000} \times 100 = 28\%$$

The balance sheet

A balance sheet is a picture of what a firm owns and owes on a particular date. It owns assets and these are divided into *fixed assets* and *current assets*.

> **Tangible items** are things that you can touch and see.

Fixed asserts are tangible assets which are used in the business over a long period, e.g. land and buildings, motor vehicles, etc.

Current assets constantly change as they are involved in continuous business activity or transactions; the stock, for instance, is constantly changing as you sell more goods and the bank account changes as bills are paid or cheques are received.

Debtors are customers who have bought goods or received a service from the business and therefore owe the business money.

The balance sheet is traditionally arranged in an inverse order of liquidity. This simply means that the items which would take longest to turn into money are put at the top and the items which can quickly be turned into money are at the bottom. This is so that calculations can be made to show how easily debts, etc., can be turned into cash and how easily bills can be paid.

The *liabilities* side of the balance sheet shows what the business owes and indicates to whom the business is responsible for its debts. This side would include the capital as the business owes the owner his or her original investment. Net profit adds to the amount the business owes the proprietor.

Drawings are amounts taken from the business for the owner's use.

Creditors are suppliers of goods and services to whom the business owes money.

The accountant constructs a balance sheet using both the trial balance and the net profit from the profit and loss account.

A frequently used analogy is that the balance sheet is a snapshot of a business at a point in time, while the trading and profit and loss account is a video running till the next snapshot.

Note from the balance sheet that the left-hand side shows what the business owes. The right-hand side shows what the business owns or is owed.

Working capital

This represents the finance which needs to be readily available to meet current expenditure. Working capital is:

Current assets − current liabilities

For example, John Ashwell's working capital is:

$$3325 - 1500 = \pounds1825$$

Any firm with a negative working capital, or a small working capital, would be in a precarious position if it had to meet its debts quickly.

Firms must pay particularly close attention to the problem of working capital because whilst they may have a lot of money tied up in fixed assets, they might end up having to wind up their affairs because of a lack of short-term funds.

Other figures used in accounts

Stockturn or rate of stock turnover

This shows how often the stock turns

Balance sheet of John Ashwell Ltd. as at 31 December 19—

CAPITAL	15 935		FIXED ASSETS	
Add NET PROFIT	4 490		Land and buildings	25 000
	———		Motor vehicles	3 000
	20 425			
			CURRENT ASSETS	
Less drawings	600		Debtors	1 500
	———		Closing stock	1 500
	19 825		Bank	325
LONG-TERM LIABILITIES				
Mortgage	10 000			
CURRENT LIABILITIES				
Creditors	1 500			
	———			———
	£31 325			£31 325

over each year. An increasing stock turnover means increasing profits, important comparisons can be made with previous years. Different types of businesses will have different rates of stock turnover; for example, a greengrocer is likely to have a high rate of stock turnover and a furniture shop is likely to have a slower rate of stock turnover. Any decrease in the rate of stock turnover could represent a decrease in sales activity and steps would need to be taken to increase sales.

Stockturn is:

$$\frac{\text{Cost of sales}}{\text{Average stock}}$$

Average stock is:

Opening stock + closing stock ÷ 2

For example, John Ashwell's average stock is:

$$\frac{3000 + 1500}{2} = 2250$$

His stockturn is:

$$\frac{7500}{2250} = 3.33$$

Therefore, John Ashwell turns over his stock every 3.6 months. To calculate this we must divide 12 months by his stockturn of 3.33.

Return on capital
This will show whether the business is justified in continuing or whether the business ought to cease operations. If the return on capital is low, the entrepreneur might consider alternatives. For a limited company the return will be in the form of a dividend upon an investment.

Return on capital is:

$$\frac{\text{Net profit}}{\text{Capital invested}} \times 100$$

John Ashwell's return on capital is:

$$\frac{4490}{15935} \times 100 = 28\%$$

Management control and budgeting

Management accounting is used to help managers to make decisions and to enable them to plan and exert control. Profit and loss accounts, balance sheets, cash flows and interpretations are used by management accountants but these only apply to the business as a whole. Management accountants take the process further and set up budgets for different areas of activity. These set objectives and create financial plans for future periods.

Costs play an essential part in all this. Costs can be either variable or fixed. *Variable costs* change directly in relation to output and would include, for example, raw materials or the wages of machine operatives. *Fixed costs* do not change directly with output and are often referred to as 'overheads'. These might include salaries of office staff, factory rent and rates, etc. *Marginal costs* and *average costs* can also be useful to the manager. Marginal cost is the cost of producing one more unit of output, while average cost is the total of all costs divided by the total number of units of output.

Breaking-even is where the total costs equal the total sales revenue. If the costs exceed the total sales revenue, losses will be made; if the sales revenue exceeds the costs, profits will be made. (See Fig. 9.2.)

Break-even analysis enables business people to understand the impact of their sales upon their profits, predict the relationship between their fixed and variable costs, and foresee the effects of changes in costs and prices.

If sales fall below the break-even point, losses are made; if they exceed the break-even point, profits are made. If a company's production is beyond the break-even point and sales are below the break-even point, it will be left with unsold stock. If the selling price changes, the break-even point will have to move.

Taxation

It is not possible to cover the area of finance without some mention of taxation. Direct taxes are paid to the Department of Inland Revenue as a result of income. They include in-

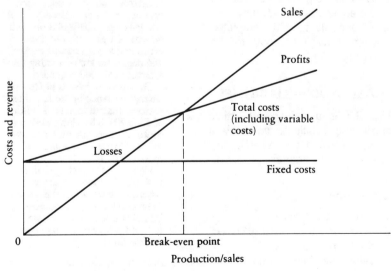

Figure 9.2 Example of a break-even chart.

come tax on money earned and corporation tax on company profits.

Indirect taxes are imposed as part of a payment for goods and services. Value added tax (VAT) is levied on most goods and services at each stage of production at a set rate. Customs and excise duties are charged on many imported goods and also on some home-produced products such as alcohol, cigarettes and petrol.

CASE STUDY—CASH FLOW

You are the accountant for a small firm. The firm is expected to take cash receipts of £50 000 per month for the first six months of the year. Its raw material and labour costs are also expected to be constant at £40 000 per month.

The firm wants to buy a new machine in March for £30 000. Fill in the firm's projected-cash-flow table (Table 9.1) from January to June starting with a balance of zero.

Questions

1. What would be the balance carried forward to July?
2. What is the purpose of doing a projected-cash-flow analysis?
3. What could make the projected cash flow turn out to be wrong?

CASE STUDY—LIABILITIES

Fig. 9.3 is a newspaper article about the liabilities faced by a rugby club and the steps it may take to solve its financial problems.

Questions

1. What is a 'liability'?
2. What are Hull Kingston Rovers' total liabilities?
3. What are their current liabilities?

Table 9.1 Table for the firm's projected cash flow from January to June.

	Jan	Feb.	Mar.	Apr.	May	June
Balance b/f from last month						
Receipts						
Raw materials and wages						
New machinery						
Balance c/f to next month						

Hull KR may be forced to sell ground

RUGBY LEAGUE
By Paul Rylance

HULL KINGSTON ROVERS, one of rugby league's most successful clubs, may have to sell their Craven Park ground and find a new home to avoid being forced into liquidation.

They are casualties of the Safety of Sports Grounds Act, which has imposed stringent new standards, and the money simply cannot be found. Already Hull KR have spent £108,000 on their 60-year-old ground, but their licence is due for renewal in April and engineers are predicting that a further £145,000 is needed.

The auditors have told Rovers, champions twice in the last three seasons, that they have liabilities of £500,000. The club's ability to continue "depends on being able to meet current liabilities of almost £300,000".

Colin Hutton, the chairman, yesterday blamed the safety regulations for the club's predicament. "The first lot of work included reinforcing a wall and then we had to build a barrier to stop people leaning on the wall.

"The estimates are £100,000 to improve the west stand, £25,000 for the east stand and £20,000 for general rewiring. If our worst fears are realised and we are ordered to carry out the extra work then we will have no alternative but to sell up and move out.

"Craven Park covers more than seven acres and is in a prime residential area, so we would expect to sell for a great deal more than we owe. We could build a completely new ground, and we are at present having informal talks with Humberside County Council about an alternative site.

"The money we have spent already will be lost, but at least it will have kept us in business until the end of the season."

Figure 9.3 Newspaper article on Hull Kingston Rovers' situation. (*Source: The Independent*)

4. What are included in their total assets?
5. Are their assets greater than their liabilities?
6. Why do they have a problem?
7. What solutions would you suggest the club take?

QUESTIONS

1. Complete the following sentences using the words below.

Balance sheet
Asset
Liability
Net profit
Gross profit
Debit
Credit
Trading account
Profit and loss account
Expenses
Capital

(a) The sum of money contributed to a business by its owners is known as ....

(b) A snapshot of a company's position at a particular moment is known as a ....

(c) An account that is owed money is said to be in ....

(d) An account that owes money is said to be in ....

(e) Lighting and heating are examples of ....

(f) An .... is something owned by a business or owed to a business.

(g) Expenses are deducted from gross profit to arrive at net profit in the ....

(h) .... will be greater than ....

(i) The .... is calculated to show gross profit.

(j) A .... is something owed by the business.

2. Your friend intends to start a small business. Explain to him the need for:
   (a) A business plan
   (b) A cash-flow forecast
   (c) A bookkeeping system

3. Find out the differences between the following:
   (a) Capital and revenue expenditure
   (b) Hire purchase and credit sales
   (c) Cash flow and funds flow
   (d) Fixed assets and current assets
   (e) Fixed costs and variable costs
   (f) Direct and indirect taxes

4. From the following information, prepare the trading and profit and loss account of P. Green for the period ending 31 December 19—.

Opening stock	£3600
Sales	£18 000
Purchases	£9000
Closing stock	£4300
Rates	£90
Salaries	£2100
Advertising	£600
Insurance	£27
Sundry expenses	£33

5. Organize the following figures into the balance sheet of N. Long as at 31 December 19—.

Capital	£11 000
Net profit	£2210
Drawings	£400
Creditors	£1000
Buildings and land	£8000
Motor vehicles	£800
Debtors	£1400
Closing stock	£210
Bank	£3400

Find the *working capital* and the *return on capital employed*

and comment upon your findings.

6. Bulco Ltd has plans to expand its production. Next year it hopes to produce 30 000 units and sell them for £8 each. Variable costs are £4 per unit and fixed costs are £50 000.

   Draw a graph to find the break-even point for Bulco Ltd. Calculate the total costs.

7. Give a list of fixed assets you might include in the following types of business:
   (a) A disco
   (b) A driving school
   (c) A corner shop
   (d) A manufacturing firm
   (e) A cinema

8. Why does a firm need liquid assets?

9. Draw up what you consider to be:
   (a) A healthy balance sheet
   (b) An unhealthy balance sheet

COURSEWORK

1. Ruth Downes goes to see her bank manager to ask for a loan to set up a mobile disco. She has had some experience of helping a friend run a disco and has made a good return each time she has worked.

   She has done some research and estimates that she will get three bookings a week which will bring in £1000 per month. The initial cost of her equipment is £4000 and a friend has offered to lend her a van if she pays for petrol.

   She has worked out her monthly expenses as being:

Petrol	£30
Stationery	£5
Advertising	£20
Maintenance of equipment	£50

New records £50
Other expenses £45

She has asked the bank for a loan of £5000 to establish herself. The repayment terms would be £220 a month over two years.

(a) You are Ruth's bank manager. You know that she lives at home with her parents and has no pressing financial commitments. Show in detail how you would arrive at a decision whether to grant the loan.

(b) What potential pitfalls would you warn Ruth about? Are there any factors she has not taken into consideration?

(c) Do you think that Ruth is making a sensible decision bearing in mind that she will have to sacrifice a steady job in the Civil Service that pays £600 a month after tax?

2. You have been called in by a retailing business to advise it on the state of its balance sheet. Write a summary of the position of the business and list your recommendations.

3. What is the state of a balance sheet?

If you run a mini-company or enterprise, do an analysis of the balance sheet. Alternatively, see if you can get the figures from a small local business. What scope is there for improvement?

4. How do we set out a trading account and profit and loss account?

See if you can obtain the relevant figures from a firm and then set them out as a trading and profit and loss account.

5. How do we rank assets in order of liquidity?

Visit the premises of a local business and by observation try to rank its assets in order of liquidity. This could be done as a class exercise so that a lot of information is brought together. You can then analyse the information to find out which sorts of business have a high ratio of fixed to variable capital. You can then take this further and look at causes, problems, advantages and disadvantages, etc.

Balance sheet of YZ Retailers

FIXED ASSETS		CAPITAL	5 000
Buildings	20 000		
Equipment	10 000	LONG-TERM LIABILITIES	
		Mortage	16 000
CURRENT ASSETS		Long-term loan	8 000
Debtors	3 000		
Stock	3 000	SHORT-TERM LIABILITIES	
Bank	100	Creditors	7 000
	36 100		36 000

10 The personnel department

Human needs at work

People spend a considerable part of their lives at work. It is not surprising therefore that we come to expect a certain amount of satisfaction from the jobs we do. To some people work is a great pleasure, giving them a great sense of personal fulfilment, but for others it is just a necessary way to make a living.

The following is a list of some of the things different people might look for in a job:

1. A good rate of pay
2. Good opportunities for promotion
3. Long breaks and holidays
4. Prestige
5. The opportunity to combine work and family life
6. Job security
7. Friendship with workmates
8. Opportunities to be creative
9. A degree of independence
10. Responsibility

Generally, satisfaction will be greatest for individuals who have the greatest freedom to choose a job and this will be those who have had the opportunity to acquire the most widely accepted range of qualifications and skills. Most jobs have some

---

The **personnel department** of a firm is concerned with all matters relating to interpersonal relationships within a firm. This includes hiring, dismissing, training, discipline, pensions, wage negotiations and other matters.

---

disadvantages but workers will enjoy work if these disadvantages can be minimized.

Recruitment

In the UK, the most common way of finding a job is by directly contacting a firm or place of employment. Sometimes people apply for a job as a result of a personal contact such as a relative already working for a firm.

Recruiting through newspaper advertisements

Newspaper advertisements are an obvious place to scout for jobs. A good newspaper advertisement gives a substantial amount of information. Personnel managers place adverts in the most suitable medium. Jobs demanding limited skills can often be advertised locally, whereas jobs requiring specialist skills needs to be advertised in specialist media. Adverts for teachers, for example, will appear in *The Times Educational*

Figure 10.1 Advertisement placed by Leigh Rugby League Club in a Welsh newspaper—the aim was to attract quality players in an area where such players abound. (*Source: Western Mail*)

Supplement, and adverts for doctors' posts will be advertised in *The Lancet.* (See Fig. 10.1.)

When recruiting labour the personnel manager will therefore do the following:

1. Target the recruiting campaign at the most suitable audience
2. Advertise in the most cost-effective way (i.e. use the cheapest method possible to get the right sort of people)

To ensure that a newspaper gets the right response it will be necessary to make at least some of the following points clear (see Fig. 10.2 on page 94):

1. Where the job is
2. How much the job pays
3. What qualifications are required to do the job
4. What the job involves
5. What fringe benefits are available
6. How to go about applying for the job

The personnel manager will then sift through the applications. He or she will look for candidates with the necessary experience who express themselves clearly and in an organized way.

Only once the personnel manager has chosen the candidates he or she wants to interview (see Fig. 10.3 on page 94) will references be sent for.

The sort of application that the personnel manager might select is shown in Fig. 10.4 on page 95.

Some businesses ask applicants to fill in a printed application form (see Fig. 10.5 on page 96). This is so that the personnel department can standardize the details of the applicants and ensure that it gets particulars

BOOKKEEPER
REQUIRED CENTRAL LEEDS (1)

Janet Davis Advertising Agency, starting salary £6000 per annum. (2)

We are looking for a bookkeeper who has had experience of (3) (4)
handling the purchase ledger and other account books and
is familiar with operations leading to a trial balance.
The successful applicant will be entitled to luncheon (5)
vouchers and transport expenses to work.

Please apply in writing to Mrs. S. Grose (6)
Personnel Manager, The J. Davis Advertising Agency,
Prince Street, Leeds, LSU 9BJ.
(Please state names and addresses of two referees.)

Figure 10.2 Advertisement appearing in a West Yorkshire evening paper. (The numbers in brackets refer to the list of points a job advertisement should include.)

hunters to meet personnel staff at the relevant firm for an interview.

Some firms regularly use this method of recruiting labour because it is a cheap and quick way of reaching an interested audience.

In the Midlands, a scheme has been introduced allowing unemployed people to find a job from the comfort of their armchairs. Under the scheme, launched by Central Television and the Department of Employment, after the end of normal programmes, up-to-date job vacancies are shown in teletext form. Jobseekers can then enquire by telephone about the jobs that interest them, without having to go to a jobcentre. An advantage of this scheme is that it reduces wasted travel expenses and it is a particularly useful scheme for the disabled.

such as National Insurance number which will later be needed to make payments. A further reason may be to establish quickly whether the applicant is capable of filling in an application form.

Other methods of recruiting
Jobcentres
The Department of Employment is responsible for the running of jobcentres which can be found in a prominent position in major towns. The jobcentres run window displays of jobs, and people seeking work are encouraged to come in and look at the cards with details of job vacancies which are on open display (see Fig. 10.6 on page 97). The jobcentre staff will arrange appointments for job-

Private employment agencies
There is a wide range of private employment agencies, which help businesses to recruit staff. Fields in which these agencies are particularly common are secretarial work, high-technology areas, nursing and casual work. A firm looking for staff will approach an agency, which will supply workers who are interviewed either by the agency or by the firm. The agency will take a commission on the salary of the worker. In the case of secretarial staff, wages will often be paid by the employing firm to the agency who will then pay the worker.

Figure 10.3 Personnel director Mary Macnamara interviews an applicant for a job. (*Source:* Kim Hooper, Reading)

The work of the personnel manager

The number of people working in the personnel department varies with the size of the company. Fig. 10.7, on page 97, summarizes the work of the personnel department.

```
                                              158 Franklin Road,
                                              Harrogate,
                                              Yorkshire,
                                              HG1 SEN


                             (Telephone:   0423 886412)

Mrs S. Grose,
J.Davis Advertising Agency,
Prince Street,
Leeds, LSU 9BJ                               10 August 19__


Dear Mrs Grose,

     With reference to your advertisement in the 'Evening Post' of the 8th August
for a Bookkeeper to Trial Balance, I would like to apply for the vacancy.

     I am 34 years old and have worked for several years in the Accounts Department
of Heels Department Store in Central Leeds.  I have been in charge of the purchases
section there and have regularly prepared the trial balance.  The firm is currently
re-locating in Glasgow and it is impossible for me to move with them because of
family ties.

     I have been an active member of the social club at Heels and am currently
acting treasurer of this body.

     I was very interested in your job advertisement and would be pleased to attend
an interview at your convenience.

     My referees are Mr S. Heel, Managing Director, Heels, and Mr S. Bartholomew,
Accounts Manager, Heels.

                             Yours sincerely,

                             Elizabeth Howard

                             (Elizabeth Howard)
```

Figure 10.4   A personnel manager will be attracted to a letter that is well written and well presented, as this one is.

Staffing

New workers must be given a written contract of employment within 13 weeks of starting the job, but the employer and employee are said to have formed a contract even before the written contract has been drawn up and signed. In law, the contract is established when the following take place:

1. The workers agrees to work for the employer.

2. The employer agrees to pay the worker a wage or salary.

Under the Contract of Employment Act 1972, the written contract must include the following:

1. Title of the job
2. Date the job starts
3. Hours of work
4. Rate and method of pay
5. Holiday arrangements
6. Period of notice that must be given
7. Pension-scheme arrangements
8. Rights concerning trade unions
9. The organization's discipline rules

The personnel manager will agree a date with the employee for work to start and the contract becomes binding from this date.

To motivate the work-force a good employer will try to foster a good relationship. Factors which could act as 'motivators' include the following:

HUNTLEY, BOORNE & STEVENS LTD.
APPLICATION FOR EMPLOYMENT — HOURLY PAID EMPLOYEE
(Please complete this Form in your own handwriting)

Surname:	Christian Names:
Address:	Position required:
Age: Date of Birth:	Married Single Divorced Widowed Dependants:

Name and Address and Telephone No. of person to be informed in case of emergency.

Relatives with Company:	Place of Birth and Nationality:
Education Details:	Details of any apprenticeship served:

Previous employment with the Company (if any):

Have you ever suffered from –

(a) Accident of serious illness? ....
(b) Dermatitis or skin condition? ....
(c) Hay fever or asthma? ....
(d) Fainting or giddy fits? ....
(e) Epilepsy? ....
(f) Heart or chest conditions? ....

Are you a Registered Disabled Person? If so, Registered No..........................
Date of Expiry: ....

Are you prepared to work shifts?

PRESENT OR PREVIOUS EMPLOYMENT
Last or present employer: .... Clock no. ....
.... Foreman: ....
Occupation: .... Rate: ....
Length of Service: .... Date left: ....
Reason for leaving: ....

Date: Signature of Applicant:	

For Office Use Only

Remarks: ....
....

Engaged as:	Clock No.:	Department:
By:	Wage Rate, etc.	
Starting Date:		
Date	Signature of Interviewing Officer:	

Figure 10.5 Huntley, Boorne & Stevens regularly takes on new employees and so issues a standard application form.

1. Rates of pay which are above the average for the industry or for workers with similar skills
2. Allowing reasonable time for holidays, breaks and relaxation
3. Good consultation to be maintained with employees about conditions of work
4. Flexibility about workers' personal problems—such as a bereavement in the family
5. Profit-sharing schemes perhaps involving workers becoming shareholders
6. Workers being made to feel that they are responsible to the owners of a company

Training

This is another major area of the personnel function. New workers in a firm are usually given an induction programme in which they meet other workers and are shown the skills they must learn. Generally the first few days at work will simply involve observation, with an experienced worker showing the 'new hand' the ropes. Many large firms will have a detailed training scheme which is done on an 'in-house' basis. This is particularly true of larger public companies such as banks and insurance companies. In conjunction with this, staff may be encouraged to attend college courses to learn new skills and get new qualifications. Training thus takes place in the following ways:

1. On the job—learning skills through experience at work
2. Off the job—learning through attending courses

Promotion within a firm depends on acquiring qualifications to do a more advanced job. In banking, for instance, staff will be expected to pass banking examinations. At the same time, a candidate for promotion must show a flair for the job. It is the responsibility of the training depart-

Figure 10.6 Jobcentre advertisement for a sales assistant.

ment within a business to make sure that staff with the right skills are coming up through the firm or being recruited from outside.

As well as sending staff to local colleges and universities, the firm may use a government-run training centre. These are run by the Training Commission and provide specialist training in centres all over the country.

The business might also contribute to a national training scheme such as the Youth Training Scheme whereby the government subsidizes the firm to employ and train school-leavers.

Safety

The personnel department will also normally be concerned with safety at work. This might involve the employment of a specialist safety officer. There are many hazards in the workplace and the safety officer has a particularly difficult job in making sure that the firm complies with the law on health and safety. Unions are also particularly concerned with this issue, so it will involve a lot of detailed discussion.

The three main laws concerned with health and safety are described below.

The Factories Act 1961

This Act covers most businesses that use mechanical machinery and therefore includes a wide range of premises, including garages, printing works, building sites and engineering establishments. Some of the important provisions of this Act are as follows.

1. Adequate toilet and washing facilities must be provided.
2. The inside of buildings must be properly heated and ventilated.
3. Floors, stairs and passageways must be free from obstructions such as boxes and furniture.
4. Floors must not have slippery surfaces.
5. Machinery such as presses must have fenced screens to prevent serious injury.

6. Fire escapes must be provided and kept in good order. Fire doors should not be locked or obstructed.

The Offices, Shops and Railways Premises Act 1963

This is particularly important in relation to office and shop conditions.

1. Temperatures must not fall below 16 °C (60.8 °F) in places where people work for any length of time.
2. There must be adequate supplies of fresh or purified air.
3. Toilet and washing facilities must be adequate for the number of employees and kept in a clean state. There must be running hot and cold water with soap and clean towels.
4. Suitable lighting must be provided wherever people walk or work.
5. The minimum amount of space for each person is 12 square metres of floor area.

The Health and Safety at Work Act 1974

This Act establishes a responsibility of both employers and employees to provide safe conditions at work. The *employer's duty* is to ensure as far as is reasonably practical, the 'health, safety and welfare at work of all employees'. The *employee's duty* is to take reasonable care to ensure both his or her own safety and the safety of others who may be affected by what he or she does or does not do.

Employers or employees who do not abide by these rules can be punished in a court of law.

An example of an area covered by the Act is protective guards for cutting machines such as food-slicing machines and industrial presses. Accidents occur if the guards are faulty or if they are removed.

The Act also lays down training

Personnel work includes:

Figure 10.7 The functions of the personnel department.

standards for workers in potentially hazardous occupations.

Generally the workplace must be designed in such a way as to minimize the risk of accidents.

This Act is backed up by a Health and Safety Executive which includes representatives of employers, employees and local authorities. Health and safety inspectors are appointed with responsibility for making sure that the law is being observed.

Not only must the safety officer be aware of general laws but there are also specific laws and codes relating to specific industries. For example, there are laws relating to workers in mines, the explosives industry, and textiles. On top of this, many industries establish their own safety regulations, often in conjunction with trade unions. A firm's personnel officer will normally attend conferences and refresher courses on safety as a regular feature of his or her work.

Welfare

The final major responsibility of a personnel department looked at in this chapter is the physical and general well-being of the work-force. This will involve social facilities and activities, lighting, heating and ventilation, canteen facilities, Christmas activities, complaints at work and many other related areas.

Members of the personnel department should know quite a lot about the employees of the firm. Not only will they meet them through recruitment and training, but they will also make it their business to keep records relating to employees' families, absences from work, qualifications, problems at work, chances of promotion, salary and other matters. The personnel officer may, for example, arrange for a card and flowers to be sent if an employee has a baby.

Staff appraisal is a feature of promotion in modern companies, and

the personnel department will be responsible for organizing this. In some companies employees are given the opportunity to discuss their career with their immediate superior in order to see where they are going and to discuss their ambitions. In return they should get a report on how they are doing at work and some advice on how to further their careers.

One area of particular importance for the personnel officer is to make sure that there is no discrimination in the workplace. Discrimination against anyone on the grounds of their sex, race, colour or national origin is illegal, whether it be in recruitment, conditions of work, promotion, training or dismissal. Job advertisements must clearly not discriminate (see Fig. 10.8). It is then necessary to make sure that interviews are fair, pay is equal for similar work, there is no sexual or racial harassment; that, in fact, there is no discrimination of any sort. If there is a case of discrimination it can be taken to an industrial tribunal or a body such as the Race Relations Board.

An **industrial tribunal** is a set up to investigate grievances at work whose decision is binding on parties. It is made up of a legally qualified chairperson, an employers' representative and a trade-union representative. Industrial tribunals sit regularly in all areas of the country.

Redundancy

This occurs when a business or firm closes down, when part of a business closes down, or when particular types of workers are no longer required. It has been a common feature of the 1980s for managers and workers in the public and private sec-

Figure 10.8 Job advertisements must not suggest that someone of a particular sex (except for certain jobs), race, colour or national origin will be preferred.

tors of the economy. On being made redundant, a worker has certain legal rights to compensation. To receive redundancy pay, a worker must have been with a firm for at least two years.

Dismissal of staff

Over the years an elaborate system for the dismissal of staff has developed as a result of the large number of cases that have been before industrial tribunals or other courts. The heart of the matter lies in the difference between what is termed *fair dismissal* and what the court regards to be *unfair dismissal*.

The period of notice that an employee must be given when being laid off is stated in the contract of employment which, as we have seen, is a legal document.

The Employment Protection Act 1978 lays down minimum periods of notice that must be given when a worker is being made redundant provided that the worker is not being sacked for misconduct. One week's notice is required for employees who have worked for the employer for four weeks; two weeks' notice is required for those who have worked for two years. For every extra year employees have worked, they must be given a further week's notice. Anyone who has worked for at least 26 weeks can ask for a written statement explaining why he or she has been dismissed.

An employer might pay off the worker for the remainder of the contract rather than expecting him or her to finish the job. This is a common practice, for example, with football managers when the board of directors requires an immediate change of manager.

Fair dismissal

It is up to an industrial tribunal to decide on the 'fairness' of a dismissal. A worker can be 'fairly' dismissed without notice. This would involve proving a case against the worker on grounds such as:

1. Wilful destruction of company property
2. Sexual or racial harassment
3. Continuous bad timekeeping
4. A negligent attitude at work
5. Inability to do the job which the employee was appointed to do
6. Sleeping on the job

Some of these may lead to instant dismissal where there has been gross misconduct, e.g. theft from a factory. Sometimes an employee may get a written warning before being sacked.

Unfair dismissal

Dismissal for the following reasons would be 'unfair':

1. *Pregnancy.* You can only be sacked if you are unable to do your job properly, e.g. a shelf stacker.
2. *Race.* A worker cannot be sacked on grounds of race.
3. *Homosexuality.* If a worker is a homosexual there is no reason why he or she should be sacked unless it can be proved that it affects his or her standard of work.

4. *Union membership.* An employer cannot sack a worker for belonging to a trade union.
5. *Criminal record.* If an employer does not find out about an employee's criminal record until some time after employing him or her, the employer cannot sack the worker on these grounds *unless* it was a very relevant crime, e.g. a cashier who has a record of stealing the petty cash.
6. *Religion.* An employee cannot be sacked on grounds of religion.

Women at work

The *Equal Pay Act 1970* aimed to eliminate discrimination on grounds of sex in relation to pay, overtime, piecework rates and holiday entitlements. The Act gave all employees the right to equal treatment to that given to an employee of the opposite sex in the same employment who is doing the same or 'broadly similar' work. This Act was amended in 1984 to include equal pay for work of equal value.

The *Sex Discrimination Act* 1975 made sex discrimination unlawful in employment training and related matters. This Act was updated in 1986 to remove restrictions on women's hours of work which had prevented them from taking on manufacturing jobs involving shift or night work.

The main problems for women as a group at work have been low pay and a concentration in low-paid occupations. Economic expansion in the UK from the 1950s onwards created more and more jobs for women. There has been a growth particularly in the proportion of married women at work, so that over half now work.

Women have been finding work in hard times because of the nature of the work they do, i.e. part-time work. Between 1979 and 1987 women's employment in Western Europe rose by 7 per cent while men's has fallen by 2 per cent.

Women have taken on the part-time jobs which are available. In Belgium, Denmark, West Germany and the UK, women do over 80 per cent of all part-time jobs. The growing service industries are the main employers of part-time workers. Part-time workers are especially low-paid, but this is not the only reason for women's generally low pay. Another factor is that men's earnings are boosted by shiftwork, overtime and productivity deals. Such payments make up a quarter of men's earnings and only one seventh of women's. The 1986 amendment to the Sex Discrimination Act may help with this.

Major problems for women are that they tend to work in industries where unions are weak and because of family commitments they are unable to work overtime. Women are concentrated in a very narrow range of occupations. It is catering, cleaning, hairdressing, bar work and other services which occupy over half of all women manual workers, and office work employs a large proportion of non-manual workers. The 1984 amendment to the Equal Pay Act, which allows for job evaluation to see if work is of equal value, is seen as an important change.

The effect of the passing of the Equal Pay Act and the Sex Discrimination Act was to raise women's pay to 75 per cent of men's; however, by 1984 it had fallen back to 59 per cent of men's earnings in non-manual work and 61.5 per cent in manual work.

A feature of the UK in recent years is that women now have more qualifications, which should lead to advancement in earnings. Women with better qualifications are choosing from a wider range of careers. Women now own a quarter of all

American small businesses. The women graduates of the 1960s went into a small number of occupations, often teaching. The graduates of the 1970s are branching into medicine, law, banking and insurance amongst other areas. In the UK 47 per cent of medical-school graduates are now women. Between the mid-1970s and mid-1980s the proportion of women members of the Chartered Insurance Institute rose from 4 per cent to 14 per cent, and the proportion of women solicitors from 6 per cent to 17 per cent.

It is the fastest-growing industries that are taking most women into their senior ranks, e.g. the information industry (including public relations, computer services and the press), financial services, tourism and design. The parts of the economy where women are rarest—upper and middle management in medium-sized and larger companies, especially in manufacturing—are generally those now entering into relative decline.

Job splitting and job sharing

The practice of job splitting is most common in large offices where the employer finds it impossible to recruit full-time staff. A common arrangement is for the employer to employ staff who work alternate weeks. Another arrangement is for staff to use the same desk and equipment for different hours of the day.

Job sharing occurs when two employees agree to share a job. An example of this would be if 20 posts were offered, to be taken on by 40 workers who would share out the responsibility for each job as a pair. Job sharers are entitled to the full rights of a full-time worker such as rates of pay, maternity leave, holidays and sick pay. Job sharers are entitled to the same rights as full-time workers.

The Race Relations Act 1976

This Act sought to eliminate discrimination of all kinds on the grounds of racial origin. It is illegal to discriminate in training, recruitment, employment and promotion.

CASE STUDY—JOB SATISFACTION (1)

The following is an extract from an interview with a worker on the production line at a car factory:

'I find work here really boring. The pay is good but it has to be because the work is so tedious. I just try to think about what I'm going to do at the weekend or how I am going to spend my money. I feel that I am stuck with this job because there is nothing else going and all the time I am counting up the money against the hours. The problem is that we have to repeat the same task time after time and we don't get the chance to put something of our own personality into the work. I would like to be a footballer but I would never make the grade.'

Questions

1. Why do you think that job satisfaction might be low in a production-line job?
2. What sort of compensation might an employer have to offer for low job satisfaction?
3. How might it be possible to increase job satisfaction for production-line workers?

CASE STUDY—JOB SATISFACTION (2)

The following is an extract from an interview with a textile worker who had been made redundant (from *Redundant Women* by

Angela Coyle, The Women's Press, 1984):

'Roger Firth rarely had to recruit labour on the open market. Once employed, their people tended to draw in members of their own family. When people said that the factory was like "family", there was some measure of truth in that, as well as indicating their attachment to the factory.'

'I enjoyed every minute, because all my friends were on that section. We used to have a right laugh and joke and I miss them all now. We could chat when we were working, that's what I liked.'

Questions

1. What elements of job satisfaction are expressed in the above extract?
2. Why did the firm find it easy to recruit labour?
3. Would you expect wages to be high or low in the above firm?

CASE STUDY—CONTRACT OF EMPLOYMENT

The document in Fig. 10.9 is the first part of a copy of a contract of employment produced by Huntley, Boorne & Stevens.

What other details would you expect to be included in the contract under the Contract of Employment Act?

CASE STUDY— REDUNDANCY

In December 1980, the Harrogate and Castleford factories of the clothing manufacturing firm of Roger Firth were closed down. Roger Firth was a traditional men's

HUNTLEY BOORNE & STEVENS LIMITED
PARTICULARS OF TERMS OF EMPLOYMENT
HOURLY PAID EMPLOYEES

This document defines the terms and conditions for hourly paid employees of Huntley Boorne & Stevens Limited and is compiled in accordance with the requirements of the Contracts of Employment Act 1972 and the Amendments thereto under the Employment Protection Act 1975.

To: (Name) ....

of (Address) ....

....

Job title: ....

This Contract to take effect as at ....

your employment with Huntley Boorne & Stevens Limited having commenced

on ....

1. REMUNERATION

Your rate of pay and overtime rate is as established by the Domestic Agreement between the General and Municipal Workers' Union and the Company.

A copy of this Agreement is available for reference in the Personnel Department.

Your current rate of pay is £_____ per week of 40 hours, made up as follows:

....

and is paid weekly in arrears, normally on the Thursday.

Each payment will be accompanied by an itemised pay statement.

The pay week commences on Monday morning and ends on Sunday midnight.

In addition to the above rate of pay, the Company operates an Incentive Bonus Scheme for direct operatives. A copy is available in the Personnel Department for reference.

Figure 10.9 The first part of a contract of employment produced by Huntley, Boorne & Stevens.

garment manufacturer producing overcoats, raincoats, jackets and trousers. In the 1970s, men's fashions had moved away from these products towards sports coats, anoraks, bomber jackets and jeans. On top of this, garment manufacturers were faced by increasing competition from low-cost manufacturers from areas like South East Asia. In 1974, the firm had merged with the textile conglomerate Carrington Viyella and had gone some way to produce more fashionable clothes. However, the firm had to resort to periodic short-time working and under the merger scheme, Carrington Viyella were looking to make cutbacks to reduce spare capacity.

The redundancies were officially announced on 2 December 1980 and employees at Harrogate received 10 weeks' payment in lieu of notice and were paid up until 2 March 1981, whilst employees at Castleford received four weeks' payment in lieu of notice and were paid up until 2 January 1981. The manufacture of coats and jackets was transferred from Harrogate to Roger Firth, Northern Ireland.

Source: Redundant Women
by Angela Coyle,
The Women's Press, 1984

Questions

1. What is meant by 'redundancy'?
2. Why were the workers at the Harrogate and Castleford factories of Roger Firth made redundant?
3. Would you expect all workers to be entitled to redundancy pay? Explain the law relating to the payment of redundancy money.
4. What is meant by payment in lieu of notice?
5. How would you expect the redundancies to help the firm?

CASE STUDY—THE SEX DISCRIMINATION ACT

The advertisement in Fig. 10.10 is commonly displayed in the job-advertisement columns of newspapers.

SEX
DISCRIMINATION ACT, 1975

No job advertisement which indicates or can reasonably be understood as indicating an intention to discriminate on ground of sex (eg by inviting applications only from males or only from females) may be accepted, unless

1. The job is for the purpose of a private householder or
2. It is a business employing fewer than six persons or
3. It is otherwise excepted from the requirements of the Sex Discrimination Act.

A statement must be made at the time the advertisement is placed saying which of the exceptions in the Act is considered to apply.

In addition to employment, the principal areas covered by the section of the Act which deals with advertisements are education, the supply of goods and services and the sale or letting of property.

It is the responsibility of advertisers to ensure that advertisement content does not discriminate under the terms of the Sex Discrimination Act.

Figure 10.10 An advertisement commonly displayed in the job-advertisement columns of newspapers. (*Crown copyright*)

Questions

1. What is the purpose of the advertisement in Fig. 10.10?
2. Collect advertisements from the press which you think comply with the rules.
3. Collect advertisements from the press which you think are trying to stretch the rules.

CASE STUDY—INDUSTRIAL TRIBUNALS

Three members of the class will represent an industrial tribunal in the following exercise. Another two members of the class will represent the spokesperson for a firm which has sacked workers for various reasons. Another three members of the class should represent workers who claim to have been unfairly dismissed. It is the responsibility of the industrial tribunal to decide whether the cases represent fair or unfair dismissal in the light of the evidence.

For each case the class must write down the name of the person whose case is being heard, his or her age and job description, the reason for dismissal and the verdict of the panel with the reason given. The normal procedure will be for the panel to ask the employer's spokesperson to present the employer's side first and then for the employee to present his or her case.

Information for the employer's spokesperson

Case 1
Name: Bill Davis
Age: 22
Position: Accounts clerk

Bill has been working at the firm for two years. He is good at his job. He has been dismissed without notice for continually being late for work. Last year he was late for work on 103 occasions. He has repeatedly been warned about the offence. This year he has been late for work on 17 occasions (by the end of March). Last week you warned him not to be late again but on Friday he was seen leaving a chemist's shop 20 minutes after he should have reported for work. He was dismissed when he then turned up for work an hour late.

Case 2
Name: Sharron Foxwell
Age: 23
Position: Gardener in a garden centre

Sharron has been working for you for two years but has never been a very effective worker. She tends to take breaks that are too long and has a fairly casual attitude. She is now pregnant (two months) and so you have informed her that you no longer require her services—she has been dismissed immediately.

Case 3
Name: Sarah Groves
Age: 24
Position: Printer

Sarah has been working for the company for six years but is known to have a grudge against the supervisor. They have not been on speaking terms for several years. Last week somebody sprayed an abusive message with an aerosol on the canteen wall. Sarah was suspected and sacked immediately.

Information for the employees

Case 1
Name: Bill Davis
Age: 22
Position: Accounts clerk

You have been working at the firm for two years. You have been dismissed without notice. You are a single parent and have to take your child to a nursery every morning. Unfortunately the nursery is rarely open on time and this frequently makes you late for work. You cannot afford to pay someone to take your child to the nursery. You have been warned about your lateness but you feel that the personnel manager is picking on you, because other workers are also late and they are rarely told off.

Last Friday your child was sick. You left the child at your mother's and picked up some medicine, but by the time you got to work the personnel manager was standing there waiting for you to tell you that you were fired. You were so angry that you just walked off.

Case 2
Name: Sharron Foxwell
Age: 23
Position: Gardener in gardening centre

You have been working for two years. You enjoy the work very much and get on well with your fellow workers. You have just become pregnant and have been joking about it at work. You wanted to work for another four months, to have a few months off and then come back to work. It came as a bombshell to hear that you were being laid off because pregnant women were not allowed to work in the centre.

Case 3
Name: Sarah Groves
Age: 24
Job: Printer

You have been working for the company for six years. You enjoy work but there is one supervisor who really has it in for you and you don't get on at all. Last week you were present when a friend sprayed some graffiti about the supervisor on the canteen wall. You were blamed and as you would not split on a friend you have been given the sack.

QUESTIONS

1. Complete the following sentences using the words below.

Personnel
Jobcentres
Contract of employment
In-house training
The Health and Safety at Work Act
Industrial tribunal
Sex Discrimination Act
The Factories Act
Health and safety inspectors
Employment Protection Act
Equal Pay Act

(a) One effect of the .... is that jobs must be advertised in such a way as to show equal favour to both men and women.

(b) .... applies to all premises using mechanical machinery.

(c) When workers learn skills at the workplace, this is known as ....

(d) The .... department of a firm has responsibility for the safety, training, recruitment and welfare of employees.

(e) The Department of Employment supervises high-street ....

(f) The .... states that both sexes should get the same wage for doing the same jobs or jobs involving broadly similar work.

(g) An .... consists of representatives of the trade unions and employers and an independent chairperson.

(h) Employment starts when an employee enters into a ....

(i) The .... lays down the employer's duty to ensure safety at work.

(j) This Act is supervised by ....

(k) The .... lays down minimum periods of notice that must be given when workers are made redundant.

2. (a) You work in the personnel department of a large department store. You are preparing a job application form to send to applicants. You must design this form in order to find out as much as you possibly can about the applicants which is relevant to you giving them a job. Set out the form in a neat and clear way.

(b) Explain why you would require eight of the items of information you have asked for.

3. You are the personnel manager of a local high-street bank. You must design a job advertisement to be placed in the local paper. The job is for a school-leaver to start off a career in banking. Make sure you state the qualifications you would expect and a sensible starting salary.

4. Rank the following in order of importance to you when applying for a job:
   (a) Good rate of pay
   (b) Opportunity for promotion
   (c) Good holidays
   (d) Prestige

(e) Good fringe benefits
(f) Job security
(g) Good working environment
(h) Opportunity to be creative
(i) Independence
(j) Responsibility
(k) Short distance to travel to work

5. Figure 10.11, on page 104, is a job outline produced by the personnel manager of Huntley, Boorne & Stevens. Write a letter of application for the job.

6. Explain the main laws relating to a worker's rights at work.

7. Which of the following cases probably involve 'fair' and which 'unfair' dismissal?
   (a) John Jones is sacked for wearing a 'gay pride' badge.
   (b) The accountant is sacked for taking money out of the wages account.
   (c) A young apprentice is sacked for deliberately sabotaging a machine.
   (d) Melissa O'Rourke, a company wages officer, is sacked when she becomes pregnant.
   (e) The works manager is sacked for regularly pinching women's bottoms at work.
   (f) Two members of the night shift are sacked for sleeping at work.

8. Explain the function of an industrial tribunal.

COURSEWORK

1. How do local firms check the time worked by employees? Do a study of the different methods used to check different workers.

2. How do local firms motivate workers? Do a study of the monetary and non-monetary

JOB TITLE:	Machine Operator
FUNCTION:	Aerosol Department.
RESPONSIBLE TO:	Aerosol Operators Manager
AGE INDICATOR:	18 or over.
HOURS OF WORK:	Monday to Wednesday 2.00 p.m. - 12.00 midnight
	Thursday 2.00 p.m. - 11.00 p.m.
DATE OF APPOINTMENT:	As soon as possible.
CLOSING DATE:	12th November, 1986.
APPLICATION TO	Applications in writing to :

Mr A. Robinson,
Personnel Manager.
Huntley, Boorne & Stevens,
Headley Road East,
Woodley.

A. Robinson,
Personnel Manager.

AR/BRB. 5.11.86

Figure 10.11 Job outline produced by the personnel manager of Huntley, Boorne & Stevens.

Shop staff win test case for equal pay

By Barrie Clement
Labour Correspondent

SHOPS in Britain could face thousands of equal pay claims from women workers after two former employees of a store in Londonderry, Northern Ireland, won an important test case for compensation.

The women, who worked as "stockroom assistants" at a Wellworth store owned by the multi-national Dee Corporation, won an undisclosed sum from the company after being paid less than three male colleagues doing similar work. The action was brought under the new equal pay for equal value legislation.

Miss Majella Ward and Mrs Patina McCarron, unloaded pallets and occasionally lorries, checked the goods against delivery notes and classified them. They earned an average of £75 a week while the men earned £83.

At an Industrial Tribunal in Belfast, the company originally argued that the two groups of employees did different work, but later conceded the case brought by the Equal Opportunities Commission.

The Dee Corporation, which owns 1,000 retail outlets, employed the services of a management consultancy to work out a new wage structure last year in response to the women's allegation. But it resulted in the original gap of £9 becoming £12. The company has now agreed to commission a new job evaluation scheme.

A spokesman for the Dee Corporation yesterday said that the company did not accept that the outcome of the tribunal affected work already being done by the company to rationalise working and grading agreements.

Figure 10.12 Newspaper article on an equal-pay case. (*Source: The Independent*)

incentives used by firms to encourage work.

3. What does a personnel manager/union official do? Find out the typical working pattern of these employees.

4. How do local firms train workers? Do a study of the in-house and outside training of workers done by a local firm.

5. How do people find work?
   Interview people to find out what methods they used to find work. Interview a personnel manager to find the most effective methods of recruiting labour.

6. What is the purpose of an industrial tribunal?
   Study articles in newspapers to monitor cases which have been before industrial tribunals. Study the work of a local industrial tribunal.

7. What happens when workers become redundant?
   Study the local newspaper for an example of a firm laying off workers. Interview the firm to find out the causes of the cutbacks and how the workers were laid off. What scope is there for the redundant workers to find alternative employment in the area?

8. What is the purpose of a job centre? Interview the local job centre manager to find out how it functions and what it does.

9. Study the article in Fig. 10.12. Prepare a report arguing the case for and against the idea of equal pay for equal value. (The report is to provide the basis for a class discussion on the issue of equal pay.)

11 Industrial relations in the workplace

In the previous chapter we looked at the main areas in which the personnel department operates. In this chapter we will be looking at the way in which the personnel department and the trade unions communicate with each other to handle industrial relations.

> **Industrial relations** are concerned with communication between the representatives of employers and the representatives of employees.

The article in Fig. 11.1 was printed in the *Harrogate Advertiser* at Christmas 1986. It showed a difference in the interests between management and trade unions. Successful industrial relations involves striking a balance of interests between the two parties.

From the employer's point of view, industrial relations is about having the right to manage—the ability to plan for the future so that a company can continue to be a success, to make profits for its shareholders, and to keep its employees motivated.

From the employer's point of view, industrial relations is about securing the best possible living standards and conditions of work for its members. Unions know that decisions that a firm makes will affect the livelihoods and opportunities of workers and their families. So in addition to trying to improve the standard of living of their members, unions will press for a greater say in how the firm or organization is run.

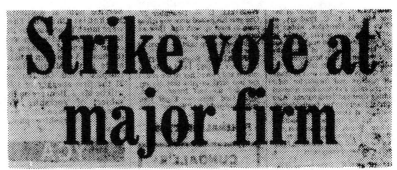

SHOP FLOOR workers at Starbeck engineering firm, Octavius Atkinson, have voted to go out on strike.

After a secret ballot the 206 strong workforce voted by an overwhelming majority to reject a four per cent pay offer and take industrial action — starting after the Christmas break on January 5.

District secretary of the Amalgamated Engineering Union, Mr. Malcolm Bushby, said: "The strike ballot was the result of a final wages and conditions offer made by the company which was rejected by the membership."

Mr. Bushby said the company was informed of the decision last Friday and there had been no response since then.

Octavius Atkinson managing director, Mr. Michael Reffitt, said it would be difficult to assess the effect of the strike until after the Christmas shutdown.

"We are always ready to talk to the unions — even on Christmas Day — if they want to talk," he said.

Mr. Reffitt confirmed the company had made a pay offer of four per cent in line with the rate of inflation.

"We have a disagreement with our shopfloor members due to the fact that we have offered four per cent and they are looking for more.

"The question is what happens on January 5.

"We would hope that during the week starting January 5 we would be able to reach agreement. At some stage we have got to get together and talk to resolve our differences."

Figure 11.1 Newspaper article on an industrial dispute. (*Source: Harrogate Advertiser*)

The main actors concerned with industrial relations

The union side

The president of the union
The president is elected nationally to represent the whole membership in negotiations with employers, government and other unions. In the union called SOGAT 82 this role is performed by the General Secretary. (See Fig. 11.2.)

The full-time official
An official is appointed and paid by the union and will cover a number of firms in a particular area. The officer has close contact with union headquarters.

The convenor
Originally the convenor was the shop steward who called for union meetings in a large workplace. Today the term simply means the senior shop

Figure 11.2 Brenda Dean, General Secretary of SOGAT 82 (*Source:* Guardian Pictures Desk)

steward. It is an important post and most convenors hold the job for long periods of time.

The shop stewards
Factories in many trades were traditionally divided into shops, e.g. the cutting shop, the sewing shop, etc. Each shop would elect at least one steward to represent them in the workplace. The work would be part-time and hardly ever paid.

The management side

The board of directors
This is a committee chosen by the shareholders to represent their interests.

The managing director
This is the senior director with the responsibility for the day-to-day running of the business.

The personnel manager
As we have seen, this is the manager responsible for recruitment, training, welfare and safety. The personnel manager will be at the hub of day-to-day dealings with the unions.

The charge hand
This is a working supervisor responsible for a particular group of employees in an organization.

Day-to-day industrial relations

On a daily basis the main industrial-relations bargaining takes place between the personnel department and a shop stewards' committee. Normally they would meet regularly once a week and thrash out issues such as the following:

1. Pay
2. Bonuses
3. The working environment
4. Disputes
5. Work schedules
6. Grievances
7. Health and safety at work
8. Hours
9. Production targets

Major industrial-relations issues

As well as local bargaining which is concerned with small-scale industrial relations, larger issues may be thrashed out on an industry-wide scale. Wages for State employees, for example, are normally agreed upon at an annual pay award. The parties involved will normally be the central executive of a union and employers' leaders.

> An **executive** is a body given the power to put decisions into effect, i.e. to make things happen.

Union structure

This varies in different industries but a typical form is shown in Fig. 11.3. Groups of workers are members of a branch. They choose branch officials to represent them. The branches also choose representatives to represent them at a regional committee. Regional groups then choose representatives to go to an annual conference. The annual conference makes decisions relating to the industry and chooses a full-time body of officials known as the national executive. The top official in the union is the president.

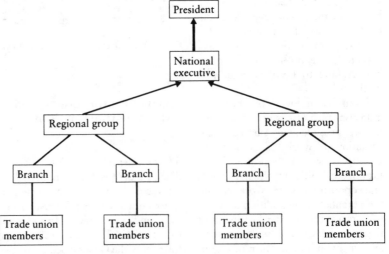

Figure 11.3 A typical union structure.

A good example of union industrial structure is in the National Union of Mineworkers. The local branch is based on the colliery, the unit of operation in mining, and the branch personnel deal with the day-to-day problems, disputes, grievances and many minor issues that can arise. Shop stewards as such are not found in the mining industry and the branch is based on the pit and includes in its membership all manual and craft grades; the branch officers undertake the duties allotted to shop stewards in other industries. There is a single line of communication from the branch up through the area coalfield office to the national centre, and similarly from centre to branch.

Craft unions	Industrial unions	General unions	White-collar unions
Musicians' Union	National Union of Mineworkers	Transport and General Workers' Union	National Union of Teachers
Pattern Weavers Society	National Union of Railwaymen	General, Municipal, Boilermakers and Allied Trades Union	Banking, Insurance and Finance Union
Associated Metalworkers' Union			

Figure 11.4 Examples of the four types of trade union.

> **Official union action** is action which has been approved by the union's executive.

Unofficial union structure

Unofficial action takes place when members carry out actions not approved by the union. Examples of this might be when local stewards call out workers in a lightning strike. In fact, in the UK, most industrial action is unofficial but only short-lived. This was particularly true in the late 1970s in industries like car manufacture, in which shop stewards had a lot of local influence. Union funds cannot be used for unofficial action, because it is not officially approved. Unofficial action will generally take place if local unionists feel that the national union is out of touch with their feelings or if they want to take prompt action.

Types of trade union

There are four main types of trade union (see Fig. 11.4):

1. Craft unions
2. Industrial unions
3. General unions
4. White-collar unions

However, it is important to point out that many unions do not fit easily into a particular class. Often they have characteristics common to more than one class.

Craft unions

The earliest type of union in this country was the Craft union. These unions were made up of highly skilled craftsmen in a particular trade. Often these groups were mutual benefit societies before the welfare state came into being. Subscriptions could be quite high and in return the union would provide sick pay, unemployment pay, a pension and other benefits. These unions are less important in the UK today. Their membership is relatively small.

Industrial unions

Industrial unionism is common in many European countries, notably West Germany. The economy is divided up into industrial sectors, and workers in each sector belong to the industrial union for that sector. The National Union of Mineworkers is often quoted as an example of an industrial union. (However, in 1985,

a rival union, the Union of Democratic Mineworkers, was formed and, on top of this, there are smaller unions such as the pit deputies' union, NACODS.) The advantage of an industrial union is that it caters for all workers in an industry whatever their job. Negotiation with employers is greatly simplified and all workers are united in their efforts.

General unions

These are some of the largest unions in the UK today. They recruit workers from several industries. They include semi-skilled and unskilled workers. A particular advantage of this form of union is that it gives strength to workers who would have little power on their own. It gives them the opportunity to belong to a well-funded and organized body.

White-collar unions

> **White-collar workers** are non-manual workers such as civil servants, bank workers and teachers, as opposed to **blue-collar workers**, who do manual work.

White-collar unions have been the most rapidly expanding groups in the 1970s and 1980s. This has happened with the growth of the tertiary sector of the economy and the expansion of large bodies of office staff in insurance companies, banks, company administration units, the Civil Service, etc.

Union finance

Unions get the bulk of their finance from members' subscriptions. They will also have a portfolio of investments which can be quite substantial if they pay pensions to members. Unions will also try to build up a capital stock in order to pay out strike pay and organize publicity in the event of industrial action.

Day-to-day union expenditure goes on the maintenance of union buildings, staff salaries, publicity, administration and running expenses such as telephone and electricity bills. Frequently unions will also run an education section and will make donations to other groups such as workers in similar trades overseas. Some unions will also make a contribution to the Trades Union Congress (TUC).

Forms of union action

Unionists have a number of types of action available to them to put pressure on employers.

Picketing

Primary picketing is legal. This involves members of a union who are on strike standing outside a firm's entrance and trying to persuade other workers not to cross the picket line.

Secondary picketing is not legal, and involves workers from one firm trying to dissuade workers at a firm not involved with the strike from going to work. Secondary picketing

takes place when unionists try to spread the impact of their action.

Withdrawal of goodwill

This involves workers becoming obstructive about things which need co-operation.

Go-slow

Workers take their time over the work they are doing.

Work-to-rule

Workers stick strictly to the book of rules relating to their particular job in order to reduce efficiency. For instance, railway workers may check that every carriage door is firmly closed at each station.

Ban on overtime

Workers refuse to work more than the hours laid out in their contract of employment.

Official strike

Workers cease work with the authority of the union.

Unofficial strike

A group of workers cease work without the official approval of the union.

Sit-in

Occasionally the workers occupy a factory. Similarly, if a factory has been threatened with closure, the workers may remain at work operating a work-in whereby they refuse to stop work.

Blacking

This occurs when members of a firm refuse to handle particular materials or work with particular machinery.

The closed shop

Unions can put pressure on management to operate a closed-shop policy whereby all workers must belong to the same union. Sometimes the

employers actively encourage this set-up because it is easier to bargain with just the one union.

Demarcation disputes

Sometimes unions have disputes with each other about 'who does what' at work. Unions are sometimes very protective about the work their members should rightfully be doing.

Forms of employer action

The employers can put pressure on trade unions to accept their authority in a number of ways. The most obvious way is to threaten to hold back privileges such as bonuses. Employers can also threaten to close down a plant which they regard as uneconomic. They may put forward the argument that a pay rise would lead the firm into a situation of being uncompetitive or that it would cease to make a profit. If there is little alternative employment in the locality such arguments will have considerable force.

Employers have open to them some other weapons:

The sack. The employer ceases to employ certain workers (although as we have seen in the previous chapter, workers have legal rights to compensation).

Suspension. Workers can be laid off without pay. This could be to allow further thought on a matter in dispute, or it could be used as a punishment.

Lockouts. Employers refuse to allow the workers on to the premises to work.

The Trades Union Congress (TUC)

This is the annual meeting of the trade-union movement. All the major trade unions are members of the

TUC and send a number of delegates to the conference depending on the size of their membership. The annual congress takes place in September every year, at seaside resorts like Scarborough and Blackpool where there is a lot of hotel space after the holiday season is finished and where large conference halls are available. The conference lasts for a week and during this time a number of motions and issues are debated.

The TUC appoints full-time officials including a president and vice-president, and has its own substantial headquarters offices. The TUC is an important organization because it reflects the general feelings of the trade-union movement. It is particularly active in the field of negotiation in industrial disputes. It offers advice and assistance to unions with problems and tries to iron out difficulties that arise between unions. It acts as a pressure group trying to influence government and employers on a wide range of issues.

The annual congress covers a wide range of issues. It is a false conception to assume that the TUC is simply concerned with wages. The congress will discuss matters as different as education, the Third World, privatization, AIDS and alcohol.

The TUC despite its importance has very little power. Individual unions are not bound by its decisions and the only threat it can use is to expel a union from membership.

Professional associations

Many workers belong to professional associations. These are organizations that do many of the same things as trade unions but are not registered as trade unions. They tend to cover better-paid white-collar workers. An example is the British Medical Association which is the body that negotiates on behalf of doctors. Professional associations also try to establish standards for members and to insist on a high level of competence for membership.

Employers' organizations

Like trade unions, employers' organizations fulfil a wide range of functions but the main one is collective bargaining. Faced by large and powerful trade unions small employers would be at a disadvantage if they had to stand alone. An employers' association may bargain on behalf of all firms in an industry. Other functions of employers' organizations include the following:

1. Pooling ideas and funds for industrial research
2. Collectively setting up training centres
3. Discussing common interests such as the threat of foreign competition
4. Providing a collective voice to raise industry-wide problems with government and other bodies

The Confederation of British Industry (CBI)

The CBI is the employers' equivalent of the TUC. It is a body with permanent officials which meets annually in conference. The leader of the CBI is its elected director-general. The CBI will be represented on government and other working parties investigating matters related to industry. Leaders of the CBI, TUC and government will periodically meet to discuss industrial strategy.

The CBI produces a number of publications related to industrial issues such as health and safety, international trade policy, etc. It is regarded as the mouthpiece of employers generally and its views on economic issues, such as taxation, investment and unemployment, are closely followed by the press and the government.

The government and industrial relations

This topic is dealt with in more detail in the chapter looking at the government and business (Chapter 13). Government has passed laws on a wide range of issues relating to industrial relations including the following:

1. Health and safety at work
2. Discrimination
3. Training
4. Employment of the disabled
5. Employment of young workers
6. Dismissal and redundancy
7. Pay
8. Industrial action
9. Restrictions at work such as the closed shop

> A **closed shop** is an agreement between employer and employees that it will be a condition of employment that an employee belongs to the appropriate trade union.

The Advisory, Conciliation and Arbitration Service (ACAS)

This body is available for use by both employers and employees. It was used frequently in the miners' strike of 1984–5 and the teachers' action in 1986–7.

> **Conciliation** is the process of trying to get each side calmly to appreciate the other's point of view.

ACAS is managed by a council of nine members—three chosen by the TUC, three chosen by the CBI and three who are independent.

In an industrial dispute in which there is deadlock, the parties might ask ACAS to help. Sometimes the parties might allow ACAS to look at the issue and come up with a solution that is 'binding'. At other times, ACAS might simply be asked to make recommendations.

> **Arbitration** is the process through which parties in a dispute allow a third party to come to a decision.

CASE STUDY—A DAY IN THE LIFE OF A SHOP STEWARD

Mrs Sylvia Holt is a machine operator on production lines making metal packaging at Huntley, Boorne & Stevens. She has been with the company for 16 years. She is also a shop steward for the General, Municipal, Boilermakers' and Allied Trades Union.

7.15 a.m.	Clock in for work.
7.30 a.m.	Start work on line.
8.55 a.m.	A worker complains that her bonus has been underpaid. She explains to me what job she was doing and how many trays she had done. I explain the situation to the supervisor who then takes it further.
9.05 a.m.	I return to my job.
9.20 a.m.	Supervisor returns informing me that the worker is owed £1.05.
9.45 a.m.	Tea-break—I also inform the worker of the amount she is owed.
10.00 a.m.	Tea-break over—start back on the line.
11.05 a.m.	Another worker

comes to me. He has caught his trousers on a broken wooden box. I take him down to the personnel department to report the accident. He is given the option of buying a new pair with the firm paying a percentage, or getting them repaired at the firm's expense. I then go back up on to the shop floor and investigate whether the broken box can be repaired or needs to be thrown away.

12.20 p.m.	Lunch-break.
12.50 p.m.	Lunch-break over—start back on line.
14.00 p.m.	A worker tells me he has been working alongside two other men for over a week and that they have been offered one hour's overtime a night, but he has not been offered any. I tell the worker to go back to his job and assure him that I will go and see the supervisor. I explain the situation to the supervisor and I am told that the worker is only helping out in that department. I then state that if he is good enough to work on the line in the daytime with them, helping out, it is only fair that he should be offered the overtime as well. The supervisor agrees and the one

hour overtime is given. I then inform the worker of his overtime.

14.20 p.m.	I return to my work.
16.30 p.m.	Clock out—day is over.

Questions

1. What do the letters GMBATU stand for?
2. What type of union is this (craft, general, white-collar or industrial)?
3. Does Sylvia work full time for the union?
4. What is the leading shop steward in a large workplace called?
5. How many hours did Sylvia work in the day illustrated in the case study?
6. Who does Sylvia represent?
7. Who does Sylvia negotiate with in the case study?
8. Would you regard Sylvia as holding a powerful position? Explain your answer by reference to the text.

CASE STUDY—INDUSTRIAL RELATIONS AT HUNTLEY, BOORNE & STEVENS

There are six trade unions represented at Huntley, Boorne & Stevens at Woodley in Reading. The six unions represent the following categories of worker:

1. Factory operatives
2. Engineering staff
3. Print workers
4. Managerial staff
5. Studio designery
6. Clerical workers

The personnel manager Alan Robinson meets representatives of these unions as and when required. In a meeting there will be between two and five union representatives and the personnel manager. Representatives of the different unions meet separately with management rather than as a joint committee. Most meetings will concern issues such as safety standards, conditions at work (the canteen menu, state of toilets, etc.) and discipline at work.

Negotiation with all the unions except the print workers (National Graphical Association) is done at a factory level. Negotiations with the NGA are done on a national level. Pay negotiations within the factory take place with the individual unions separately.

Questions

1. Why does Alan Robinson meet with the union representatives?
2. What issues are the concern of day-to-day industrial relations?
3. What difficulties do you think are posed by having six separate unions?
4. Why do you think workers are grouped into six unions?
5. The six unions are the GMBATU, AEU, MATSA, SLADE, NGA and ASTMS. Try to find out which union represents each group of workers mentioned in the text.

QUESTIONS

1. Complete the following sentences using the words below.

Shop steward
Unofficial strike
President
General union
White-collar union
Craft union
Industrial union
Branch
Official strike

(a) A strike that is recognized by the executive of the union is known as an ....
(b) A .... is made up of highly skilled workers.
(c) Local workers in a particular union are members of a .... of the trade union.
(d) The executive officer who acts as the figurehead for the trade union is known as the union ....
(e) An .... tends to be short and can flare up with little notice.
(f) Factory-floor workers will be represented by a .... in day-to-day negotiations with management.
(g) A .... is made up of workers from several different industries.
(h) Clerks, teachers and bank employees would all be examples of workers who could be members of a ....
(i) An .... is made up of all the workers in the same industry.

2. The following are all examples of industrial action that could be employed by a trade union:

- Strike
- Work-to-rule
- Blacking
- Overtime ban

Explain which you would use in each of the following situations and why you would use the particular method. (You might also wish to use an alternative strategy.)

(a) You are the shop stewards' leader in a company producing confectionary. Your firm has an important order to meet for an overseas buyer. Currently your firm is refusing to allow a 6

per cent wage increase which is the equivalent to the rise that workers in a competing firm have just been given.
(b) You are the shop stewards' leader in a firm that has just introduced some new highly advanced machinery. The machinery will increase output but the management is expecting workers to use it at the old wage rates. Introducing the new machinery will make it necessary to make 10 workers redundant.
(c) You are the union representative in a large office. It is a particularly hot summer and you have asked for an extra quarter of an hour break in the middle of the afternoon. The management side argues that this is not necessary.
(d) You work in a leisure centre in which there are only a few members of your union. The management is insisting that you work at the weekend as well as during the week.

3. Suggest how each of the following might 'work to rule'.
(a) Check-out operator at a supermarket
(b) School caretaker
(c) Schoolteacher
(d) Dustbin collector
(e) Footballer
(g) Actor

4. Find an example of a local industrial dispute in the newspaper. Interview two members of the class, one acting as the spokesperson of the union, the other as the management representative. Tape-record the interviews. Do they give a balanced view?

COURSEWORK

1. An important part of course-work is learning how to ask the right questions in a business context. This piece of course-work is concerned with preparation for a practical investigation of business activity. In particular, we are looking at the internal and external pressures within a business leading to an industrial-relations problem.

   This exercise should be tackled as a class activity.

   Study the article in Fig. 11.5 relating to Octavius Atkinson in Harrogate. What questions would you ask in order to find out why a conflict of interests had arisen between the two groups? Split the questions up into those that you would ask the management and those that you would ask the work-force. Is there any similarity in the questions you would ask the two groups?

   Having established the set of questions you would like to ask, apply them to local industrial-relations issues. Does a common pattern emerge in local issues or not?

2. Study a local dispute over pay. Generally in these disputes a great deal of attention is given to statistics such as price changes, productivity, comparable earnings, etc. Find out the main figures which the different sides in a dispute are quoting. Discover the sources of these statistics and how much weight each side gives to the other's figures. How reliable and useful are the figures which are used?

3. For this activity the class must be split into two groups. One group represents the management negotiation team of the West Wales Assurance Company and the other group represents the union negotiators.

The union and management are worried about absenteeism and illness. The work-force has been suffering from headaches, dry skin and a general feeling of drowsiness at work. Outside experts have been called in and they have reported on a number of 'building-related illnesses' (see Fig. 11.6). The building is air-conditioned, windows cannot be opened and the air that is recirculated makes workers feel sick and drowsy.

The glue in the carpet contains formaldehyde, which causes headaches, and the photocopier produces toxic fumes. Water in the pipes has become contaminated and produces bacteria which seep out into the air system. Eye complaints stem from the various chemicals present in the air which react with the rays that come from fluorescent lighting.

Crunch talks at strike firm

CRUNCH talks were due to be held yesterday in a bid to try and resolve a strike which has stopped production at a Harrogate engineering company.

More than 170 steelmen from Octavius Atkinson, in Prospect Road, Starbeck, went out on strike on Monday over a pay dispute with management.

Pickets at the factory gates yesterday morning said their shop stewards had agreed to meet with management for the first negotiations since the strike began.

The results of the negotiations would then be put to the striking workforce by union leaders at a mass meeting at lunchtime today.

The dispute started just before Christmas, when a four per cent. pay offer was rejected by the workforce in a secret ballot.

The unions want an £18 a week rise and say the four per cent. offer — amounting to £3.50

By RICHARD SPENCER

a week—is an "insult."

Pickets on duty at the factory gates have turned away delivery lorries all week and production inside has ground to a halt.

"The lads thought the pay offer was not enough," explained shop steward, Mr. Bob Roddam.

"There have been flat weeks for the past eight months and the men haven't been earning bonus or overtime payments.

"Average earnings are less now than they were three years ago and we are prepared to stay out until we get a reasonable offer.

"The flat wage rate is so low a married man is entitled to a Family Income Supplement.

"This is not a militant place but we have

been pushed into taking action."

Octavius Atkinson's managing director, Mr. Michael Reffitt, said there were about 40 men in the factory carrying out maintenance and a limited amount of work.

Mr. Reffitt warned that if no agreement could be reached the dispute could hit the order book.

"We are dealing with a very serious situation. In today's market there is the risk that clients may decide to cancel orders.

"We won't turn away orders but we can lose them very easily."

Mr. Reffitt said annual pay and conditions negotiations had not been concluded but were broken off by the strike decision before the company had made its final offer.

Mr. Reffitt said he was "anxious" to reach a settlement with the striking workforce and put an end to the damaging dispute.

Figure 11.5 Newspaper article about a dispute at Octavius Atkinson in Harrogate. (*Source: Harrogate Advertiser*)

Figure 11.6 Some causes of 'building-related illnesses': 1. Contaminated air from the air-conditioning. 2. Chemicals in the air reacting with the rays from the fluorescent lighting. 3. Windows that cannot be opened. 4. Toxic fumes from the photocopier. 5. Formaldehyde from the glue in the carpets. 6. Bacteria from contaminated water in the pipes.

You are told that this sort of situation is not uncommon in modern offices. In 1984, there was an outbreak of illness at the Public Record Office in West London. The problem was traced to the air-conditioning system. More than £100 000 was spent on the clean-up and the building was closed for 10 weeks.

Each side must decide what the key issues are. Why is the situation a problem to the people you represent? What solution would you like to see? Try to negotiate the problem.

4. Interview a shop steward to find out what he or she does at work. Pose the assignment as a question: 'What contribution does the shop steward make to industrial relations?' A similar assignment can be done with a personnel manager.

5. Carry out an investigation of the framework for industrial relations at a plant or factory. A suitable question to pose might be, 'What is the framework within which industrial relations take place at the X plant?'

12 Business in an international setting

Business activity takes place against a background of world trade.

1. Many businesses based in the UK are owned by overseas shareholders or are offshoots of foreign companies.
2. Many UK firms buy raw materials and supplies from overseas.
3. Many UK firms face overseas competition.
4. Many UK firms sell their products or services overseas.
5. Many UK businesses have offshoots overseas and foreign companies have UK shareholders.

In recent years we have become particularly aware of the impact of the world market on business life in the UK. The 1970s and 1980s were periods of world recession and many UK businesses suffered.

Imports and exports

For centuries Britain has been a country that relies on international trade. We purchase goods and services from other countries and in return we sell them goods and services produced here.

> An *import* is a purchase by UK citizens from overseas. An *export* is a sale by UK citizens to a member of another country.

Visible and invisible trade

For the purposes of classification we call the tangible goods that we trade visible items. We call the services that we trade invisible items.

Why do countries trade?

Countries trade in order to benefit from each other's resources and skills. In the UK we are highly effective at producing whisky (mainly because of climate), Land-Rovers (because of skill and efficiency) and insurance policies (because of long years of experience). We are not so effective at producing rice (because of climate), motorbikes (because of lack of efficiency compared to other countries) and snow tyres (because of lack of experience).

International trade is an example of an area in which specialization is advantageous. A tennis player might not only be good at her sport but also be a first-class accountant. However, she concentrates on her tennis and hires an accountant to do her bookwork because tennis is her best line. It would take her a week to do all her paperwork. In this time she would lose £5000 in earnings whereas it only costs her £800 a year to hire an accountant. In the same way in the UK we concentrate our resources into our most efficient lines of production such as banking, insurance and microtechnology. By trading these goods on world markets we are able to purchase items which we could only produce in an inefficient way when compared to other countries such as cricket bats, pineapples and washing machines.

Other reasons why we trade include the following:

1. Some items such as scarce minerals are impossible to obtain in the UK.
2. To foster good relations with other countries.

3. To earn foreign currency.
4. Because we cannot fully supply our own market in many items.

The balance of payments

Exports bring currency into the UK whereas imports lead to an outflow of currency.

The UK has always done well on her invisible account. This is because we developed a world-wide reputation for commercial services. Some of our major invisible earnings come from the following:

1. Selling insurance policies overseas
2. Bank services to foreigners
3. Carrying goods for foreign companies by sea and air
4. Tourists spending money in the UK
5. Money earned on investments overseas in the form of interest and dividends

On the news every month we hear that the UK has made a surplus on invisible trade showing that we have sold more invisible services than we have bought. The figures for a particular month might be, for example:

Invisible exports   £100 billion
Invisible imports   £80 billion
Invisible surplus   £20 billion

At the same time the UK frequently makes a loss on her visible trade. In the early 1970s when the price of oil rose dramatically, the UK had a massive visible trade loss. However, as we began to sell our own oil this loss began to fall and oil has been of great benefit to the UK balance of payments. Unfortunately, however, the rise in oil prices led to a

Table 12.1 How the current trading account of the balance of payments is made up of the visible and invisible balances.

Visible exports	500	Invisible exports	400	Total exports	900
Visible imports	650	Invisible imports	200	Total imports	850
Visible balance	− 150	Invisible balance	+ 200	Current balance	+ 50

big fall in world trading because high fuel costs meant that people in industrial countries had less to spend on other goods and, because fuel goes into producing all goods, prices rose. The fall in world trade led to a fall in demand for manufactured goods like cars, carpets, textiles and chemicals. For the first time since the industrial revolution the UK has started to import more manufactured goods than it sells.

> The **visible trade balance** = sale of visible goods − purchase of visible goods

The current trading account of the balance of payments is made up of the visible and invisible balances, as shown in Table 12.1.

Ways of solving balance-of-payments problems

While it is typical today for the UK's visible balance to run at a loss this is greatly helped by our surplus on invisibles. There are no easy ways of solving balance-of-payments problems. Because we are a member of an international community, actions we take at home will have effects on other countries and their actions will affect us. The following are ways of improving the balance of payments:

Becoming more competitive
If we produce more up-to-date products than other countries, produce goods more cheaply, offer better after-sale service, and meet required

deadlines, then we will find our products selling well.

Import tariffs
If we tax foreign imports then they will be more expensive to home buyers, who will switch to buying more goods produced in the UK. However, the danger of such a policy is that other countries will retaliate, and tariff barriers around the world reduce world trade so that everyone loses.

Import quotas
We sometimes limit the quantities of foreign goods entering this country such as Japanese cars and East European suits. This can either be done by a voluntary agreement between trading countries or by law. Once again such a policy leads to retaliation and foreign companies get round it by setting up factories in this country.

Subsidies
The government could give financial assistance to UK companies to enable them to sell their products more cheaply. Once again this normally leads to retaliation and the breakdown of trading.

Exchange control
In most countries the central bank which is controlled by the government keeps the central pool of foreign currency. If the government wants to cut back on imports it will instruct the central bank to reduce the amount of foreign currency it will supply. Usually this will mean that the central bank will only readily

supply currency to important users. For example, importers of important raw materials will find it easy to get hold of foreign currency whereas citizens wanting to holiday abroad may find that they can only take out of the country a limited amount of foreign money.

Buying home-produced products
The government might run a campaign encouraging citizens just to buy their own home-produced products. This has been done in the UK from time to time and is used throughout the world as is illustrated by the photograph from Pakistan in Fig. 12.1 on page 116.

Trade restrictions

The direct impact of international trade is that it exposes businesses to foreign competition. This can be a major problem if businesses are competing with subsidized imports or with dumped products.

> **Dumping** occurs when a firm sells goods at lower prices overseas than in its home market. It is an illegal practice.

Another major problem for firms is in exporting to markets that are protected by customs duties and taxes.

The impact of foreign competition

Business must operate today in a situation in which transport costs between countries have fallen dramatically. Modern-day businesses therefore must compete in an international context. This becomes obvious when we ask questions such as the following:

Figure 12.1 Pakistan encourages its citizens to buy home-produced goods. (*Source:* Denis Doran)

1. What are the major cars sold in Britain today?
2. What are the main types of television sets sold?
3. Which firms dominate the UK computer market?
4. How many foreign banks operate from the City of London?

British Coal is an example of a business organization that has faced very powerful foreign competition. In the late 1980s the price of oil has fallen so that coal has found it more difficult to compete with alternative fuels. On top of this in 1986 the average price of UK coal was around £44 a tonne which was nearly double the world price for coal.

The problems of exporting

Most of the UK's exports continue to go to Western Europe and North America. Our major market is the European Community which

accounts for nearly half of our trade. The percentages of UK exports going to various areas of the world in 1986 were as follows:

EC	46
North America	17
Western European (non-EC)	12
Middle East and North Africa	7.9
Other developing countries	8.4
Other developed countries	4.8
Communist countries	2
Latin America	1.4
Other	0.2

The European Community is a **free-trade area**. This means that there are no customs duties on goods that are traded between these countries.

Wherever firms export goods, they must get the following right:

1. Price
2. Quality
3. Delivery

The exporters must know their market. Information about overseas markets can be obtained from two main sources:

1. The government
2. Banks

The government and banks play a major role in overseas trade because of their experience. They will help to organize finance, give advice, help with insurance and assist with foreign currency.

It is not surprising that some businesses are reluctant to engage in international trade. Problems include:

1. Uncertainty
2. Language differences
3. Differences in tastes
4. Paperwork
5. Customs duties
6. Extra transport and insurance costs

The student should try to think these through in terms of, for example, sending to Italy a vanload of fashion dresses made in the UK.

Documents and payment in international trade

The exporter needs to do substantial paperwork because a lot of documents are needed.

One of the most important of these documents is the *bill of lading*. This document has two purposes.

1. It forms a contract between the exporter and the shipping company. The ship's captain will sign it to show the state of the goods when he or she takes them aboard. If they are undamaged he or she will sign to say it is a 'clean bill'. If they are not in perfect condition the captain will note their condition on the bill (a 'dirty bill').

2. A copy of the bill is sent ahead of the goods by air to the importer. This paper gives the importer proof that he or she is the owner of the goods. When the goods arrive in port the importer can present the document and claim the goods. (See Fig. 12.2.) If the goods are sent by air the document is called an air waybill and the importer must prove his or her identity to claim the goods.

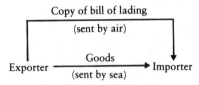

Figure 12.2 A bill of lading is sent by air so that the importer can claim the goods being sent by sea.

Open-account payment

International trade payments can be made in a way which is similar to trading within a country. The Irish Whiskey Company regularly sells goods to an importer in Canada. At the end of each month the importer is sent a statement of account. The importer arranges for the sum of money to be withdrawn from her account with the Royal Bank of Canada and transferred to the Bank of Ireland branch in Dublin used by the Irish Whiskey Company.

Bills of exchange

With many trading deals, more risk is involved than in the home trade. The bill of exchange is a common way of making payment for credit deals. The exporter sends goods to the importer and only expects payment after a certain period—generally three months but sometimes one month or six months.

The exporter draws up the bill of exchange and sends it to the importer, where it is signed for and accepted.

Fig. 12.3, on page 118, shows a bill of exchange made out for £5 117.65 which must be paid within three months of being presented. The bill has been drawn up by Edward Angus of Scottish Cosmetics Ltd (the exporter) and has been signed and accepted by Sonia Ramos of the US Import Agency, Boston (the importer).

The exporters, having sold goods on credit, might find themselves with a cash-flow shortage. They need money to carry on business and yet they have to wait for payment for goods sold on credit. To ease this problem they could do one of the following:

1. Sell the bill of exchange for less than its face value to a bank or other body dealing in money. There is a well-organized market in bills of exchange.
2. Borrow money from a bank using the bill of exchange as security for the loan (see Fig. 12.4 on page 119).

Other documents used in international trade

Exporters can get tied up with endless paperwork. Small companies might employ a specialist firm to handle their paperwork. Large firms have a specialist exporting department but today's uncertainty regarding the exchange rate has encouraged many multinationals to set up plants and offices overseas. Documents used in international trade include the following:

1. *Invoices.* International-trade invoices are similar to those used in the Home Trade.
2. *Certificates of insurance.* These cover various risks, mainly risks involved in transport.
3. *Certificates of origin.* Because the amount of import taxes paid varies according to where goods have come from, most shipments of goods must carry a certificate of origin for inspection by customs officers.
4. *Import licence.* This is issued by the importer's government giving permission for goods to be imported.
5. *Export licence.* This is needed for certain goods such as firearms and works of art.

The government and exports

The government of nearly every country tries to encourage exports for the following reasons:

1. They create business contacts and opportunities to make further sales
2. They help to create jobs
3. They earn foreign currency

The British government organizes trade fairs and 'British Weeks' overseas. It provides information and advice about foreign markets and currencies, and vital statistics about trade. It helps with the translation of documents and materials.

The Department of Trade also runs the Export Credits Guarantee service. The Export Credit Guarantee Department performs two important functions:

1. It provides grants and low-interest loans to help exporters get contracts off the ground.
2. It provides an insurance service against non-payment of debts by the importer (see Fig. 12.5 on page 119). Non-payment may be caused by war or bad relations between countries or by civil unrest in the importing country.

CASE STUDY—TRADE, BUSINESS AND THE INDIVIDUAL

The international situation has an enormous impact on an economy.

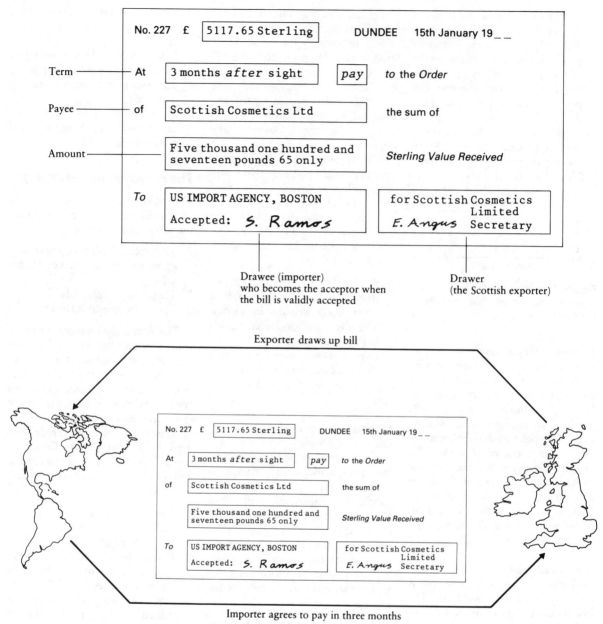

Figure 12.3 An example of a bill of exchange, and how it works.

The state of the economy influences the individual business and the state of the business affects the members of the business organization. Below is an article by Andrew Horvaat which appeared in *The Independent*.

Japanese city on a knife edge

Kikuhei Sakatsume and his wife Mitsue have spent the past 41 years putting the finishing touches to stainless-steel cutlery. Sitting on either side of an electric motor in a wooden shack behind their house, the Sakatsumes press every knife, one by one, against two grindstones. "I do the blades and my wife does the handles," said Mr. Sakatsume, who is aged 65. "But if our income goes down

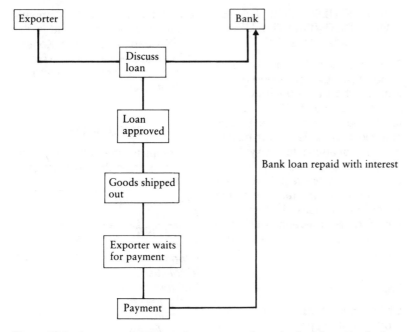

Figure 12.4 An exporter may have to borrow money from a bank while waiting for the payment promised in the bill of exchange.

If an overseas buyer failed to pay you, would you see red?

In the event that a buyer is unable to pay you, getting angry will be the least of your problems.

One bad debt can cause havoc with your cashflow and turn the tide on profits.

The non-payment of, say, a £20,000 contract could erode the profits on a much larger piece of business. All that work wasted when the £20,000 could have been covered for as little as £80.

In such an unpredictable trading environment, the cost of ECGD insurance seems a small price to pay compared to the damage caused by a bad debt.

ECGD is used by 4 out of every 5 companies who insure their export sales, and can tailor a competitively priced package to suit your individual needs.

See your local ECGD Regional Director, **ECGD** before you see red. Export with confidence.

Figure 12.5 Advertisement for the Export Credit Guarantee Department. (*Crown copyright*)

much more, we'll close shop and live off our pensions."

In Tsubame, the Sakatsumes are considered lucky. They get the equivalent of a penny a knife, and if they are unhappy, they can quit any time. A year and a half ago, the

Sakatsumes got about 1.5 pence a knife, but "what with the high yen, the factories have asked us to work for less," said Mr. Sakatsume.

Were it not for the sudden decline in the value of the dollar, few

people in Tokyo would pay much attention to this city of 45 000 people on the rainy, economically under-active side of the mountains that divide the main Japanese island of Honshu. But since the decision in September 1985 by the finance chiefs of the five big Western industrialized democracies to lower the value of the US currency, Tsubame has been front page news.

Heavily dependent on exports, too poor to be able to diversify into other fields, Tsubame is a Japanese nightmare come true. According to the Ministry of International Trade and Industry, Japan's production of cutlery—almost all made in Tsubame—declined by 35 per cent last year. Virtually every big cutlery manufacturer in the city had become eligible for government help.

Tsubame's plight is at once symbolic and real. At a time when Japan has become synonymous with the latest in high technology, Tsubame is one of 55 export-dependent cottage-industry areas which turn out everything from toys to artificial pearls, products which can no longer be made in Japan at a profit. The city represents the poor, isolated aspect of Japan which many Japanese and most foreigners had forgotten.

To Japan's makers of steel, ships and household electronic products, Tsubame is cause for concern. At the Ministry of Labour in Tokyo, officials estimate that the high yen has driven around 50 per cent of Japan's leading manufacturers to move part of their production operations overseas. Those that are not moving factories abroad are cutting domestic production and starting to procure parts from abroad.

Toshiba announced last month that it intends to increase overseas production from just under £1bn in 1986 to the equivalent of £1.5bn by next year. Labour Ministry officials say that 38 per cent of manufacturers have reduced their workforces as a result of recent changes due to the high yen.

Questions

1. The high price of the yen made Japanese goods expensive in 1987. Why is this particularly a problem for a country like Japan?

2.

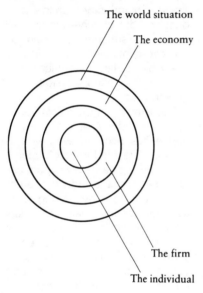

Figure 12.6 Diagram for question 2.

What do you think Fig. 12.6 is meant to represent? Explain it in your own words.
3. What picture do you have of Japanese industry? Does the industry in Tsubame fit this picture?
4. How have big Japanese companies responded to the high price of the yen?
5. What do you think will be the impact of this for UK firms?

120

CASE STUDY—THE TRADE WAR BETWEEN THE USA AND THE EC

The European Community sets import taxes on competing goods entering the Community from the rest of the world. Before Spain joined the EC, American exporters enjoyed a sizeable export market in Spain for animal feeds. With the entry of Spain into the EC, American farmers were faced with falling demand. In retaliation the Americans increased their own import duties on various EC food products, such as cheese and wine.

Task

Divide into two groups. One group must prepare the case *for* the UK using trade restrictions. The other group must argue *against* trade restrictions.

CASE STUDY—SOUTH KOREA

Over the past 20 years, South Korea has gone from being a nation of poor farmers to the most advanced of Asia's newly industrializing countries. Its prosperity has come from buying Japanese components, turning them into finished goods—and selling the results to America. Yesterday it was textiles spun on Japanese looms from Japanese synthetics; today it is personal computers with Japanese semiconductors inside them.

Questions

1. Where is Korea?
2. Draw a map showing the flow of parts from Japan to South Korea and of goods from South Korea to the United States.

3. See if you can find a comparison of income per head in the USA, Japan and South Korea.
4. Find out what goods sold in your local shops come from South Korea.

QUESTIONS

1. Complete the following sentences using the words below.

Bill of exchange
Bill of lading
Certificate of origin
Export
Import
Visible trade
Invisible trade
Exchange rate
Discount
Export licence

(a) A UK product sold to a foreigner is called an ....
(b) The sale of whisky to Japan is an example of ....
(c) An importer would present a .... at the docks to claim the goods.
(d) A .... makes it clear where goods first came from.
(e) A foreign product brought into the UK is known as an ....
(f) The .... is the rate at which one currency will exchange for another.
(g) When a bill of exchange is bought for less than its face value it is bought at a ....
(h) To take a valuable painting out of the country you would need an ....

(i) A .... is used to sell goods on credit.

(j) Selling banking services to a foreigner is an example of ....

2. Work out the visible balance, the invisible balance and the current balance from the following figures:

Visible imports	1200
Invisible exports	1000
Visible exports	1000
Invisible imports	600

3. Give six examples of visible and six examples of invisible items of trade.

4. Which of the following statements are true?
   (a) The UK always runs a surplus on visible trade.
   (b) The current balance will always be a negative figure.
   (c) The UK earns a lot of money from invisible trade.
   (d) Interest, profits and dividends from overseas are a visible trading item.
   (e) The UK buys imports from Third World countries.
   (f) The UK was one of the founder members of the EC.
   (g) The EC is a free-trade area.

5. Explain the following trade restrictions:
   (a) Subsidies
   (b) Quotas
   (c) Tariffs

6. Explain what is meant by 'dumping'. Find a reference in a newspaper to a case of dumping.

7. Study Fig. 12.7.
   (a) What is the worker in South Korea able to offer consumers in this country?
   (b) Why do we purchase imports from South Korea rather than manufacturing the goods ourselves?
   (c) What benefits will this worker get from our buying South Korean products?

8. List eight problems that are faced by exporters. Given these problems, why do firms export?

9. How can a rise in exchange rates affect businesses in this country?

Figure 12.7 Assembling a computer in South Korea. (*Source:* David Hayes)

COURSEWORK

1. Why does international trade take place?

Split the class into groups. In your groups discuss where things come from and why. Make out lists like those in Fig. 12.8. Try to make some notes which will help you answer the questions that follow.

(a) Choose one item which is *not* produced in the UK and explain why not.

(b) Choose one item which we consume in the UK which is not imported and explain why.

(c) Choose one item which you have found that is produced in the UK and abroad. Explain why this situation arises.

(d) With the help of your answers to questions 1–3, explain the main reasons for international trade.

(e) With the help of an atlas, complete a world map using a key to show where the goods on your list come from.

(*Source:* Peter Radband)

2. What paperwork is involved in exporting?

Imagine that you are exporting to Australia 200 packing cases of Scottish whisky. Explain what paperwork would be required and make out the necessary documents. (Word processing would help with this work.) How would the paperwork be different if the goods were sent to France?

FOOD AND DRINK

1 Tea from Sri Lanka

2 Milk from _____

3 _____

4 _____

5 _____

SMALL CONSUMER GOODS

1 Camera from Russia

2 Telephone from _____

3 _____

4 _____

5 _____

TOYS AND HOBBY EQUIPMENT

1 Lego from Denmark

2 Bicycle from _____

3 _____

4 _____

5 _____

ELECTRICAL GOODS

1 Video from Korea

2 _____

3 _____

4 _____

5 _____

GARDEN AND MOTORING

1 Lawn Mower from Germany

2 _____

3 _____

4 _____

5 _____

RAW MATERIALS

Can you find where these come from?

1 Wool from Australia

2 Oil from _____

3 _____

4 _____

5 _____

Figure 12.8 Produce lists like this of where different products come from.

13   The government and business

This chapter looks at the inter-relationship between government and business in a general way. We are not concerned with listing every single Act of Parliament or each government operation. The details of government policy change regularly and it is more important for the student to be aware of *why* the government becomes involved, the *ways* in which it might become involved and the *effect* this has on business activity.

Central government governs the whole country. Citizens choose Members of Parliament. The MPs belong to political parties which have leaders. Central government passes new laws in Parliament. Civil servants run the day-to-day activities of the State such as collecting taxes. **Local government** looks after only a small part of the country, e.g. a county like Somerset or a heavily built-up area such as Manchester. Citizens vote for councillors to represent them at local-government level.

Why does the government get involved in the economy?

To understand fully the part played by the government, take a walk in a group along a road outside your school or college. List ways in which the influence of government makes its presence felt. For example, who has paid for the roads, street lighting, and maintenance of the pavements and parks? Why are drivers wearing seat belts and why are lorries only allowed up to a certain size? The list that you come up with will be extensive and you should come up with many items that you might not have thought of simply by sitting in the classroom.

1. Some goods and services are provided by the government because it is felt that all citizens are entitled to a share in the public provision of such items. For example, most people in the UK believe that all children should have some form of health care and education.
2. Some goods and services which everyone benefits from can only be produced by the government if they are going to be properly provided. An example of this is the police force.
3. Some people believe that the government should try to reduce inequality. This might involve taxing some people at a higher rate than others and giving more benefits to those who are worse off. Of course there are others who believe that inequality is not such a bad thing because it gives people a motive to try to better themselves.
4. The government might also try to make the economic system run more smoothly. For example, it passes laws against monopolies and to protect consumers and it takes measures against pollution and other antisocial practices.

A very important role played by the government is to set the 'rules of the game' within which business activity takes place.

These rules are constantly changing and when they do some people will lose out and others benefit. It is important to bear in mind the following questions:

1. Who makes the rules?
2. Why do the rules change?
3. How do they change?
4. Who loses and benefits when they change?

Questions

Who would lose out and who would benefit as a result of the following changes in the rules? (It would also be worth trying to work out why some of these rules might have been changed.)

1. A new law is passed so that lorries have to contain a tachograph showing how many hours a lorry driver is at the wheel at one time.
2. The government passes a new law making Sunday trading legal.
3. The government publishes a list of drugs and medicines limiting the types that doctors can prescribe on the National Health Service.
4. The government passes a law laying down tighter controls on safety standards at sporting grounds.
5. The government passes a law making it compulsory for all businesses to publish their accounts for public inspection.
6. The government passes a law allowing doctors to advertise their services in newspapers.

The ways in which the government becomes involved in the economy

There are a wide number of areas in which government involvement in the economy is particularly felt and you should have a general understanding of these broad areas. Many of them are covered in greater detail in other sections of the book.

Major areas include the following:

1. Employment policy
2. Industrial policy
3. Regional policy
4. Inflation policy
5. Trade-union policy
6. Education policy
7. Taxation policy
8. International policy
9. Establishing the rules of the game

Government policy is an area of the course where it is particularly useful to take up-to-date notes on developments from newspapers.

Employment policy

In the 1920s and 1930s unemployment in the UK created terrible human, social and economic problems. Living through this period made a very big impact on people who were later to be in a position to make policy decisions. After the Second World War politicians of all parties saw full employment as being a major goal of government policy. A major policy used between 1945 and 1979 was for the government to spend money to try to boost jobs in the economy. The government built up its spending projects so that eventually about half of all the money spent in the country came from government sources. The government also became a major employer of labour and took a stake in several companies including Rolls-Royce and British Leyland.

After 1979 the Conservative government tried to reduce the part

the State played in running the economy. It believed that the best way of creating and keeping jobs was to allow businesses to compete because this will make them more efficient. In the 1980s the government pulled back from major spending policies to create jobs yet at the same time there were a host of small-scale projects, often run by local government, to create jobs.

On a national level interesting schemes of the 1980s have included the following:

1. *The Youth Training Scheme*. This guarantees a period of work experience and training for all school-leavers. The scheme subsidizes employers who take on workers under the scheme.
2. *The Enterprise Allowance Scheme*. The government pays wages to unemployed people setting up their own business for the first year of its operation.
3. *The Restart Scheme*. This provides training for the long-term unemployed. Unemployed people are invited to discuss their situation with the view to retraining for work.

Questions

Between 1945 and 1979 governments believed that government spending could play a major role in creating employment. After 1979 the government tried to reduce its share of spending. Why do you think this change came about? How do you think this might have affected the following people?

1. A taxpayer
2. A miner in a loss-making pit
3. An unemployed person
4. A firm making machinery

Industrial policy

British industry depends crucially in

many fields on having government as its partner. Michael Heseltine (an industry minister in the mid-1980s), writing in March 1987, said, 'This government, like all its predecessors for at least the last fifty years, is up to its neck in the business life of this country, stimulating one enterprise here, stifling another there and interfering everywhere.' It would be worth while for a class of students to check out this statement by following the television mid-evening news for a week and recording references to the government's relation with business.

The government plays a major part in approving and participating in major projects concerned with developing the UK's economic infrastructure.

> The **infrastructure** is the skeleton at the base of the economy, e.g. motorways, power stations, etc.

Examples of decisions that the government has made during the mid-1980s are decisions about the Channel tunnel and the new Severn road bridge.

The government has a partnership with industry in some research and development projects. In mid-1987, for example, Rolls-Royce was able to get a multi-million-pound grant from the government to launch a new super-fan engine.

The government also subsidizes particular projects and industrial sectors. An example of this is the grants given by the government to farmers to employ certain traditional farming methods.

The public sector of the economy is also important as a creator of employment, output and incomes. British nationalized industries alone employed over a million workers in 1986–7. These industries include

British Rail, British Coal, British Steel and many others. Over the years government objectives for the nationalized industries have changed. Since the Second World War these industries have increasingly been expected to show profits on investments although they still get a subsidy for social benefits (e.g. running some cross-Pennine railway services where other forms of communication are difficult).

The most recent policy for nationalized industry has been that of privatization. This involves selling off shares in State industries so that they become part of the private sector. One of the main arguments for this is to make them more competitive so that they cut out inefficient parts and expand efficient ones. There is the belief that if a business is open to the threat of 'bankruptability' then it will be spurred on to greater efforts.

Regional policy

Central-government policy in relation to the regions is covered in the chapter on external influences on businesses. In the UK today there is also a very strong thrust of policy at a local level. Local councils compete with each other to create employment within their region. This leads to extensive advertising of regional advantages. Councils will research the employment needs of the local situation and will organize the building of office and factory units to encourage industrialists in.

Areas which are situated in government-designated development and enterprise zones will be at a considerable advantage but it must be remembered why these areas are designated as needing help in the first place.

Inflation policy

Inflation is all about rising prices, but we must bear in mind that different prices affect different people in different ways.

Questions

If the price of petrol went up how would this affect the following people?

1. A pensioner living in an old people's home
2. A mobile-discotheque owner
3. Someone living on an agricultural commune
4. An insurance agent

The government, however, is concerned with the general level of inflation. It becomes concerned if prices generally start to rise, because of the following consequences:

1. UK goods become more expensive and difficult to sell.
2. People become unsure about prices and this can cause uncertainty and unrest. For example, workers might want more wages to keep up with price rises.
3. Some people lose out whilst others benefit and this might not be thought to be fair. For example, somebody who lends £10 at a time when this would have bought two records would not be happy to find that when the money was repaid to him or her it would only buy one record.

The government can use many different policies to deal with inflation. This book is only interested in them in the way they affect business. Policies that might affect business would include the following:

Raising interest rates
This policy would make it more expensive for business to obtain money. This increased cost could and does help to cause bankruptcies.

Discouraging spending
If the government carries out policies that cut back on the spending of money, such as making it more difficult to buy goods on hire purchase, this will inevitably hit the sales of a lot of businesses.

Controls on wages and prices
If the government sets limits on the amounts by which firms can raise their prices or on wage increases this will have a number of effects including reducing the ability of a firm to make profits and its ability to hire workers.

Trade-union policy

Different governments have different policies on trade unions. Some people think that trade unions have too little power while others think that they have too much power. In the 1980s there have been several rounds of trade-union laws and most people would recognize that these have reduced union power.

In 1987 the government introduced the following further new proposals:

1. Union officials should be elected by secret postal ballot.
2. Union officials should have to be re-elected every five years.
3. The closed shop should be outlawed.
4. A Commissioner for Trade Union Affairs should be appointed by the government to help union members take action against their union.

Question
Do you agree with the above proposals?

Education policy
Education is seen in the UK as having an important contribution to make to business life. The government plays a part in researching the contribution education can make and in encouraging schools to move in various directions. In recent years the

government has subsidized the use of computers in schools and encouraged the teaching of business studies and information technology.

In 1987 the government was trying to encourage a partnership with industry to set up 20 City Technology Colleges which would run independently of local government. These colleges would be set up in areas of existing industrial decline. Inevitably such policies will benefit some groups while others lose out. (Try to make a list of winners and losers.)

In the late 1980s the government is trying to steer schools in the direction of a core curriculum whereby all students will have to do certain subjects up to the age of 16. The government also hopes to test pupils at certain set ages in both primary and secondary school.

Taxation policy

Businesses can make valuable contributions to the community by the taxes they pay. Businesses in return benefit from government spending on projects like airports, roads, research and development, aid to developing countries and many other items.

The four main taxes that affect business are:

1. Profits taxes
2. Value added tax
3. Customs and excise duties
4. National Insurance

Profit taxes

Someone who is a sole trader or in a partnership will pay income tax, while companies pay corporation tax on profits over a certain amount.

A director in a limited company would pay income tax on his or her salary and on any sum of money withdrawn from company funds.

Value added tax

The standard rate of value added tax is 15 per cent in the UK. If a small firm bought in £1000 of inputs in a year and sold its output for £11 000 it would have added £10 000 to the value of the product. It will then add 15 per cent as value added tax on the value it has added to the goods or services. In total therefore it will hand over £1500 of tax to the government which it charges to its customers' bills.

Firms send the VAT payments to the government every month or quarter. A firm that buys goods or services with VAT on them can claim the VAT contribution back. For example, Sally Jones Ltd hires a solicitor to help with some paperwork. The solicitor charges £1000 + £150 VAT. Sally Jones Ltd will hand over the VAT but the amount can be reclaimed from the government at a later date.

Customs and excise duties

Customs duties are duties charged by the government to protect home industries. They would normally be placed on goods from non-EEC countries that compete with UK goods.

Excise duties are taxes placed on goods for the purpose of raising revenue for the government. Taxes are a great bone of contention with many businesses. For example, the UK whisky and cigarette industries have formed strong pressure groups arguing that they are over-taxed.

Questions

Study Fig. 13.1.

1. What percentage of a bottle of whisky goes in tax?
2. If a bottle of whisky cost £7, how much of this would be paid to the government in tax?
3. Who loses out from the tax?
4. Who benefits from the tax?
5. Is the tax high or low?
6. Is it a fair tax?
7. Should changes be made to the tax?

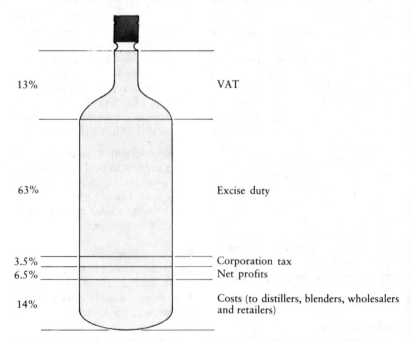

Figure 13.1 Diagram showing what percentage of the price of a bottle of whisky goes to different recipients. (Figures supplied by Scottish Whisky Association, 1987)

National Insurance

As well as deducting National Insurance from wages, employers also have to pay a contribution to the National Insurance Fund.

International policy

This topic has been dealt with in the chapter looking at business in an international setting (Chapter 12). The government may try to promote trade, encourage exports or reduce imports.

Governments of all political parties believe that a healthy world market is good for the UK and that we have an important contribution to make in helping in the development of other countries.

An important principle laid down in recent EC policy for its aid programme is that aid should not be limited to sending small amounts of surplus grain and dairy products to poor countries (which tends to damage the markets there for the products of local farmers). Instead we should use the same money to buy from, and thus support, poor-world farmers with surpluses available for sale.

Establishing the rules of the game

The government sets the rules of the game in many areas of business life. A few examples of these would be rules on the following matters:

1. Setting up a business and making information available
2. The protection of records and data
3. Health and safety
4. Monopoly and competition
5. Noise, nuisance and other social costs
6. The rights of buyers and sellers

The student only needs to have a general awareness of these rules because the actual fine detail is often very extensive. Health and safety

regulations, for example, stretch into thousands of pages.

It is worth while, however, for the student to look at a particular subset of rules and follow through the effect of changes in the rules. Interesting examples are changes in competition rules and consumer-protection laws.

It is interesting, for example, to note that until the 1960s consumers in this country had very little protection in law. Nowadays there is a mass of laws covering various areas and there is a detailed literature on this subject.

The effect of government activity

This will vary from business to business but inevitably all businesses will come across the government in a wide range of areas. We can therefore see that the government is a key

institution in the external environment of the business and that government laws have a great influence on the internal activities of businesses.

The main areas of government spending

Government spending has become an important fact of life in the twentieth century and, with the growth of welfare services, the amount spent has continued to increase. The biggest single item of government spending is social security, of which the largest part is pensions. In the UK today we have an increasing number of elderly people and this group of people will continue to need an increasing share of resources for the remainder of the century.

Table 13.1 lists the main areas of government spending, and states for each area whether central or local government is mainly responsible.

Table 13.1 The main areas of government spending, and whether central or local government is mainly responsible for them.

Spending programme	Is central or local government mainly responsible	Examples of spending
Social security	Central	Pensions, unemployment pay
Defence	Central	Army, Navy, Air Force
Health and personal social services	Central and local	National Health Service, Social services
Education and science	Central and local	Schools, colleges, research
Industry, energy, trade and employment	Central	Development grants, training schemes
Law, order and protective services	Local	Police, fire and prisons
Housing	Local	Repairs to council houses
Agriculture, forestry fisheries and food	Central	Subsidies to farmers
Overseas aid and overseas services	Central	Aid to poor countries and contributions to EEC
Transport	Local	Roads
Other environmental services	Local	Refuse collection, parks
Arts and libraries	Central and local	Libraries
Government lending to nationalized industries	Central	Lending to British Coal
Other	Central and local	Help to Wales, Northern Ireland and Scotland

Saved from the scrap-heap

Joan M. Clayton decided to go it alone — with some very professional help

LAST Monday I became a budding playwright — by courtesy of the Government. The Manpower Services Commission pay me £40 a week to stay at home and write. Other women have been launched as dressmakers, minicab drivers and florists. We have one thing in common — we were all on the dole.

Most of my life, I have been a journalist in trade and industry. My job as a newspaper editor was a gallop of daily deadlines strung together with work and worry. So when my boss asked me first thing one morning: "Could you come into my office?" I said: "Do I really have to, can't it wait till this afternoon? I've got to get some copy to the printer on the 11.30 train." But it couldn't.

The news was that the Editorial Department had been dissolved as of now. I was redundant.

The world suddenly stopped. "So what's new? There's over three million others in the same boat out there," I told myself — but that is no comfort when you have to think about the mortgage.

I tried for other jobs. But it seems that employers consider that anyone over 35 has one foot in the grave. After a crushing number of rejections my chin was on the ground.

I tried for "bit" jobs, like publisher's proof reader and creative writing tutoring in adult education. But all I got was understanding, sympathy and encouragement — and you cannot pay the mortgage with any of those.

The Department of Employment are strong on information. Among the multiplicity of free leaflets at the Job Centre I found *Action for Jobs*. This details employment, training and enterprise programmes offered to the unemployed. There are many of them.

But what caught my eye on page 28 was a question: *"Want to start a new business or work for yourself but can't afford to lose out on unemployment benefit payments until you get off the ground?"* Yes, that's me, I thought.

I was tenuously thinking that if I could not find someone to employ me, I could jolly well work for myself. I would love to have a shot at writing radio plays. But you do not get Unemployment Benefit for sitting at home slaving over a hot typewriter — you have to be job hunting.

People who have been unemployed for 13 weeks can apply to the MSC for an Enterprise Allowance as a financial cushion for the first year of self-employment. The scheme gives women and men with initiative a chance to show they are not scrap-heap material.

From my local Job Centre I got a detailed Guide to the *Enterprise Allowance Scheme*, and the news that the MSC run fact-finding EAS seminars at selected Job Centres. I was told

there was a seminar locally in a couple of days — but first there were a few questions. Was I receiving Unemployment Benefit? Yes. Had I already started the business I wanted to follow? I had hardly had time, as I'd been out job-hunting.

That was one of the first hurdles. They will not consider anyone who had already started. Was I between 18 and state retirement age? Yes. Could I raise £1,000 to invest in my business as capital? Again yes.

I was then told to turn up on time at the seminar and be prepared for the session to take at least two and a half hours. I was one of 30 people who attended — from business types in city suits to people in punk gear.

I must say the MSC were not only thorough but the staff were helpful and knowledgeable. One chap briefed us on the many stipulations for qualification.

For instance, you must be an EC national, you must work full time in your new business and the enterprise must be agreed by the MSC (ie. it can't be involved with politics, religion, gambling, pornography, or other obscene material).

Other requirements are that you can't consider taking over an existing business, you must set up in Great Britain, and you aren't an undischarged bankrupt.

Faced with the reality of working for themselves, some people's spirits quailed

---

He also pointed out pitfalls such as the fact that your NHI credits cease when your Unemployment Benefit ceases. So you need to buy weekly self-employed stamps costing £3.75 each.

For me, the plus points of EAS are that the payment is £40 a week compared with £30.80 Unemployment Benefit, and it wasn't necessary to sign on at the DHSS office every other week.

In addition, the EAS Scheme allows eight weeks' sick pay and five hours a week training. This, as well as four weeks' holidays (whilst on Unemployment Benefit you can't take holidays without sacrificing payments as you are, of course, to be available at all times to take up work).

The second half of the seminar was a valuable talk by a consultant from the Small Businesses Service pointing out such risks as over-investment and competition in the marketplace.

He covered obligations of the self-employed including legal, VAT and health and safety regulations. And there's tax, of course — you have to pay

income tax on the Enterprise Allowance, just as you have to on Unemployment Benefit.

It sounds basic but it is helpful to be reminded about keeping accounts for the Inland Revenue, how to work out charges, overheads, cashflow and how banks can help.

And at the end we were told that once started up in business, everyone is entitled to three free, private counselling sessions with a consultant. Counsellors provide information on a wide variety of management questions and give practical and confidential advice. They can help you to draw up a business plan, advise on raising money, choosing premises, planning your marketing etc — all things the beginner entrepreneur needs to know.

After the briefings came question time. Everyone there got more than satisfactory answers in easy-to-understand language. At the end of the seminar everyone received application forms, which all but a few of us completed. I suppose face to face with the reality of working for themselves, some spirits quailed.

Then came the wait while applications were assessed. I had to send them the synopsis of my first play.

Three weeks later I had to go for a personal interview. A brief discussion, a few more questions, a look at some documents, and I was accepted.

I had to agree that I had read and understood the Enterprise Allowance Scheme Guide and satisfied all the eligibility conditions, and sign an agreement. The MSC will make sure I abide by it by sending one of their staff to visit me after I've been on the Scheme for about three months. I'll also be asked to sign declaration forms to say that my circumstances haven't changed roughly every three months.

I was given a date upon which to start up in business (it's always a Monday). After collecting my fare refund I tore back home to take my other half out for a celebration meal.

EAS has given my self-confidence a positive shot in the arm. Initially I had little hope of being accepted on the Scheme — but I *was*. Now I'm trying hard to justify the whole thing — I'm on the last lap of my first play.

I urge people in a similar situation to give it a try. Don't automatically assume that your enterprising idea won't qualify. Among the businesses started on the scheme are catering, fashion, beauty, sandwich delivery, curtain maker, herbalist, dress maker, hand-made chocolates, picture framing, gardener, cattery, acupuncture, personnel consultant, hand knitter, jewellery repair, antiques, textile design — even a songwriter.

All Job Centres can give details and addresses of the 75 Job Centres throughout the UK which specialise in the EA Scheme.

Study the newspaper article in Fig. 13.2.

Questions

1. How much does the government pay people on the scheme per week?
2. Where would you find information about the scheme?
3. How long must you have been unemployed for to qualify for the scheme?
4. How much of your own capital must you be able to put into the scheme?
5. What sorts of enterprise would not be accepted for the scheme?
6. What would you have to sacrifice if you went on the scheme?
7. How does the scheme allow for sickness and training?
8. What problems would someone be faced with in setting up his or her own business?
9. What back-up help do you get if you join the scheme?
10. Give some examples of businesses that have started up in this way.
11. What would your main difficulty be if you wanted to apply for an Enterprise Allowance?
12. What would be the main advantage of starting up in this way rather than going it alone?
13. Do you think it is a good idea? Are there any drawbacks?

Figure 13.2 Joan Clayton joined the Enterprise Allowance Scheme and wrote a newspaper article about it. (*Source: The Independent*)

QUESTIONS

1. Complete the following sentences using the words below.

Central government
Local government
Infrastructure
Youth Training Scheme
Enterprise Allowance
  Scheme
Nationalization
Privatization
Value added tax
Customs duty
Excise duty

(a) The .... guarantees all 16 year olds a period of work experience and training.

(b) The .... of a country is the skeleton of its economy.

(c) .... is a tax levied on the difference in value between a firm's input and its output.

(d) .... is responsible for major national policies.

(e) .... involves the transfer of ownership from the public to the private sector.

(f) A government levies .... to protect its home industries.

(g) The .... enables someone to claim a subsidy while starting up his or her own business.

(h) .... is responsible for making some of the rules in a local area.

(i) An .... is levied to raise revenue for the government.

(j) .... involves the government taking over private firms and industries.

2. Study the statements about the government in the UK in Table 13.2. Copy out the table and tick the boxes which you think apply. (A—a statement based on fact; B—a statement based on opinion; C—something that can be proved; D—a political statement).

3. Suppose that the government increases its spending by building a new airport. What effect will this have on the following?

(a) Businesses in the area that are not directly involved with building the airport

(b) Long-term unemployed workers in the region

(c) School-leavers in the area looking for their first jobs

(d) Citizens living in the area of the new airport

(e) The firm that plays the major part in constructing the airport

(f) Companies that make building and construction equipment

4. Study the article below:

Firm fined over lead levels in toys

Thousands of Thomas the Tank Engine toys had to be recalled from the shops after it was found that they contained 90 times more than the allowed lead level.

The importer, ERTL (UK) Ltd, was fined the maximum £2000 by Devon magistrates. 130 000 of the toys were brought in from China in 1985. The company pleaded guilty and was made to pay court costs of £1400.

The prosecutor said that responsibility rested fairly and squarely on the shoulders of the marketing company.

(a) Why is the government involved in the above case?

(b) How is the government involved in the above case?

(c) What action is being taken against the firm?

(d) Do you regard this as sufficient action against the firm?

(e) What do you think the consequences would be of the government not being involved in such cases?

5. The following example illustrates the adding of value in the process of producing a product. We are assuming that VAT has not as yet been charged.

Table 13.2 Table of statements about the government in the UK.

	A	B	C	D
(a) The government carries out a high proportion of all spending in the UK.				
(b) The government spends too much.				
(c) The government should spend more on unemployment.				
(d) Inflation is a major problem.				
(e) Over a million workers are employed by nationalized industries.				
(f) It is necessary to subsidize traditional farming methods.				
(g) Trade-union officials should be elected by secret postal ballot.				
(h) The whisky industry is taxed too highly.				

Jean produces £100 worth of wheat from seed that she got for nothing. Michael buys the wheat for £100 and grinds it into flour which he sells for £300. Melanie buys the flour for £300 and sells it to Stan for £350. Stan buys the flour for £350 and converts it into bread which he sells for £450.

How much value added tax would each one hand over to the government?

6. List and explain four business taxes that a firm may have to pay to the government.

7. List six rules that the government makes which affect business activity.

COURSEWORK

1. The article in Fig. 13.3 is used to illustrate changing rules. Before starting on the piece of work you should be some research into the arguments for and against privatizing bus routes.

   (a) On what basis would you expect bus services to have run prior to privatization?

   (b) Make a list of all the groups which you think will have been affected by the change of rules that has taken place.

   (c) Which of these groups would you say have benefited from the rule change and which have lost out?

   (d) Write a short paragraph to put forward the case of each group.

   (e) Split the class into at least five sub-groups to represent interest groups involved and have a discussion to try to argue out the issue.

   (f) Do you think that the community was better off or worse off as a result of the rule change

   (g) Each member of the class should write up an individual report covering in detail all the points brought up by the above. This should be a summary of the issue making it clear that all points of view have been understood and accounted for. This report should provide the basis for a class discussion of the issue.

2. What would be the benefits of a government subsidy?

   The aim of this piece of work is to consider the needs of a town. Barnsley is a town in South Yorkshire that has depended on mining and its associated industries for the creation of employment and income for a long time. In 1987 Barnsley had an unemploy-

Children 'casualties of Dales bus war'

By HARRY HARDCASTLE

EARLY-MORNING passengers bound for Harrogate from Nidderdale—including schoolchildren—are 'casualties of a bus war', Summerbridge parish council heard on Tuesday.

The West Yorkshire Road Car Company and Wrays Coaches, of Summerbridge and Harrogate, are in competition for passengers on the Pateley Bridge-Harrogate route.

Coun. Nevin Ward told the parish council that the rival companies' buses were competing for the downdale passenger trade before 8 a.m. from Monday to Friday.

"Recently we have had buses coming through the village so early that our schoolchildren going to Harrogate have missed the bus," he said.

"Its become the same for everybody—no-one knows just when the buses will pass through the village on the way to Harrogate.

"In fact, we now see coaches hopping round each other—if one company's bus is at a bus stop, the other company's bus races to the next one where there are people waiting."

The council chairman. Coun. David Smith, said: "It appears to be a free-for-all. We can complain to the bus companies but we know the problem will not go away while they are seeking to make their journeys profitable."

He said the bus services in rural areas had been discussed at last week's Yorkshire Local Councils' Association, and the Rural Community Council was wanting information about gaps in the daily public transport service and wanted suggestion for improving the services with the aid of county council grant aid.

Coun. Kathleen Hulme said the worst gap in the services was that between 12.30 p.m. and 3.20 p.m.

"There are no buses in between those times, either up or down the dale, and it creates problems for people wanting to visit Harrogate hospitals. It also ruins social life because people without cars cannot get to afternoon functions away from their own locality.

"Also anyone going by bus to Harrogate in a morning can't get a bus back until late afternoon."

Borough councillor Richard Whitefield said the county did have some finances for grant aid to bus services which would not be viable otherwise. "It's a matter of making the needs known," he said.

The council agreed to inform the Rural Community Council that an early-afternoon service, and a late-night service was needed. The last buses up and down dale start from Harrogate and Pateley Bridge at 6.20 p.m. and on Saturdays at 5.20 p.m.

Coun. Hulme said: "I wish we could get the companies to stagger their services—it looks ridiculous to have buses arriving in twos and threes as at present."

A spokesman for the West Yorkshire Road Car Company on Wednesday said the company's morning service had started at Pateley Bridge at 7.40 for a long time, and was changed to 7.35 a.m. in last October's reorganisation.

"We issued circulars on our buses informing passengers well in advance of our change in the morning timetable," he said, adding that he had no knowledge of drivers racing each other.

The managing director of Wrays Coaches, Mr. Malcolm Wray, said on Wednesday: "We started off with our Daleslink service morning and evening.

"Our morning service was starting from Pateley Bridge at 7.45, but then the West Yorkshire Road Car Company put on a service starting at 7.40, from Pateley. To be fair we moved ours to start at 7.40 a.m., but now West Yorkshire has moved its starting time to 7.35 a.m.

"I must admit that our drivers began to leave earlier than 7.40 for a day of two when the competition began, but I have now laid down the law—start at 7.40 prompt."

Figure 13.3 Newspaper article illustrating some possible effects of bus privatization. (*Source: Harrogate Advertiser*)

ment rate of 23 per cent but was not at the time designated as a government development zone. Between January and June of 1986, 34 firms enquired about setting up in Barnsley. Nine of these were looking for properties in a development zone (which Barnsley could not offer) and six more wanted financial subsidies from the council. Barnsley is shortly to get a subsidy from the European Commission in recognition of its particular problems.

Between January and April 1986 the number of people out of work compared with each vacant job in Barnsley averaged 79.5 compared with a UK average of only 18.6.

Grants of up to £3000 per new job would come to Barnsley if it obtained development-area status. Since 1985 Barnsley has experienced the largest increase in unemployment rates in the country, raising it from twenty-seventh to seventh place in the league table of unemployed rates in England.

(a) Barnsley has been trying to acquire development-area status. What further information would you like to know if you were going to make the decision?

(b) What is a development area?

(c) Study a map showing the development areas of Britain (these change from time to time but you should find an up-to-date map in your local library). Find where Barnsley would be on this map. Does it currently receive any form of government assistance?

(d) What factors might encourage the government to give development-area status to Barnsley?

(e) What factors might discourage the government from giving development-area status to Barnsley?

(f) Set out the front sheet of a newspaper which you can call the *Barnsley Chronicle*. Set out some headlines and write some stories illustrating how the following might feel about Barnsley's request for development-area status:

  (i) A coal miner whose pit is about to close
  (ii) A retired pensioner
  (iii) The manager of the local football team
  (iv) The owner of a successful supermarket
  (v) A local building firm
  (vi) The owner of a firm that has just set up in a neighbouring town

3. What are the effects of a change in the rules?

Study a local example of the effect of a change in a law. This could be a law made nationally or a local by-law. Who gains and who loses? What are the general effects of the change?

4. What are the effects of consumer-protection laws?

Consumer-protection laws will only be really effective if consumers are aware of their rights and producers comply with the laws. Interview some consumers to test their awareness. Interview some shopkeepers to test their awareness and how they comply with these laws. You could also find out how Trading Standards Officers operate to see how effective they are in checking on standards. In order to carry out this assignment you must first of all research consumer-protection laws. The Trading Standards Office have produced a very good pack of information.

5. How do business taxes affect a local firm? This is a subject that would have to be talked through with a firm's accountant.

6. How does the government interfere with the economy in any one week?

This could be the subject of a groupwork exercise based on newspapers. Sub-groups within the class could look through one day's newspapers and report back their findings.

14   The consequences of business

The idea of efficiency is of central importance to the well-being of members of a community. However, the issue of efficiency becomes more complicated when we recognize that a community is made up of many different interest groups. It might be a good idea to build a motorway to a growing industrial area. It is not such a good idea if the route of the motorway goes through your front door.

We therefore need to look at the social benefits and the social costs of business activity to get a clearer picture of net benefits.

> **Private benefits** are all the benefits to an individual or group resulting from a particular activity, e.g. the revenue from a new factory.
> **Private costs** are all the costs to an individual or group resulting from a particular activity, e.g. the cost of building and running a new factory.
> **Social benefits** are the private benefits, plus all the good effects for other members of the community resulting from a particular activity, e.g. jobs created in the new factory.
> **Social costs** are the private costs, plus all the bad effects for other members of the community, e.g. the extra traffic congestion caused by workers travelling to the new factory and lorries distributing goods, etc.

The benefits of business activity

Many people involved in business and industry see its fundamental importance as the creation of wealth. Industry provides all the goods and services that we need. Almost everything that we see around us has been produced by industry—even much of our food.

Industry reacts to people's changing wants and produces the products that people are prepared to buy. Sometimes industry creates new demands for products by developing new products and marketing them. For instance, society did not know that it wanted the video recorder. The product had first to be invented, then tested and researched. Finally, it had to be marketed. When the product became popular it was obvious that it would be a commercial success but in the meantime industry had to develop the product.

> The wealth of a society is the stock of possessions—money, houses, stocks and shares etc. owned by members of that society. To this we should add human wealth, that is, the economic skills of the people which depends on such things as education and training.

In modern society, products are often highly complex and may be assembled thousands of miles apart. The modern motor vehicle is an example of a product whose components are built in many different plants before being finally assembled. Workers often have only a very limited knowledge of what they are producing. In a similar way, consumers may have only a sketchy idea of how modern complex products are made and brought to market.

Industry brings together productive resources to produce wealth. In so doing it produces the following major benefits:

1. Industry provides employment. Millions of people are employed in industry and commerce. Some of them are employed in enjoyable, creative work whilst others work in boring, unimaginative environments where work is a burden rather than a pleasure.
2. Industry creates income. The factors of production that produce goods earn factor incomes. Shareholders receive profits, landlords receive rent, lenders receive interest, workers receive wages, etc.
3. Industry creates products. Value is added at each stage of production. A simple example of wealth creation is the carpenter converting relatively inexpensive material into furniture. The difference between the cost of the wood and the price of the finished article is the wealth which he or she has created. (See Fig. 14.1.)
4. Industry improves living standards. Table 14.1 shows that most people became materially better off between 1974 and 1984, and indeed most of us are materially better off today than ever before. However, in this chapter, we shall go on to consider some costs of growth such as pollution of the

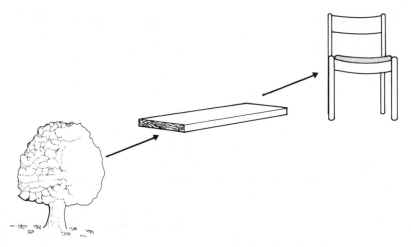

Figure 14.1 Industry creates wealth by adding value to raw materials. (*Source: Understanding Industry*)

Table 14.1 How standards of living improved between 1974 and 1984. (*Source: Lloyds Bank*)

	1974	1979	1984
Dwellings per 1000 population	349	370	381
TV sets (licences) per 1000	308	327	330
Private cars (licences) per 100	244	261	283
Telephones per 1000	337	440	520
Refrigerators, percentage of households owning	82	83	94
Civil servants per 1000	12.3	13.0	11.1
Pupils per teacher	20.8	19.1	17.8
Real personal disposable income per head (1984 prices)	£3422	£3811	£3898

environment. We might question whether the modern worker in Tokyo, New York or London is really better off with more material possessions in situations of noise, smoke and high crime figures.

5. Industry makes it possible for people to enjoy more leisure. Because of industrial growth, people have more free time on their hands. Hospitals, schools, museums and the many welfare functions we have come to expect, are all supported from the wealth created by businesses in the public and private sectors of the economy.

The costs of business activity

When a firm produces something it has to bear in mind a number of internal costs:

1. Production costs
2. Marketing costs
3. Financial costs
4. Administration costs

In addition to these, there are external costs, which are costs which go beyond the balance sheet of the firm. These costs are sometimes known as externalities or spillover effects.

> **Externalities** = social costs − private costs

Pollution

The most obvious social cost of business activity is pollution.

Water pollution

It has been standard practice for a long time for industry to locate by canal, river and sea. Industries such as paper production, chemicals and breweries not only use water in the manufacturing process, but also pour out their effluent into rivers and the sea. Perhaps the most notorious example of this type of activity is the dispersal of waste products from the nuclear-fuels industry. We have purification and filtration plants where water is treated, but it is difficult to break down the effects of industrial chemicals which destroy water life.

In Hungary, France, West Germany and other European countries firms are charged heavily for causing water pollution. This puts heavy pressure on firms to clean up their water.

Of course one problem of checking on water pollution levels in order to tax firms that pollute is the cost of administering the system. In the UK, we tend to prosecute firms that break water safety laws. Fines can be imposed and imprisonment ordered in serious cases.

Air pollution

This has been dramatically illustrated by several events in the mid-1980s. In December 1984, there was a leak of poisonous gas from a Union Carbide plant at Bhopal in India. More than

2000 people died and at least 10 times this number suffered from breathing and eye complaints. The Carbide plant was part of an American multinational producing pesticides to spray on crops. Subsequent investigations have led to a questioning of safety standards at the plant.

Perhaps even more dramatic was the nuclear disaster at Chernobyl in 1986. Here we have an example of a growing centrally planned economy trying to push through the growth of new power sources rapidly. Again, the safety standards of the nuclear reactor were highly questionable. Wide tracts of land have been made uninhabitable and a cloud of nuclear waste was carried airborne across northern Europe. The reindeer herds of the Laplanders have been declared inedible for several years, threatening the ruin of a whole economy. Livestock of Welsh hill farmers was banned from sale in the market-place because of heavy contamination.

Emissions from UK factory chimneys and power-stations are recognized as major sources of the 'acid rain' which results in the destruction of forests and pollution of lakes in Scandinavia and Germany.

Dereliction

If we consider the decision to build a new mine, or to drill for oil or natural gas, we can see that this might destroy areas of natural beauty in a non-reversible way. Furthermore, when business pulls out of an area, the effects can be worse, for not only do jobs disappear but the community is also left with derelict land which is unpleasant to look at and sometimes dangerous. These dangerous remains include disused railway tunnels, mine shafts, quarries and old buildings. Generally it has then been left to imaginative local councils to redevelop the sites as parks, boating lakes and sites for new industry.

Traffic congestion

The development of the pace of modern business life has put enormous pressures on our road networks. In 1986, the M25 orbital road around London was opened. By the time it was made fully operational it was inadequate to meet the need for a circular road. It has been described as the longest traffic jam in Europe.

Motor vehicles cause accidents, pour out noxious fumes and are noisy. One way of calculating the cost of modern roads is to compare house prices near a large road with those of similar housing which is placed further away from the road in the same locality.

Long-term waste

British Nuclear Fuels plc reprocesses nuclear waste at its plant in Sellafield. This waste is collected from the UK's second-generation power-stations. A report produced in 1986 shows that if these power-stations were shut down immediately, it would take 10 years to reprocess the existing spent fuel.

Highly radioactive spent nuclear fuel is transported by road or rail in nuclear-waste 'flasks'. The resulting waste is then either dumped in the sea, or buried in stores underground. It is argued that in this way we are storing up problems for the future.

Noise

This is another external effect of business. Concorde is a great flag-flyer for British Airways. It is also a considerable nuisance for those citizens who live close to its take-off and departure points. Noise from road and rail traffic can also be a considerable nuisance to householders.

In the UK, noise nuisance is controlled through by-laws made by local authorities covering a wide range of matters from noisy animals and fireworks to radios and televisions. People can be prosecuted for

continually making noise. In the same way, the activities of businesses and construction firms are controlled and certain areas may be designated by the local authority as Noise Abatement Zones.

Food additives

In modern society presentation and value for money are part of the marketing package of many foodstuffs. Artificial colourings and flavourings are used as well as synthetic ingredients. The medical profession have pointed out the dangerous spillover effects particularly in areas such as hyperactivity in children.

Insufficient testing of products

In order to capitalize on market leadership some firms have put products on the market without sufficient background testing. A classic example of this was the production by the Distillers Company of a drug used by women to reduce the effects of morning sickness in pregnancy. The spillover effect was the terrible side-effect of thalidomide children.

Weighing up costs and benefits

At the end of the day, society benefits if resources are used efficiently. When business makes a decision it weighs up the costs and benefits in private terms. It does so because its prime consideration is its shareholders. The government is more likely to use cost-benefit analysis, for instance in deciding whether to build a new road.

Cost-benefit analysis has been used to weigh up building a new London Underground line, the siting of the third London airport, subsidies to firms in depressed regions, even the building of fences to stop sheep from straying into the streets of Merthyr Tydfil.

In carrying out a cost-benefit analysis of building a new training centre for unemployed workers, you would have to find out who would benefit and who would lose out. You would then have to make measurements in money terms. You would have to ask someone who would benefit how much he or she would be prepared to pay to see the project carried out. You would then have to ask someone who would lose out the minimum sum he or she would be prepared to accept as compensation for the project taking place.

We then add up all the gains and all the losses. If the gains outweigh the losses the project passes the test.

Pressure groups

Businesses have to operate against a background in which they are faced by many different competing interests.

Internally the business needs to make a profit for shareholders and the shareholders need to be kept content with the way the business is being run. Externally the business has more to contend with.

1. Perhaps the biggest pressure is actually to sell its products. Consumers do not have to buy a product.
2. The business is faced by the pressure put on it by its competitors. Competition is often a spur to business efficiency.
3. The government also exerts pressure on business to produce within certain standards.
4. Businesses also have to respond to the influence put on it by organized 'pressure groups'.

Types of pressure group
The two main types of pressure groups are:

1. *Protection groups.* These are set up to fight a specific issue such as danger on a local road caused by construction traffic building a

local airport. In other words, local residents are protecting their interests against an outside threat.
2. *Promotional pressure groups.* These are more formal groups which are sometimes highly organized and fight campaigns on a wide range of issues. Examples of the latter would include Greenpeace and Friends of the Earth. Businesses might also find that a political party exerts strong opposition to some of their activities, e.g. selling produce to South Africa.

Consumer pressure groups
A well-known and powerful consumer group is the Consumers' Association, which produces the magazine *Which?* The group is funded by subscriptions from members who buy the magazine. The Consumers' Association uses its funds to test a wide variety of products on which it then produces reports in its monthly magazine. It also produces books on consumer-related matters.

The influence of the Consumers' Association goes beyond its publication of *Which?* because its reports are frequently reported in the national press. Consumer programmes also get a fair amount of time on national television, the most famous being Esther Rantzen's 'That's Life'. Typical media coverage involves the investigation of complaints, and the comparison of goods and services.

Nationalized industries also have consumers' councils, examples of which are the Post Office Users' National Council for the Post Office and the Central Transport Consultative Committee for British Rail. The government makes provision for the continuation of these groups when industries are privatized.

Consumer boycotts
Consumers sometimes are organized into groups to stop buying certain

products. In 1986, Barclays Bank sold off its South African subsidiary. Throughout the 1970s and 1980s opponents of apartheid put pressure on Barclays customers to use other banks. It is arguable that this sort of pressure helped finally to influence Barclays' decision. In a similar way, animal-rights pressure groups have used advertising campaigns and more direct persuasion to stop consumers using animal furs and the products of modern factory farming.

As an extension of these activities sabotage has been used as an extreme form of protest against some forms of industrial production. Within the area of animal experimentation in the food, chemical and drugs industries, there are several animal-rights protest groups (each with its own way of protesting) including the Animal Liberation Front and the National Anti-Vivisection Society. Quite clearly this can cause adverse publicity for businesses operating in this area and raise operating costs. Animals have been freed and premises attacked and businesses have had to spend money on the employment of security, such as the specialist security firm Control Risks which specializes in risk assessment and kidnap negotiations.

Local lobbying
There are several reasons why local residents may want to put pressure on a business to change its operations including:

1. Traffic danger
2. Emission of fumes
3. Emission of fluids
4. Litter and noise
5. Safety hazards such as tips, pits, etc.

Normally, a pressure group will develop out of letters to the press and protest meetings. The pressure group will then try to encourage the firm to change its policy, after which point it will put pressure on local and central government to influence the activities of the firm. Enlightened firms will try not to antagonize local feelings, which brings adverse publicity for the business.

Other organized pressure groups

Sometimes groups run themselves in a highly organized way to influence public opinion. They will try to get a wide number of people to accept their views in order to exert pressure on the business community. Trade unions use this method of persuasion quite often. Groups like the teachers, the miners and the print workers have used national advertising to try to win support from the public and from political parties for their cause. Picketing and industrial action are another way of trying to put pressure on business.

The employers' organization, the CBI, and the unions' organization, the TUC, also exert influence. An example of this was a report published in December 1986 by the TUC, circulated to businesses, trying to discourage the use of alcohol during the working day.

Other promotional pressure groups, such as the campaign for lead-free petrol and the anti-smoking lobby, use similar techniques. Sometimes groups use less peaceful methods to impress their views on the public. Demonstrations, protest marches and sit-ins often lead to publicity on television and in the press.

Business responses to pressure groups

There are a number of ways business can respond to pressure groups.

1. It can ignore them, using the argument that consumers can choose whether to buy the product, and in the meantime make sure that production takes place within the bounds of legal requirements.

BRITISH NUCLEAR FUELS PLC

request the pleasure of your company to view their Sellafield Exhibition Centre.

Open from 10am–4pm every day of the week,

Easter–end of October

or 10am–4pm Monday–Friday,

November–March.

Exhibition Centre, British Nuclear Fuels plc, Sellafield, Cumbria.
(Off the A595 at Calderbridge between Millom and Whitehaven)

Figure 14.2 The wording of an invitation that formed part of the publicity campaign by British Nuclear Fuels plc to counter the publicity given to anti-nuclear pressure groups.

---

2. It can run a counter-campaign to win public support. This is the policy which has been used by British Nuclear Fuels plc. 'Come to Sellafield. Look around the place. See for yourself how safe it is.' This, loosely paraphrased, is the message of a multi-million-pound advertising campaign which has been commissioned by British Nuclear Fuels. The campaign is appearing on television as well as in newspapers.

3. It can take advice from consumers in order to compromise and win public support in this way.

Employment and unemployment

Another consequence of business is the creation and destruction of employment. There are more people working in the UK today than ever before as a consequence of the rise in population. Business has con-

tinually to expand to take on extra people. At the same time, the sorts of skills required are continually changing. Almost 70 per cent of the employed and self-employed in Britain now work in services and between 1965 and 1978 nearly two million additional jobs were created in this sector.

At the same time, many jobs have been lost in agriculture, mining and manufacture. The UK's manufacturing base has been steadily declining for a long time. In the 1950s, exports of manufactures were three times bigger than imports. Today, we import more manufactured goods than we export. Factors causing this decline have been low quality and an over-concentration on producing low-value products which many other countries now also produce.

Unemployment can be seen as a consequence of the failure of business to keep up to date. In the annual review of government-funded research and development 1986, the government's chief scientific adviser warned that 'industry is not spending enough on research and development to bring new products and processes to the market'. He went on to say that, 'history shows that we are a very innovative nation; what we lack is development—the knack of exploiting the ideas that we produce'.

A contrasting view of modern unemployment is that it is a consequence of new technologies. A recent report by the West German Kommerzbank estimated that every robot employed in industry today replaces three workers on average, and that by the late 1980s the second generation of 'intelligent' robots will each replace between five and ten workers in certain assembly jobs. In the service sector too, job losses are being felt, as with CHAPS (a new automated way of clearing cheques in the City of London), which has already made the activities of 8000 messengers unnecessary. The estimates suggest that information technology will replace about 10 per cent of jobs by 1990. However, we are also told that it will create another 6 per cent of jobs, and if the development of the UK's microchip revolution makes us more competitive we should actually create more jobs than we lose.

We can thus see that the relationship between business development and unemployment is a complicated one. What is clear is that in the UK today a higher level of skill is required in workers.

In the early 1980s, for every 100 unemployed general labourers there was one job vacancy. For every 100 unemployed electronic engineers there were 87 vacancies. As a rule of thumb, higher levels of skill are being required in both factory and office, and people are expected to have a wider range of skills.

A further problem is that regional imbalance is a consequence of the way that business locates in profitable areas and later abandons these areas if locational advantages decline. Firms might choose locations in East Anglia and the South East on the basis of private costs and benefits. However, the greatest benefits to society might be reaped from locating in an unemployment blackspot like Central Scotland, South Wales, the North East, the North West or Northern Ireland.

School-leavers form the age-group with the highest rate of unemployment (over 30 per cent). Other groups particularly hard-hit are older workers and those in racial minority groups.

Business and communities

Centres of population develop around work. As these centres become established, a community comes into being. Very strong communities develop where people share similar jobs, working together and experiencing similar life-styles. Mining communities, farming communities and fishing communities, for example, are well known for the strong bonds that tie people together.

In modern society, people tend to move further to get work and modern housing estates are characterized by people doing a wide range of different jobs. Inevitably this tends to reduce the bonds that hold people together.

Conservation

Modern business depends on the use of non-renewable resources, particularly in the use of energy. Modern technology is particularly dependent on three main fossil fuels—oil, coal and natural gas. Together they account for over 90 per cent of the world's energy supplies.

A **non-renewable resource** is one of which only a limited stock exists (not necessarily totally discovered) on the planet of which no new stock is being created.

Some commentators are very worried about the way in which non-renewable resources are being used up. D. H. Meadows and his associates, in their book *The Limits to Growth*, argue that if resources continue to be used up in the way they are today, then within the next hundred years a crisis will occur because certain resources are limited, namely:

1. Arable land
2. Coal
3. Oil
4. Aluminium
5. Copper
6. Iron
7. Other minerals

The problem of conversation is both a national and an international one. Businesses are more concerned with relatively short-term profits than with the future of society. Multilateral agreements have been signed between countries limiting whaling and fishing. On a national scale, governments have used subsidies as a means of encouraging farmers to preserve hedgerows and use more traditional methods of farming. Commercial farming has tended to encourage farmers to use chemicals as pesticides and fertilizers to increase yield per acre. Pollution of water by nitrates has increased since the Second World War as

"The current financial year has started well with total turnover for the first six months up 14.0% compared with the same period last year at £4,614 million. Excluding sales by companies acquired since the first half of last year, turnover grew by 10.7%.

Turnover from telephone calls grew by 9.4% to £2,423 million. Our inland telephone call volumes increased by 7% and international call volumes were up by 11%.

We earned £1,006 million before tax which represents an 11.5% increase compared with last year. Operating costs, excluding those of new acquisitions, increased by 10.4%.

Earnings per share in the first six months were 20.0% higher at 10.2p and we have declared an interim dividend of 3.35 pence (net) per share which will be paid to investors on February 23, 1987.

Your Board has confidence that satisfactory progress will be maintained through the rest of the year.

Our continuing strength makes it possible for us to invest more than ever before, to improve the service we give our customers and to secure the future prosperity of our company for shareholders and staff alike.

Our total investment in fixed assets for the year is planned to be over £2,100 million – up more than 35% on 1984, the year in which the company was privatised."

Sir George Jefferson, Chairman

INVESTING · FOR · A MORE · MODERN · NETWORK

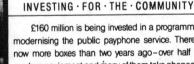

Over £450 million of investment is planned this year on modern digital exchanges which are now being installed at the rate of one every working day. We have already laid over 100,000 miles of optical fibre – proportionately more than any other country. All this will improve the capacity and quality of the network and result in faster, clearer calls across the country.

INVESTING · IN · NEW · SYSTEMS · AND · SERVICES

We are spending over £100 million this year to develop our directory enquiry and customer service systems. This is part of a continuing £700 million computerisation programme.

INVESTING · FOR · THE · COMMUNITY

£160 million is being invested in a programme for modernising the public payphone service. There are now more boxes than two years ago – over half have modern equipment and many of them take phonecards. Every public payphone is now fitted with a device to help people with hearing aids and the new phone booths are easier to use for people in wheel chairs.

Figure 14.3 Advertisement produced by British Telecom.

INVESTING · IN · RESEARCH

Many technical improvements now being introduced have been developed in our own research laboratories, the work there being part of our £180 million annual research and development programme.

Overall a record investment by British Telecom this year. A massive ongoing programme to transform our systems and services and to achieve our objective of matching the best telecommunications company anywhere in the world.

British
TELECOM
Investing for growth

farmers have ploughed more and more fertilizers into the land. This is particularly true in areas of heavy cereal production. Rain has then washed the chemicals into the water supply. The Wildlife and Countryside Act has provided scope to compensate farmers to encourage them to consider the environment rather than simply to aim for profit.

Over the last few years, report after report has stressed the gravity of world utilization of resources. One of them, *Global 2000*, concluded that we face a world 'more polluted, less stable ecologically, more vulnerable to disruption than ever before'.

> **Ecology** is the relationship between living things and their environment.

CASE STUDY—BRITISH TELECOM

The article in Fig. 14.3 highlights some of the overall achievements of British Telecom in 1986.

Questions

1. Who owns British Telecom?
2. Who benefits from British Telecom?
3. What is meant by the 'turnover' of the business?
4. How does the business cater for growth?
5. In what ways is British Telecom improving its service?
6. Who will benefit from these developments?
7. What questions would you ask the Chairman to find out about benefits not listed in the article?

CASE STUDY—CITIES FOR PEOPLE

Study the article in Fig. 14.4.

Figure 14.4   Advertisement produced by Friends of the Earth.

Questions

1. What are the benefits of the motor car?
2. What costs of the motor car are mentioned in the article?
3. Draw up a report weighing up the costs and benefits of motor cars. (This report should form the basis for a class discussion.)
4. What is a pressure group?
5. What is the pressure group in the above advertisement?
6. Find out more about this group.

CASE STUDY—CHERNOBYL

Six months after the nuclear disaster at Chernobyl, the plant was once again producing nuclear power.

The Russians estimated that it

cost $3 billion to clean up the site and rehouse the refugees in a new area. They were quite open in admitting that the design had been wrong and that human error had been involved.

The accident occurred on 26 April 1986 but within months the plant was back in production.

The Russians expected to build a further six pressurized water reactors by 1990. The damaged reactor, unit 4, at Chernobyl was encased in concrete. After the accident, Chernobyl employed 3500 workers who worked in two-week shifts and lived 20 miles away from the plant to reduce the danger from radiation.

The costs will be felt for a long time. Electricity prices were set to rise by over 10 per cent in the Soviet Union and in early 1987 there was a severe energy shortage. Street lighting was run at a dim level. The Russians were forced to make changes to 14 plants similar to Chernobyl.

Questions

1. What are the benefits of the nuclear-energy programme to the Russian economy?
2. What have been the costs of the Chernobyl disaster?
3. Is it possible to measure these costs?
4. Who should be responsible for these costs?
5. What pressures would you expect to have been put on the Russian government as a result of this disaster?

CASE STUDY—TROLLEY FOLLY

Study the article in Fig. 14.5.

IT'S WAR on the trolley wallies!

Reading Borough Council is set to take action against stores which own the wire eyesores discarded around the town.

They have taken on the powers outlined in The Berkshire Act of 1986 to help deal with the problem.

And if you think the council's off its trolley, think again. Already the problem of abandoned trolleys has been "drastically reduced" thanks to the Cleaner Reading Campaign.

But now the wheels are in motion to step up action against the little metal monsters, which can turn up in the most unlikely places.

Reading Borough Council wants a shopping showdown with stores in the Reading area, and have invited them to a special meeting at the Civic Offices in January, and want all stores using trolleys to attend.

The council hopes that using the powers outlined in Section 13 of the Berkshire Act will help curb the problem of discarded trolleys.

They explain: "This Section allows the borough council to carry out its own collection of trolleys left abandoned on the streets and to make a charge to return these to the stores.

"The main responsibility for the retrieval and control of the use of shopping trolleys rests with the shops providing them for customer use.

"The borough council expects frequent collections in areas of high use and from the surrounding area with attention to a wider area as well."

The act empowers the council to move in if regular collections from stores in the area are not up to scratch and if trolleys have become so damaged they cannot be used any more.

Figure 14.5 Newspaper article on an environmental problem in Reading. (*Source: Reading Standard*)

Questions

1. How has Reading Borough Council the powers to deal with the problem outlined above?
2. Who is responsible for trolley pollution?
3. Who is going to be made to pay?
4. Do you think this is a good solution?
5. In what other fields do you think this solution to social costs could be applied?

CASE STUDY—THE NATIONALIZED INDUSTRIES' CONSUMER COUNCILS

In 1987, British Rail was considering bringing back its first-class day-return tickets as a result of pressure put on it by commuters.

The first-class day-return had been stopped in 1983 but ever since there had been a storm of pressure to bring it back. An experiment was being planned in the South East to bring back the ticket and, if it went well, the ticket would go on sale nationwide. There had been a lot of pressure put on British Rail by the Central Transport Consultative Committee which is the watchdog of how BR runs its affairs.

An executive said, 'All my friends were furious when they stopped the ticket. Often we do not travel at peak times and why should we pay the full price to sit on an empty train? Many people have switched to cars.' A train driver said, 'We need all the passengers we can get.'

Mr Len Dumelow of the Transport Committee said, 'I don't see how British Rail can ignore the market. Now they are beginning to see the light but only after a long period of pressure. A study by the committee showed that first-class carriages are often underused and that there would be a big demand for the ticket.'

Questions

1. What is the consumer council mentioned in this article?
2. What does it do?
3. Does this group have any influence?
4. What sorts of complaints might you make to this group?
5. What are the advantages and disadvantages of such a group?
6. Do you think that such a group would represent everyone's views equally?
7. Do some research to find out if other students or members of the public are aware of the existence of such groups?
8. What other protection do consumers have over the activities of public corporations?
9. Why do you think that the executive quoted in the passage had such a strong view? Do you agree with him?

QUESTIONS

1. Complete the following sentences using the words below.

Conservation
Pollution
Externalities
Private cost
Non-renewable resource
Pressure groups
Cost-benefit analysis
Regional imbalance

(a) The wages a firm has to pay out are an example of a ....
(b) Businesses often have to face opposition from .... which try to influence the way the firm runs from outside.
(c) The government might carry out a .... before building a new road.
(d) .... are the difference between private and social costs.
(e) Oil is an example of a ....
(f) .... is a result of the way industry moves to the most profitable locations.
(g) Dumping of waste products is an example of ....
(h) .... involves carefully saving up resources for the future.

2. Which of the following would you classify as private costs, private benefits, social costs and social benefits, from the point of view of a firm manufacturing chemicals?
   (a) Local jobs
   (b) Wages
   (c) Purchase of raw materials

Oh deer

FROM OUR NORDIC CORRESPONDENT

Rudolph the Red-Nosed Reindeer may have an unusual glow to his nose this Christmas, if his summer home is in those areas of Norway and Sweden contaminated by radioactive fall-out from the Chernobyl disaster. Local experts think that up to a third of the animals killed in this year's autumn season will be unfit for human consumption. That is tough, but not absolutely disastrous, for the Lapp people of sub-arctic northern Scandinavia.

About 30,000 Lapps and 200,000 herded reindeer live in Norway and 17,000 Lapps and 250,000 reindeer in Sweden, where some 40,000 wild reindeer are also preserved for hunting. In both Norway and Sweden something over 2,000 Lapps make their living from reindeer-herding. They are no longer nomads; although some do follow the herds to the summer pastures (where they also entertain the tourists), all have permanent, hard-roofed homes where they spend the cold months, comparatively in the Lapp of luxury. Each year they slaughter 60,000-80,000 animals, whose lean dark meat has a specialised market.

In the late 1950s, the Lapps and their animals were exposed to high doses of strontium-90 from Russian nuclear tests. The Chernobyl fall-out, mostly of caesium-137, is about 50 times as high. The 1950s fall-out seems to have had no measurable effect on the Lapps' health. This year's exposure lasted a much shorter time, but reindeer moss may prove to have been very efficient at capturing caesium from the atmosphere, so the after-effects of Chernobyl could be long-lasting.

Sweden and Norway are taking no chances. The World Health Organisation says there need be no restrictions on eating food with radioactive levels of under 2,000 becquerels per kilogramme. Sweden has set an upper limit of 300 becquerels per kilogramme, Norway of 600. Some reindeer in Norway have registered 40,000 becquerels; but the average in the Norwegian affected areas is probably nearer 10,000, and in Sweden it is much lower.

As for the Lapps, restrictions on sales of the meat will hurt their traditions worse than their incomes. About one-third of them still speak their ancient language, which is of the Finno-Ugrian family, originating in central Asia. Its vocabulary is not extensive, and a remarkably large proportion of its words refer to reindeer and products derived from them. Now the Lapps' governments have promised to buy up the uneatable dead animals, which will very likely end up as food for mink.

Sniffing the caesium

Figure 14.6 Magazine article on an environmental problem in Scandinavia. (*Source: The Economist*)

141

(d) Heating costs
(e) Destruction of local beauty spot
(f) Revenue from selling products
(g) Waste fumes
(h) Noise from construction traffic
(i) Wider range of products on the market

3. In East Bay there is a meat-processing plant producing dog food. It employs 200 workers and is the largest local employer in a town of just 1200 inhabitants, with a 15 per cent unemployment rate.

The smell coming off the plant is very strong and is a major source of complaint for residents. House prices around the plant sell for on average £4000 less than the market value elsewhere. Wages in the factory are well below the national average.

When a residents' committee took the complaints to the firm it was told that the firm was considering closing down this factory and converting it into an automated warehouse employing six workers.

(a) List *five* social costs and *five* social benefits to the community from the food-processing plant.

(b) Would East Bay be better off if the buildings were converted into an automated warehouse?

4. Study the article in Fig. 14.6 on page 141.

Imagine that you are a Laplander writing a letter of complaint to the Russian Embassy. Structure the letter to highlight the problems of your people.

5. Fig. 14.7 illustrates just one way in which the pressure group Greenpeace highlights environmental problems. Write

Figure 14.7 Advertisement produced by Greenpeace.

Sellafield shadow over tourist trade

By Nicholas Schoon

ANY NEWS about the Sellafield nuclear reprocessing plant is bad news for the towns and villages of the mid-Cumbrian coast, even if the latest publicity is favourable.

Many, perhaps most, people living nearby have no fears about the plant and accept British Nuclear Fuel's reassurances about its safety. They also appreciate the 6,500 permanent jobs Sellafield provides, and the extra 4,000 jobs created by a £1.65bn investment programme in new plant.

But the tourists have stayed away since local beaches were closed three years ago following an accidental discharge of radioactive sludge. There was also the Yorkshire TV programme, *Windscale, Britain's Nuclear Laundry*, which revealed a cluster of leukaemia deaths in Seascale.

When Betty Roddis advertised her ten-bedroom hotel in West Cumbria in a Manchester newspaper she had 35 replies immediately. When she told inquirers she was selling the Sea Field Hotel, Seascale, nobody was interested. Mrs Roddis said: "It's all the bad publicity, all this nonsense about cancer."

The Sea Field now gets 90 per cent of its business from people working at the plant. In nearby Ravenglass, the best customer of the Pennington Arms Hotel in recent months has been the Nuclear Installations Inspectorate.

Manageress Shona Siddons said: "There isn't a tourist trade about any more in the summer, but our winter trade has improved no end from contractors working at the plant."

Takings are down in Ravenglass craft shops. One of the village's two working fishermen has retired early, and the other has sold one of his two boats — visitors are in no hurry to try the local seafood.

Figure 14.8 Newspaper article illustrating how industrial activity can affect the local community. (*Source: The Independent*)

a report on one pressure group, highlighting the methods used by the group to publicize its case.
6. What is cost-benefit analysis? Show how you would use this method to evaluate the activity of a local business.

COURSEWORK

1. Split the class into three groups to discuss the question, 'Is the Sellafield nuclear reprocessing plant a good or bad thing for local people?' (See Fig. 14.8.)
   Divide into:
   (a) Local villagers in favour of the plant
   (b) Local villagers opposed to the plant
   (c) Representatives of British Nuclear Fuels plc
2. The article in Fig. 14.9 would provide an ideal focus for a local study looking at the question, 'Should firms be made to pay for the social costs they cause?'
   Information collection could involve the following:
   (a) Direct interviews on the scene
   (b) Interviewing people mentioned in the article
   (c) Postal correspondence
   (d) Letters to the press and reading follow-up items in newspapers
   (e) Looking at parallel cases in newspapers, magazines and textbooks
   Analysis would involve answering the following questions:
   (a) Who are the major groups involved?
   (b) What are the main costs and benefits?

Figure 14.9 Newspaper article illustrating the social costs business activity can have. (*Source: Harrogate Advertiser*)

Outcry over road chaos

● TRAFFIC chaos caused by the Telecom works. (W2188)

CHAOS caused by excavations in Wetherby High Street was deplored by Wetherby and District Accident Prevention committee on Tuesday.

The local traffic warden, Mr. Ken Grey, protested that no provision was made for pedestrians while work was carried out on the footpath by British Telecom.

He had made telephone calls but there had been no action.

At 8.30 one morning there was a hole "bang in the middle" of the approach to the zebra crossing, he said. But no allowance was made for pedestrians.

Then a trench was dug by the corner of the Angel which was dangerous enough for pedestrians at the best of times.

"Nobody seems to have bothered about pedestrians," he added.

Members agreed the situation in the vicinity of the crossing must have been "very dangerous"

It was also pointed out that road works had posed similar problems. While traffic was using only one lane, it was a free for all with long queues building up.

The meeting felt there had been slackness and carelessness over this safety aspect of the operation.

Both the North Yorkshire county highway authority and British Telecom are to be told of the committee's concern and will be asked to bear in mind for the future, the safety of pedestrians.

Wetherby traders were also upset because they were not notified about the road works.

The president of the Chamber of Trade, Mr. Vincent Cargill, of Mallories, one of the properties most affected by the work, said he intended to raise the matter at the next Chamber of Trade meeting.

Mr. Cargill was disturbed that there seemed to have been no notification of the work whatsoever. It had certainly caused disruption in the town.

He added that it had affected businesses because a number of car parking spaces had been lost while the work was carried out.

He added that noise from the work had been exceptionally bad.

Mr. Melvyn Jones, of the Abbey National Building Society and A1 Insurance, was annoyed that there had been no notification.

He told the "News": "I am appalled by the lack of communication for a company which is in the communication business. It shows a singular lack of thought when it comes to communicating with other people in terms of spoiling their trade and blocking their premises, not to mention the dust and noise."

Mr. John Driver, owner of Touchwood DIY, estimated that his trade had dropped by about 50 per cent while work was going on outside his premises.

He had received no warning of the work at all, but he added: "To be fair to them they have worked to get it done. That is commendable and makes a refreshing change."

Mr. Neil Walker, of North Midland Construction Ltd., the contracting company carrying out the work, explained that it was being done to lay new ducts which would improve the telephone service to the public.

He said it was not normal practice to inform traders before work started but he had been to see one or two.

He had received a complaint about the loss of parking but pointed out that there were double yellow lines in High Street.

He added that the men were working hard to try to finish the job as quickly as possible.

(c) Can costs and benefits be quantified?

Evaluation would involve answering the following questions:

(a) Who is to blame?
(b) Who should pay?
(c) What should be done now?
(d) What should be done in future?
(e) Are social costs necessary evils?

3. Are nationalized-industry consumer councils effective? This should be a study of a consumer council.
4. What do pressure groups do? This should be a study of a pressure group.
5. What are the causes of local unemployment?
6. What is conservation? This should focus on a local issue highlighted in the press and take the form of a library-based study.

15 Services to business

The individual business is heavily dependent on other groups within its environment: the government provides it with a legal framework, consumers provide it with a market and other producers provide it with competition. Business is also dependent on business services provided by other specialist firms. Without the specialist services illustrated in Fig. 15.1 businesses could not function.

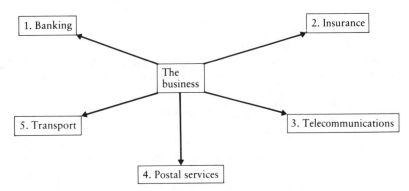

Figure 15.1 Diagram showing the services needed by business.

Banking services

Banks in the UK take the form of public limited companies. They are owned by shareholders and one of their main aims is to make a profit for these owners. The 'big four' banks in the UK are also multinationals with a wide range of financial interests. The big four are the National Westminster, Lloyds, Barclays and the Midland.

These commercial banks use depositors' money to make loans. It is by making this money work for them that banks make a profit. (See Fig. 15.2.)

Banks attract customers by offering accounts providing services or interest or both.

1. A *current account* gives the user a cheque-book but usually no interest. The value that the customer gets from the bank is the safety and easy use of the service.
2. A *deposit account* is used for saving money and pays interest.
3. A *combined deposit/current account* does both things. If the money in the account goes over a certain amount it earns interest, and a cheque-book is also used with the account.

There are many different types of banks in the UK including:

1. *The Bank of England.* This supervises the other banks and controls the banking system for the government. It issues new and destroys old notes and holds accounts for the clearing banks and the government.
2. *The clearing banks.* These are mainly made up of commercial banks and the big four plus others such as the Royal Bank of Scotland, the Co-operative Bank and the Trustee Savings Bank. Each day these banks clear the cheques between banks at the London Clearing House.

Clearing is a highly automated system of sorting cheques and settling debts.

3. *Merchant banks.* These are old-established trading banks such as Rothschild's and Schroeder's. As well as helping firms with international trade finance they also help firms to sell new shares through their contacts with other financial institutions.
4. *Money shops.* An alternative to commercial banks that has increasingly invaded the high streets of the UK are money

Figure 15.2 How banks use depositors' money to make loans to borrowers.

145

shops. They are prepared to take bigger risks but they charge a higher rate of interest.

Commercial banks provide a wide range of services to business, as described below.

A safe place for money

Banks provide a place where customers can put their money in safety. A business can put its daily takings into the bank by sending round an employee with a paying-in book. Alternatively money can be deposited after bank closing hours by placing a money pouch in the night deposit safe.

A source of loans

The banks lend money to customers. A business can arrange a suitable form of lending facility with a bank.

A *loan* enables a business person to buy a fixed asset such as a piece of office equipment or a motor car. This is an agreed sum of money borrowed and paid back over a period of, say, two to three years. The bank will only be prepared to make the loan if it is reasonably satisfied that the flow of cash coming into the business is enough to cover the repayments plus the interest charged.

An *overdraft* helps to solve any short-term financial problems, for example by enabling the firm to pay suppliers before customers have settled their bills. Other firms might use an overdraft to help buy seasonal stock, e.g. around Christmas.

The bank manager fixes a limit up to which total the firm may draw cheques beyond what it has paid into the bank. Charges are made by the bank, but only on the actual amount overdrawn on each day. The bank might ask for security ('collateral') on the loan or overdraft such as the deeds to the business premises.

A way of transferring money

Customers can use the bank to

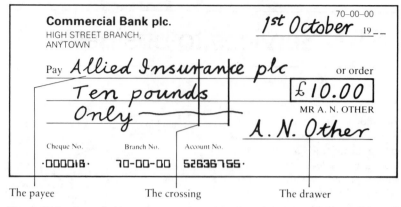

Figure 15.3 Crossed cheque.

transfer money to other people and receive money from other people. This is of great benefit to business.

Cheques

A cheque is a written instruction by the account-holder (the 'drawer') to the bank to make payment to somebody else (the 'payee').

The most common form of cheque used by a business is a crossed cheque, which takes three banking days to clear. The crossed cheque has two lines drawn down it. A crossing on its own is called a 'general crossing'. (See Fig. 15.3.)

It is worth noting some special crossings used by business (see Fig. 15.4):

1. A business might ask its customers to write 'A/C Payee only' in the

crossing. This is to ensure that the money is paid only into the account named on the cheque (i.e. the business's account). The cheque cannot be signed over (endorsed) to some other account.
2. The second crossing in Fig. 15.4 means that the cheque can only be paid in at a specific branch of Barclays, i.e. the business's branch at Woodley.
3. The third crossing in Fig. 15.4 is a warning to the person that the cheque is paid to. It warns him or her to check the identity of the person making the payment. If the cheque is stolen or dishonestly used then the person who accepted it must refund the money to the rightful owner.

Cheques are a very useful instrument for a firm. A lot of its receipts

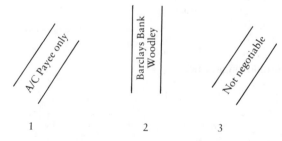

Figure 15.4 Three special cheque crossings used by business.

and payments will be in the form of a cheque.

A *cheque guarantee card* (see Fig. 15.5) guarantees a cheque up to an amount of £50. Businesses like these because even if the cheque-book and card have been stolen the bank guarantees the payment.

Figure 15.5 Cheque guarantee card.

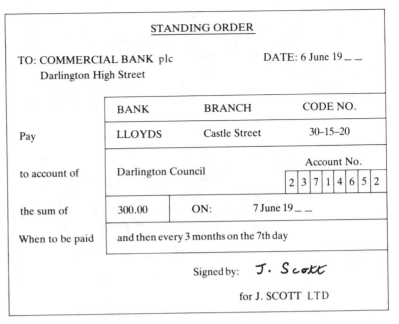

Figure 15.6 Standing order.

Standing orders

A standing order is a written order by a bank customer to the bank to make a payment of a certain amount on a certain date. The order stands until the bank customer stops it. For example, a business could pay its rates bill of £300 per quarter year in this way.

> A **standing order** involves a set amount which needs to be paid at a regular time.

The standing order in Fig. 15.6 is made out by J. Scott ordering her commercial bank to make payment for rates every quarter to Darlington Council.

Direct debits

This is similar to the standing order apart from the following features:

1. The payment can vary in amount and date.
2. The firm to which the payment is made informs the bank what the size of the payment will be.

An example of the use of a direct debit could be for the sale of a vehicle on hire purchase. The hire-purchase company would ask the customer to sign a direct-debit form giving his or her bank permission to make payments when requested to do so by the hire-purchase company.

Bank giro

A form for a single bank giro (see Fig. 15.7 on page 148) is made out to make a payment into a single account; a multiple giro makes a payment into several accounts.

A giro makes it very easy to transfer money. Anyone can transfer money into a single account simply by walking into any bank or post office and handing over cash or a cheque and filling in a giro form for the amount. A business can have its bills paid in this way. When sending a customer a bill, a business might enclose a pre-printed giro form as part of the bill. This practice is most notably carried out by the gas boards, electricity boards and British Telecom.

A multiple giro allows several amounts of money to be transferred using just one cheque. A business will pay a cheque into a bank and fill out a multiple-giro form listing the names, account numbers and banks it wants money to be paid into. This is used by firms particularly to pay wages. Very large firms now use a computerized form of multiple giro whereby they make out a computer tape of wages for the bank.

Bank drafts

A bank draft is made out by a bank and signed by the bank manager. It looks like a big cheque. It is used for making payments of large sums of money. If a business is selling an expensive item it will not accept a cheque if the customer is going to take the item away immediately. It will, however, accept a bank draft

Figure 15.7 Form for a single bank giro.

The table on the form (cash breakdown):

£50 notes		
£20 notes		
£10 notes		
£5 notes	50	–
£1 notes		
50p		
Silver		
Bronze		
Total cash	50	–

Form fields:

bank giro credit

Date   6 June 19 _ _

Code No. 31–42–57

To be used by customer for own account at other braanches/Banks

Cashier's Stamp   To

Bank   LLOYDS

Branch   WOODLEY
(Block Capitals)

Account   WOODLEY TOYS   Account No. 76015

Postal Orders
Cheques etc.
(Listed overleaf)

Rem   £   50   –

Paid in by   M. Gray.

---

because it knows that the bank manager has guaranteed the payment.

Credit cards

Most credit-card schemes are run by companies owned by the banks. These cards make it possible for people to buy goods on credit given to them by the card company. If Sandra Bailey buys £10 worth of petrol from a garage she will show the garage her card and sign a slip with the details of the sale on. The credit-card company then settles the bill with the garage, keeping back a percentage of the bill. The percentage which is subtracted will add to the credit company's profits. At the end of the month Sandra will receive a statement from the credit-card company.

The advantages to businesses of the credit-card scheme are that it helps solve their cash-flow problems (when they buy using a credit card) and allows them to make more sales (when they allow customers to pay by credit card).

Other bank services

Banks provide a wide range of other financial services.

1. They will be prepared to give financial advice to businesses.
2. They help businesses with advice and documentation on international trade.
3. They provide a factoring service for business. They will take a business's invoices off it in return for cash, and collect the money when it is due. They will do this at a price.
4. They will provide a business with a regular statement of its bank balance.
5. They will hire a safe-deposit box to a business for important documents and valuables.
6. They will provide traveller's cheques for overseas travel. These are special international cheques charged against a particular bank.
7. They offer businesses advice on legal, insurance, accountancy and tax matters.

Insurance services

Insurance is the business of taking on other people's risks.

Most businesses have valuable property and equipment and they all take risks. They can cover themselves against many of these risks by taking out insurance policies.

To take out an insurance policy costs money but if anything should happen to the business or its possessions the insurance company will compensate it. The money we pay to an insurance company is called a *premium* and we can illustrate how insurance works by making out a simple example.

Imagine that there are 20 students in a class each with a bicycle worth £40. Each year, one of the bicycles gets stolen and the unfortunate person has to pay out £40 for a new bicycle. One of the students has the idea of starting an insurance pool. The idea is that each student should put £2 into an insurance pool so that there is £40 in the pool. Whichever student loses his or her bike that year claims the £40 to buy a new bike. Every year therefore they will put £2 each in premium into the central pool of funds. Of course, if your bike is not stolen you will not get any money out of the poll but you will be a lot less worried about losing your bike.

Insurance companies are not in business to take risks. They very carefully calculate the chances of accidents happening and then set the premiums the public have to pay.

Stages in taking out insurance

Fig. 15.9 summarizes the step involved in taking out an insurance policy. When a business has chosen the insurance policy it wants, it will fill in an application form for insurance called a *proposal form*. The proposal form will ask a number of important questions so that the insurance company can work out the amount of premium that should be charged. Of course, the proposal form should be filled out with complete honesty. This is termed *utmost good faith*. Obviously the level of risk involved will determine the amount of premium to be paid.

You will only be able to insure something in which you have an *insurable interest* (i.e. something which will cause you to lose money if anything happens).

An *insurance broker* is a salesperson working for several companies. A broker does not just work for one insurance company but for many. You can choose the policy which you think will give you best value for money.

Figure 15.8 Insurance protects businesses against risks such as fire.

A business is exposed to a large number of risks ranging from fire to non-payment of debts. With all the insurance policies available, business people are able to sleep a lot more easily at night, knowing that by paying out fairly small premiums they are covering themselves against the risk of having to pay out large amounts should anything happen to them or their possessions. (See Fig. 15.8.)

Figure 15.9 Diagram showing the steps in taking out insurance.

149

A *cover note* will cover the insured until the actual policy arrives. The *policy* is evidence of a contract between the insurance company and the insured.

The details of what is covered are laid down in the *schedule*—a section of the policy which is completed to indicate the name or description of the business, the complete list of items covered, and, possibly, the maximum or minimum claim allowed. Premises insurance, for example, might cover a firm for carpets, fixtures and burst pipes to a total value of, say, £5000.

When an insurance company has to pay out money, this is called *indemnity*.

Types of business insurance

Whatever the type of business it will require a similar set of policies.

Motor insurance

Insurance will be required for the company's vehicles. It will probably insure them all together under what is called *fleet insurance*. The company will probably have *comprehensive insurance*, which covers damage to the company's vehicles and covers the company against claims made for damage caused by its vehicles.

Goods-in-transit insurance

If a firm is transporting goods, it will want to cover against them being damaged on the way.

Fire and flood insurance

The firm will want to insure against buildings, goods or machinery being damaged in a fire or by a flood.

Consequential-loss insurance

A firm might lose its profits as a consequence of a fire or other damage; for example, as a result of an explosion and fire, a hotel in Brighton had to close down for several weeks. The

Figure 15.10 A member of the public who is hurt on business premises may sue—public liability insurance protects the business against this.

Figure 15.11 An employee hurt on the employer's premises may sue—employers' liability insurance protects the business against this.

150

hotel was able to claim compensation for money lost in this period.

Public liability insurance
A firm can cover itself for the money it has to pay out if it is sued by someone who is hurt on its premises. (See Fig. 15.10.)

Employers' liability insurance
A firm can cover itself for the money it has to pay out if it is sued by one of its own employees who is hurt while working on the company's premises. (See Fig. 15.11.)

Fidelity guarantee
A firm can cover itself against one of its trusted employees stealing company funds.

Products liability
A firm can insure itself against being sued by a consumer who suffers injury or loss caused by the firm's products.

Plate-glass insurance
A firm like a jewellery shop could insure its plate-glass windows.

Freezer insurance
Firms like large supermarkets would insure against the large losses that might occur if their freezer went out of action.

Bad-debts insurance
Firms that sell goods on credit can insure against non-payment of debts. Exporters would use the government's Exports Credit Guarantee Department for this purpose.

Theft insurance
Firms can also insure against items being stolen from their shops, even by shoplifting.

Firms cannot insure against not making a profit or holding goods that do not sell—these are non-insurable risks.

Telecommunications services

Modern business relies on telecommunications services for a wide range of speedy links. Most of these are covered in the chapter on communications (Chapter 7) but some others can be mentioned here.

Telephone services
The telephone makes possible direct communications throughout the UK and international direct dialling to many parts of the world. Businesses can also make use of the following services:

1. Radiophones for communication with moving vehicles.
2. Telephone credit cards, whereby telephone calls can be charged to the phone bill when someone is travelling around.
3. Phonecards, which can be used in some phone boxes as an alternative to coins.
4. Alarm calls.
5. Business information services.

Telemessages
These allow up to 50 word messages. The firm simply telephones the operator before 8 p.m. (6 p.m. on Sunday) and British Telecom delivers on the next working day. This would only be of use to a very small firm with no other facilities.

Postal services

The Post Office provides a range of services which act as aids to business. The main service of the Post Office is in the field of communication. Up and down the UK there are numerous post offices. Some are main post offices; others, especially in villages and more remote places, are sub-post offices. The sub-post offices usually occupy part of a small general store or small independent shop.

Letter services
Letter post
The Post Office offers a two-tier system, with first- and second-class letters. A higher price is paid for faster service.

Poste restante
Packets can be sent to a Post Office in a particular town and picked up from there. This is useful if a business person is travelling and does not know the address he or she will be staying at.

Certificates of posting
The Post Office will issue a certificate to show the date on which a packet was posted. It can be used as proof of posting.

Business reply service
This service makes it possible for firms to enclose an unstamped reply card or envelope in any magazine or book or direct-mail correspondence. The firm must get a licence from the Post Office. The cards or envelopes can carry first- or second-class postage and the firm will only be charged for the replies that are returned.

Freepost
An alternative to the business reply service, this facility removes the need for the firm or business to provide a pre-printed card or envelope, and is therefore ideal for advertisers on television and radio and in the press. A firm arranges with the Post Office for the public to be able to add the word 'Freepost' to the firm's address; the firm is then charged for each letter delivered.

The service only operates on a second-class basis.

Recorded delivery
A business will use the recorded-delivery service if it needs proof that a letter has been received. The letter will be signed for on delivery. It

would be a useful way of sending a summons to appear in court or a note requesting prompt payment of a debt.

Registered post

This is a method of sending valuable items through the post. If the package goes missing the Post Office will compensate the sender for the value of the packet up to a substantial amount of compensation.

The service provides:

1. A certificate of posting
2. A record of delivery
3. Compensation for lost or damaged items

Swiftair

For an additional fee, letters can be given express air treatment for quick delivery.

Services for parcels and packets

Parcel post

The cost of sending a parcel will depend on the weight. Parcels must be securely packed or the Post Office will repack them and charge for doing so.

Express delivery

A Post Office messenger will deliver packages and letters over short distances.

Special delivery

Once a first-class letter has arrived at its town of destination it can be sped by messenger to the person to whom it is addressed.

Compensation-fee parcels

A parcel can be insured against damage in posting.

Cash on delivery

A firm can arrange for the Post Office to pick up the payment owed for an item before it is handed over. This is commonly used by companies selling goods by mail order.

Datapost

This service is particularly suitable for the delivery of computer data. It is based on an overnight delivery service. It is also used for many other types of delivery.

Franking machines

A business can hire a franking machine from the Post Office to replace sticking stamps on envelopes. A frank can be made out for any amount. The user will pay a chosen sum of money to the Post Office and then be able to frank its mail up to this amount. Most businesses have special franks created which also serve to advertise their product.

Transport

Transport is an essential service to business. The success of modern transport has followed from a clever combination of road, rail, sea and air transport. Containerization of loads has made possible the integration of these different forms of transport. Routes and services have been simplified to cut out wasteful duplication. Special types of vehicles have been designed to carry special loads.

To **integrate** means to join together.

An example of **wasteful duplication** would be two half-full airliners running the same route at the same time.

Other services to business

Chambers of commerce

Most towns and cities will have a chamber of commerce, which is a pressure group and interest group looking after the well-being of business people in the area. The group will meet to discuss matters of mutual interest concerned with developments in its area. It may, for instance, have an interest in the subjects being offered in schools or in plans to change the routes of local roads or the provision of car parks.

Chambers of trade

These are similar to chambers of commerce except that whereas the above include all sorts of business people, chambers of trade are mainly made up of shopkeepers.

Both bodies have a national committee which makes suggestions to the government and other groups.

Industrial research associations

In most major industries, leading firms club together to establish a combined research association so that they can benefit together from advances.

Industrial training boards

In a similar fashion, firms will jointly fund training initiatives such as a training school for employees.

Trading associations

Firms with common interests club together to discuss common problems such as overseas competition.

CASE STUDY—SETTING UP A GARDEN CENTRE

Alvan Whittaker is just about to open up a new garden centre in Manchester. The garden centre is made up of a complex of eight greenhouses and a large showroom area and is centred on a plot of eight acres of land. Alvan will be employing six workers and the firm will have two delivery vans. Alvan has asked for advice on insuring the business and his insurance broker has told him that the best deal will be gained from taking out a comprehensive business insurance policy which will cover all the main business risks.

Questions

1. Make a list of the main risks which you would expect to be covered under a comprehensive business insurance policy.
2. How will Alvan benefit even if he does not have to make any claims under the policy?

CASE STUDY—USING THE SERVICES OF A BANK

Tonia Yiannapas set up a taxi firm in Cardiff using the name 555 cabs because the telephone number of the firm was 555111. Her business was able to benefit from many of the services offered by her local bank. She was able to pay her rates bill by standing order and the telephone and electricity bills by direct debit. Some of her larger clients such as local businesses paid their bills at the end of the month using a credit scheme that she offered and she was able to cover herself by using the bank to factor her debts. The firm employed eight drivers who received the bulk of their wages cash in hand but were paid a monthly bonus by bank giro.

Questions

1. Explain the following services which were mentioned in the case study:
   (a) Standing order
   (b) Direct debit
   (c) Factoring of debts
   (d) Bank giro
2. Explain how Tonia might also have made use of the following:

(a) A business loan
(b) An overdraft facility
(c) A banker's draft

QUESTIONS

1. Complete the following sentences using the words below:

Cheque card
Credit card
Night safe
Factoring
Overdraft
Bank draft
Bank loan
Bank giro
Standing order
Direct debit

(a) The bank service used for depositing money after bank closing hours is a ....
(b) A business would accept a .... for £1000 in immediate exchange for a product.
(c) .... makes it possible to deposit money into any known account.
(d) .... of debts involves allowing a bank to collect payment for your invoices.
(e) A business might take out a .... to buy an expensive piece of equipment.
(f) A .... is a 'good way for a business to collect regularly debts of irregular sums.
(g) A .... would be a good way of paying regular quarterly insurance Premiums.
(h) A .... guarantees a cheque payment up to a set amount.

(i) If a business is prepared to accept payment by .... this should increase its sales.
(j) A cheap way of borrowing money to ease cash-flow problems in the short term is by ....
2. If you were going to set up in business as a small florist what business services would you require?
3. Study the advertisement for British Aerospace shares (Fig. 15.12 on page 154).
   (a) What sort of organization are Kleinwort, Benson Ltd, Hill Samuel & Co. Ltd, etc.?
   (b) What services to business do these groups offer?
   (c) What type of share is being issued?
   (d) What will be the issue price of these shares when fully paid?
   (e) If an investor wanted to buy 200 of these shares what would be the value of the cheque he or she would have to enclose with the application?
   (f) What is meant by 'privatization'?
   (g) What evidence is there in the advertisement that this issue of shares is an example of privatization?
4. Which method of posting would you use in each of the following situations?
   (a) A jeweller wants to send a small but fairly valuable item of jewellery.
   (b) Ross Frozen Foods Company needs to send documents to its travelling salesperson to await her arrival at a certain town.
   (c) Overnight door-to-door

delivery is needed of some computer data to a centre for processing.

(d) An insurance broker needs proof that she has dispatched important policies to her customers.

5. Using the *Post Office Guide*, find out the various postal rates for both letters and printed papers, both surface mail and air mail, to Australia and the United States of America.

6. You have set up a small business which involves a great deal of sending of mail and relying on people to reply. What kind of service would such a business use and why?

7. The Post Office offers a banking service. What is it called? In what ways does the Post Office banking service offer the same facilities to business as the high-street banks?

8. What do the following stand for?

(a) STD

(b) IDD

(c) COD

(d) CWO

9. Describe the services offered by British Telecom. What rival services are there?

10. Describe the Freepost and Freefone services.

COURSEWORK

1. This piece of work should be done as a groupwork exercise. The class should split into groups to explore how business services benefit a local firm. Each group should select appropriate questions. The overall question should be, 'Could business survive without business services?'

2. Study the article in Fig. 15.13. Should coal travel by road or rail from Grimethorpe?

What do you think that the view of the following individuals and groups would be on this issue, and why would you expect them to have these views?

(a) A resident living close to the road in Cudworth

(b) British Coal's transport manager

(c) A representative of Coalite

(d) The head teacher of Pontefract Road First School

(e) A local councillor who had listened to the views of all interested parties

British Aerospace
Public Limited Company

Offer
by
Kleinwort, Benson Limited
and
Lazard Brothers & Co., Limited
on behalf of
British Aerospace Public Limited Company
and
The Secretary of State for Trade and Industry

of
146,852,746 Ordinary Shares
of 50p each at 375p per share

200p is payable on application
175p is payable by 10th September 1985
underwritten by

Kleinwort, Benson Limited   Lazard Brothers & Co., Limited

Hill Samuel & Co. Limited   Morgan Grenfell & Co. Limited

J. Henry Schroder Wagg & Co. Limited

Figure 15.12   Advertisement for British Aerospace shares.

Concern over heavy road traffic

Call for switch to rail

HEAVY goods vehicles travelling through Cudworth — often as many as two a minute at peak times — are causing concern to councillors and residents alike.

Now local councillors are calling for more heavy goods from Grimethorpe, particularly coal and coke, to be taken off the roads and carried by rail.

And railmen say there is less coal and coke carried by rail than three years ago — threatening the future of the railways and causing congestion as more goods move on to the A628 Pontefract to Barnsley Road.

Suggest

In a count made in Cudworth over a 12-hour weekday period last September, a total of 904 heavy lorries were recorded in both directions. In a similar count on a day in September 1985 the figure was 788.

These figures do not seem to suggest any significant change since November 1981 when one weekday count recorded 957 heavy goods vehicles in both directions.

The most recent count made in Cudworth, however, on January 9 this year showed unusually few lorries passing through — 563 — still too many for the good of the area, according to local councillors Hedley Salt and Charlie Wraith.

Trend

Coun. Salt said "It is too early to judge anything from the latest count — it could just be a one-off. But if it did show a trend away from the roads I would welcome it very much.

"I believe there is still a lot more scope for moving coal and coke in this area by rail."

Railman Mr. Bill Taylor — an ex-chairman of Cudworth branch of the NUR — says

by Mike Hind

"British Rail have taken up two of the four tracks on the main Leeds to Sheffield line and we are concerned that the whole line could close and all the coal and coke from Grimethorpe move on to the roads.

"They are already closing the section from Cudworth to Wath Road junction, even though it is continuously welded track needing very little maintenance.

"Without a doubt there is now more going by road in this area than there was before the miners' strike — and fewer trains."

A spokesman for Coalite would not supply any figures concerning how their coke is moved. He said: "These are commercial figures which we do not disclose. But the bulk of our coke is carried by road — which is just part of a national trend towards road haulage rather than rail."

According to British Coal, between 6,000 and 10,000 tonnes of coal a day are carried from Grimethorpe, compared with between 400 and 1,800 tonnes by road.

A spokesman said: "As a result of losing some customers during the miners' strike, some coal was diverted on to the roads, but not enough to make a significant increase."

British Rail confirmed plans to close the section of line between Cudworth and Wath Junction but insisted the northern section would remain open.

Council officers suggested that traffic counts could be misleading, as the maximum legal tonnages of lorries had increased in recent years. And the counts did not take night-time movements into account either.

A Planning Department spokesman said: "We accept the need for lorries in certain cases but they do cause damage to the roads, which is just one concern in the borough.

Tied

"For many reasons we actively support the use of rail freight, particularly for bulk commodities such as solid fuel. For instance we promote the use of Section 8 grants covering 60 per cent of the costs of rail infrastructure for companies wishing to transfer to rail. But apart from that our hands are tied."

Public Services Department officers share their concern at a time when finance is short for highway maintenance. A spokesman said: "Our problems would be eased if more goods like solid fuel were transferred to rail."

OFF THE RAILS: The main line from Leeds to Sheffield — looking north towards Grimethorpe and Cudworth. "There is more scope for moving heavy goods in this area by rail," says Coun. Hedley Salt.

ON THE ROAD: Two of the many heavy lorries which travel through Cudworth each day passing Pontefract Road First School.

Figure 15.13 Transport is one of the services required by business, but it may have social costs, as this newspaper article shows. (*Source: Barnsley Chronicle*)

Index